THE INDIAN EXPERIENCE

OUR PERSONAL GUEST

Media Transasia Thailand Ltd

3rd floor, Sarasin Building

14 Surasak Road

Bangkok, Thailand

Thomson Press Hong Kong Ltd

19th floor, Tai Sang Commercial Building

24-34 Hennessy Road

Hong Kong

Publisher: J S Uberoi
Editors: Ken Barrett and Suresh Sharma
Photo Editors: Alberto Cassio and Luca Invernizzi
Design: Sam Tse
Cover Design: Alan Chan
Editorial Board: Pupul Jayakar; Sir Michael Walker;
H Y Sharda Prasad; Dr F R Allchin; Raghu Raj; H K Malik;
John Lenaghan; AshaRani Mathur

Published by Media Transasia Thailand Ltd and Thomson Press Hong Kong Ltd
in association with Air-India on the
occasion of the Festival of India.

Printed by Toppan Printing Co (HK) Ltd
Toppan Building, Westlands Road
Quarry Bay, Hong Kong

INTRODUCTION

by Mrs Indira Gandhi,
Prime Minister of India.

My father spent all his life, in and out of prison, trying to discover India. I travel incessantly and each trip brings to light some new facet. How can I attempt to describe its many-sided personality?

The articles in this book touch upon various subjects and give a glimpse of certain aspects, obviously expressing the writers' own points of view. Having only glanced hurriedly at them, I can neither endorse nor reject what they say. But I do know that India is much much more in variety and depth.

If you wish to know something about India you must empty your mind of all preconceived notions, of what you have heard or read. Why be imprisoned by the limited vision of the prejudiced? Also don't try to compare. India is different and, exasperating as it must seem, would like to remain so! You will not find any of your familiar labels useful. India is many and it is one. It has incredible diversity, yet is bound in a unity that stretches way back into unwritten history.

There is hardly a thought in philosophy, science or the arts of which you will not find some grain in India. Even the passing fashions or cults which rock the West from time to time were found in India somewhere some time and were tolerated without the raising of an eyebrow or affecting others. This is the secret of India, the acceptance of life in all its fullness, the good and the evil, and, at the same time, trying to rise above it all.

In all the ups and downs of its long history, India's culture, mores and traditions have been continuously evolving, shaped by its many experiences within itself and influences from outside. It has not hesitated to adopt, adapt and absorb new ideas. But these, like the foreigners (all except European conquerors), became merged in Indian society, became Indians, contributed to Indianness. The most remarkable thing was that through the ages, thousands of years, our roots remained strong and healthy.

Our European rulers deliberately kept their distance to emphasise their imperial status, so there was little ethnic imprint but we could not but be affected, and the British connection influenced us deeply and in many ways. British laws shaped our institutions, and literature introduced an entirely new and exciting dimension to our thinking. The British men and women who became interested in various aspects of our lives, those who helped us to discover ourselves and those who became involved in causes dear to us, are too numerous to be named.

Christianity was brought to India by St Thomas and we are told that the first Englishman to visit India was an envoy from King Alfred bearing gifts to the apostle's tomb in AD 884. Islam also became one of our religions and the Indian mystic tradition made its own contribution to the evolution of Sufism.

Almost from the first days of the Empire there were Britons who devoted their lives to the study of some sphere of activity. The works of William Jones and Wilkins blazed the trail for Oriental studies, followed by Wilson, Macdonnel, Max Muller and Berriedale Keith. But for Cunningham, Fergusson, Havell and Curzon, our archaeological treasures might have remained neglected. Archer contributed to a better understanding of art. Some of us still live and work in environs designed by Lutyens. Two India-born authors, Thackeray and Kipling, have thrilled generations with their descriptive writings. E M Forster searched for truth under the trappings of cultural difference. Margaret Noble and Edwin Arnold delved into philosophy.

Almost a century ago, Allan Octavian Hume founded my political party, the Indian National Congress, which, as off-spring often do, grew far beyond his imagination into the colossal mass movement which was to win us our independence. British liberal tradition stimulated our social reforms, fired our passion for freedom, justice and equality, and fanned the urge to struggle against tremendous odds for our ideals.

Annie Besant and Nellie Sen Gupta became Presidents of the Indian National Congress and suffered imprisonment. Charlie Andrews and Madeleine Slade were friends to Gandhi, and Elmhirst helped Rabindranath Tagore. Corbett's name recalls the teeming wild life of the time and Verrier Elwin was a guardian of our tribal riches. Many are the founders of medical or educational institutions. Besides the known are the countless anonymous missionaries, teachers, doctors, nurses and other ordinary and extraordinary people who worked in inhospitable circumstances or remote areas. This is an occasion to pay tribute to their love of India and spirit of adventure

Enough of the past. Let us cross the years to the India of 1982. It still holds within itself all the old ideas, the old racial memories and many stages of development. The Air-India jet and the bullock cart coexist as do top-level atomic or other scientists with primitive communities.

Time and again we have attempted and often attained the seemingly impossible. Independence for 400 million people without violence or hatred. Planned development in a democratic set-up. Self-sufficiency in cereals for a population that has grown to 683 million. Impressive gains in industry and science. High level institutes of civil, military, technological and scientific training. Statistics can prove the vast development that has taken place but statisticians do not bring a country to life. The observer with his preconceptions determines the area and focus of his vision.

Of all the myriad questions we ask ourselves, the most fascinating and challenging is whether, in the relentless march towards material progress, we can sustain the best of our ancient tradition, keep our closeness to nature, the spontaneity and *joie de vivre* of our tribals, the instinctive feel for colour and line of our folk artists, the skill of our artisans and more particularly, our perception of tolerance and compassion, all of which have been so integral a part of our cultural and spiritual experiences. "Nothing is changeless in this changing world." Our endeavour is to fuse the power of science with the wisdom of old insights. Keeping in step with time, the essential India will continue to cherish its eternal truths.

I welcome Britain's imaginative initiative in organising a Festival of India. For old friends, this is a return visit by India. To the generation which has grown up after Indian independence, I hope it will be an opportunity to glimpse something of the secret of India's persistence. The British are attached to history. Through our living arts, and the narrative of some of our current preoccupations, a bit of India comes to their very doors.

FESTIVAL OF INDIA: A CULTURAL RE~EVALUATION

by Mrs Margaret Thatcher,
Prime Minister of Great Britain.

The Festival of India which opens in London on March 22, 1982, is an event without parallel in the history of cultural interchange between India and the United Kingdom. Over a period of six months it will bring together exhibitions which illustrate aspects of the Indian heritage from earliest times to the present day. It will range from the way of life of a typical Indian village, specially recreated at the Museum of Mankind, to a display of the development of Indian science and technology at the Science Museum. Painting and sculpture, modern art, design, the performing arts, folk art, photography and film will all be represented at museums and galleries throughout the capital and in other parts of the United Kingdom.

I am particularly pleased to have been invited to become joint patron of the Festival with the Prime Minister of India, Shrimati Indira Gandhi — and not just because it will allow me to extend my own acquaintance with Indian culture, all too briefly but wonderfully glimpsed on my visits to India. This Festival is an important symbol of the close links between our two countries and of the mutual regard which we have for one another's achievements. It will give a new generation of Britons from all walks of life and a variety of ethnic backgrounds an insight into the best of Indian civilisation and increase their understanding of the influence it has had on the United Kingdom.

India has always exerted a powerful fascination for the British. At the time of our contacts in the late 16th and early 17th centuries our interest was at first essentially mercantile. But later, as we came to know the subcontinent better, we came to appreciate its people and civic order, its magnificent architecture, its luxuriant sculpture and frescoes, and its many other wonders. Perhaps one could also say that India, by its very contrast with our own culture, evoked in us a new perception of ourselves. At one time we were impressed by the richness and opulence of imperial India. At another, as we sought our own historical roots, it was the depth and spread of Indian civilisation and its impact on the European tradition which excited us. And during periods of turmoil, in our values we have turned to the Indian philosophical tradition for a new appreciation of meaning and harmony in human affairs.

But these perceptions represented only partial fragments of an India too complex and too diverse for us to grasp as a whole. This Festival gives us the opportunity to see the Indian experience with fresh eyes and fresh understanding. India's culture is not static; it is continuously developing and has its own dynamic relationship with the West. We shall see something of that cross-fertilisation of artistic ideas in the exhibitions of modern art, industrial design, graphic art, photography and film. We shall also see it in contemporary music, for the concert which opens the Festival will feature the renowned musician Ravi Shankar giving the first European performance of his Second Sitar Concerto, accompanied by the London Philharmonic Orchestra.

Nor should we forget India's outstanding achievement in the world of scientific endeavour. She has pioneered developments in medicine and agriculture and has a foremost position in nuclear energy, satellite technology and computer science. I am glad that this aspect of India will also be well represented in the Festival.

The Festival of India will enable us to more fully appreciate a country whose effect on our own way of life has been incalculable. It remains for me to extend my thanks to the organisations which have so generously given their sponsorship and to the many individuals here and in India who have devoted much effort to preparing and mounting the Festival. Success will attend their efforts.

CONTENTS

INDIA AND BRITAIN: YESTERDAY, TODAY AND TOMORROW

B K Nehru

When history gets written after further efflux of time has given a more objective perspective, the story of Britain and India will seem hard to believe. That a small commercial company formed in London for trading with the Indies should have established itself as the ruling power over a whole continent 6,000 miles away would sound more a flight of fancy than a statement of hard fact.

That this should have happened is a proof of the law that nature abhors a vacuum. The decay of the Moghuls created a power vacuum which was filled by the representatives of a small and distant country because they were superior to the Indians of the day in organisation, discipline, unity and fire power. Indian society of the time was tradition-bound and decadent, having lost all resilience to meet new situations; it was in no position to resist.

The idea of territorial nationalism did not as yet exist in India. The loyalty of the people was given to individual princes and dynasties. The British had little opposition on the ground that they were foreigners; they were simply the followers of another prince taking part in a many-sided civil war.

British rule in India continued as long as it did because it had the cooperation of the people. It could not have done this otherwise with so minuscule a British presence in so large an alien ocean of humanity. The moment this co-operation became unwilling, British power came to an end. It would have been possible, of course, for the British to stay on in India for another few years as the French tried to do in Indo-China and Algeria but that would have been a foolish, tragic and futile attempt. It has been well-said that nothing became Britain in India more than her manner of leaving it. It was a wise and timely decision and one of its greatest benefits has been the complete lack of bitterness between the two nations and the continuation of a very strong psychological influence of Britain in India.

No two countries can have a relationship as close as Britain and India had for so long without affecting each other in many ways. The profounder effects of this relationship were felt in India: the ideas and institutions of the rulers tended automatically to be transferred to the ruled. It was patent to the Indians that British prestige and power in the world rested, not so much on military strength as on the whole complex of social institutions and relationships (themselves a product of ethical values and intellectual processes and ideas) which make a nation great. The leaders of the subject people wished to understand how it was that an alien people should rule over them and to transfer their greatness to their own society.

The Indians were fortunate that in the European scramble for territory India was allotted to the British. Colonialism is in itself an evil system; but colonialism is of various kinds and the one from which we suffered was, in comparison, enlightened. Nothing was, of course, permitted which would weaken the Empire. But within this basic limitation, much was done, whether by design or by the compulsions of the situation, to modernise a mediaeval society.

Perhaps the most important factor of change introduced into India was the English language. To those who had the privilege of getting acquainted with it, a whole new modern world was thrown open. The avid study of English literature, British political ideas and institutions, British social customs and British history and, above all, the introduction

Below: Transfer of power — midnight, August 14-15, 1947 "..........nothing became Britain in India more than her manner of leaving it". (Photo courtesy of Press Information Bureau.)

Bottom left: The Commonwealth bond — In January 1951 at the very first Commonwealth Conference where free India was represented, HM King George VI and the Queen held a lunch at Buckingham Palace. India's Prime Minister, Mr Jawaharlal Nehru, is seen at the extreme right, next to Princess Margaret.(Photo courtesy of British High Commission, New Delhi.)

Bottom right: Trading partners: Mr R D Sathe, Indian Foreign Secretary, and Sir John Thomson, British High Commissioner in India, exchanging documents in New Delhi on April 16, 1981 after signing a memorandum of understanding on co-operation in the field of industry and trade between India and the UK. Looking on are the Prime Minister of India, Mrs Indira Gandhi and the Rt Hon Margaret Thatcher, MP, Prime Minister of Great Britain and Northern Ireland. (Photo courtesy of Press Information Bureau.)

of the scientific method and a rational approach to life introduced a ferment into the tradition-bound and authority-ridden society of India which caused, over the years, its complete transformation.

More valuable perhaps were the ideas of democracy, equality, liberty of the individual and the rule of law. None of these ideas are of native origin. None of them, except the last, (though the law itself was "rigged" in favour of the rulers) was put into practice, save marginally, by the British in India. But that these were the concepts which formed the basis of the governance of the United Kingdom — and, therefore, it was assumed, of its power — caused them to be adopted as ideals towards the attainment of which the country should work. Without the enforced exposure to these ideas which colonialism ensured, none of these would have taken the firm roots that they now have in our country.

Another great and abiding contribution of British rule to India was a modern system of administration. In India, as elsewhere in the world, the administration used to be carried out by the favourites of the Emperor. The East India Company started off with the same system of favourites of the court of directors being appointed to the Indian service. These traders subsequently had administrative duties thrust upon them; the combination of trading with administration resulted in colossal corruption, severe exploitation of the people and extreme maladministration. It was not till after the great revolt of 1857 that fundamental reform of the civil service took place substituting competitive examinations for direct nomination, giving civil servants security of tenure, prohibiting trading and increasing their emoluments so as to raise them above temptation. The Indian civil service thus constituted, developed fairly rapidly unimpeachable integrity, a strict internal discipline, great competence in the task of administration, and an attitude of service to the people. It governed the Indian Empire for the next hundred years and its successor continues to form the backbone of Indian administration today. It is a little known fact that the later reform of the British civil service had for its model the structure of the ICS.

Yet again, British rule was responsible for the growth of nationalism and the forging of the political unity of India — even though the Indian Empire had to be split into two. India has always had a cultural unity but it has only been a political unit at long intervals and for comparatively short periods of time. Loyalty was owed to the ruler rather than to the country. The reaction to two centuries of foreign domination was to develop the strength of Indian nationalism to such an extent that loyalty is no longer owed to a person or a dynasty but to the nation as a whole and any effort to weaken the unity of India finds her entire people in strong opposition to it.

No benefit is ever obtained without the payment of a price and India did pay a substantial price for being dragged into the modern age. Perhaps the worst effect that alien rule had was to destroy the confidence of the Indians in their own culture and civilisation and to give them an inferiority complex. It is necessary for the continuance of the domination of a minority — especially if it happens to be as foreign and as small as the British were in India — to convince the ruled that the rulers are superior beings and that the ruled are in subjection because they are inferior. It is interesting that before the East India Company had become paramount its representatives used to live and behave as did Indian gentlemen of a corresponding class but when the rule became absolute the whole system of life and behaviour changed to one of extreme exclusiveness. The deliberate isolation of the British from their Indian subjects, their insistence on never making any concession to the customs and manners and dress or food of the country, no matter how inappropriate their own were in a totally alien environment, was consciously designed to stress their difference and their superiority. And the racial arrogance, prejudice, and discrimination which marred the last century of British rule was a direct consequence.

All aspects of Indian culture were discouraged. The Indian languages did not grow; Indian painting, sculpture, dance and music virtually ceased to exist in British India, being kept alive only in the princely states. The enormous upsurge in Indian artistic and cultural life which took place immediately after Independence showed that the British effort at least in this direction had fortunately not succeeded.

Another price India paid for colonial rule was that its social structure became frozen at the point of time at which British rule became finally paramount. At that time, both Indian and British societies were highly class-conscious, extremely hierarchical, and believers in hereditary privilege. The natural British bias in favour of the existing structure was reinforced by the need of having to rely on a group of privileged people who could keep economic, political and social discontents in check. For 100 years, the princes and the landlords continued to dominate the Indian scene resisting, with the support of the administrative and military might of the Imperial power, all efforts at change. No wonder then that, on the advent of Independence, the power of the princes was rapidly eliminated, land was taken away from the landlords and India was transformed rapidly into a less unequal society.

India had also to pay an economic price for its subjection. Apart from the early days when the nabobs of the company indulged in open loot, the economic exploitation of India took subsequently more subtle and sophisticated forms. No matter what the rhetoric of Kiplingesque imperialism is, the fact remains that countries conquer and rule other countries in order to get economic and other benefits out of them. It is true that India was developed economically during British rule and that some of the benefits of this development remained in the country. But the whole pattern of development was designed, and subtle fiscal and financial devices were adopted, to ensure that India remained a source of raw material for the "mother country" and a market for its industrial products. Indian industry developed not on account of the encouragement of the British government but in spite of its best efforts and as a consequence of the two World Wars.

It may be that "the evil that men do lives after them but the good is oft interred with their bones." But as far as India is concerned it is fortunate that what is remembered is only the good; the evil is fast being forgotten. Though India's contacts with the outside world, which during the colonial era were limited solely to Britain, have been widened, the psychological domination of British thought and British institutions has not diminished. The English language has an irresistible attraction for the mass of the people. Very many more people know English now than they ever did under British rule and the desire to learn it is universal.

Our constitution which has adopted the British parliamentary form of government, was adopted almost unquestioningly by us mainly because we know of no other.

And though the need for fundamental changes in the methods of government is patent, the resistance to change seems impossible to overcome. The judicial system too is copied wholesale from Britain and though, being a federation, the judgments of the Supreme Court of the United States are often cited, Indian judicial decisions are influenced far more by the decisions of the House of Lords than by those of any other court in the world. Here again, though our judicial institutions are almost universally recognised as inadequate for the country, our legal profession, convinced of the perfection of the British legal system, cannot be convinced.

Our economic policies still tend to follow the tenets of Fabian socialism — though Britain itself may long have outgrown them — and our trade unions are all modelled on the British pattern. Though this pattern is doing us demonstrable harm and the modes of organisation of labour in other countries are far superior, we will not change.

Though our commercial relations with many countries have achieved an importance which they never had earlier, Britain continues to be the principal investor in India and also one of our most important trading partners. So does it continue to be as a source of supply for defence equipment; our defence forces have been modelled on those of Britain and look naturally to that country as a first choice. The same applies to industrial equipment; for, here again, the contacts and familiarisation born of 200 years of history steer us towards Britain.

Our newspapers, the radio and television are all patterned on the news media of Britain, our news still largely comes from British sources, the pre-eminence of the external services of the BBC is unquestioned, and we still tend to attach quite unusual importance to developments in British political, social, economic and cultural life — not to mention sport where cricket still reigns supreme!

How the Indo-British connection will develop in future it is naturally very difficult to prophesy. It is obvious that with the loss of Empire, Britain's geographical relationship must necessarily assert itself and she must increasingly become part of the European continent. So must India increasingly develop her relations, which used to be non-existent, with her neighbours. Her historical and cultural bonds and the facts of geography must steer her necessarily towards Asia and Africa.

The transmutation of the British Empire into the Commonwealth of Nations (which owes its existence to the remarkable flexibility and ingenuity of British constitutional experts) is a counter-influence to this natural development. But the Commonwealth bond is tenuous and as the historical links that united the Empire are weakened by the passage of time and as our various countries revert to their own diverse modes of life and government, corresponding more closely to their own genius, the strength of the Commonwealth link will be weakened.

One of the reasons for the continuance of British psychological dominance in India and her dominance in trade and industry is the fact that even after Independence a substantial number of Indian students went to Britain for advanced education. Higher courses in many disciplines are now available in India itself; the number of students going abroad proportionately (though not absolutely) is smaller. Larger numbers now go to the countries (particularly the United States) where technological advance has overtaken that of the United Kingdom. The recent great increase in the cost of education for foreign students in Britain will, of course, appreciably decrease the number who go there. This is a pity because the intangible benefits, which are great, of large numbers of the Indian elite being educated in Britain will gradually disappear to the disadvantage of both countries and of the Indo-British connection.

On the other hand, the resurgence of the Indian arts has made Britain conscious, virtually for the first time, of the great cultural heritage of India. There is increasing appreciation — as in the rest of the Western world — of Indian art, music, dance and sculpture. Nor can we neglect the influence of Indian "gurus" in the Western world, to which Britain is not impervious. The West has made enormous material advances. But the very process of economic advance seems to have created a kind of spiritual void and has given rise to a quest for the ultimate meaning of life. Perhaps because India has never been in the forefront of material prosperity, Indian philosophy and Indian spiritual thought have undoubtedly been highly developed. Nobody in the Western world, except a few specialists, was even aware of this, but the vacuum that has now been created is being filled, to some extent, by these propounders of Indian spiritual thought. There are many Indians who dislike what they consider to be the perversions of their philosophy as it is presented to the West through this channel, but the fact nevertheless remains that an interest is being created in Britain, as in other countries, in Indian modes of thought, which may well develop into a fuller understanding of the basic values of India when this interest grows into maturity.

One abiding consequence for Britain of the Indo-British connection is, of course, the existence of a considerable Indian population in the United Kingdom. This alien body is no more welcome to the British people than was its counterpart in India in the days of Empire. But no matter how this intrusion of an alien culture is resented, the contributions which Indian immigrants are making to the economic well-being of Britain is undoubted. How this body of conservative people, wedded to their own religion, customs and values and, at the moment, very resistant to change, will eventually find an equilibrium in their new environment it is difficult to say. In all probability though, they will, to a certain extent, maintain their identity. They will also merge with the other elements in their new home and form ultimately communities, such as the various national communities of the United States, following some of their original customs but nevertheless being loyal and patriotic citizens of the country of their adoption as any of the earlier occupants of the soil.

THREE DECADES OF INDUSTRIAL DEVELOPMENT

L K Jha

Between 1950, when India embarked on its first five-year plan, and the end of the seventies, the country achieved a four-fold expansion of industrial output. Over this period, steel production rose from one million to over seven million tonnes, the value of machine tools produced went up from less than £150,000 to about £7.5 million, the output of power transformers increased from about 3 KVA to over 20,000 KVA, coal production moved up from 30 million tonnes to over 100 million tonnes, and fertiliser production shot up from a negligible level to more than two million tonnes. Among products of direct interest to consumers, cotton cloth production rose from 3,350 million metres to about 9,400 million metres, while sugar output recorded a six-fold increase. As a result, starting from a position of no significance, India began to be counted among the top 12 countries of the world in terms of industrial output.

The pace and pattern of India's industrialisation over the last three decades have been influenced by a variety of factors. The public sector and the private sector, indigenous capital and foreign capital, sophisticated technology and traditional crafts, mammoth corporations and cottage industries have played their part within the policy framework outlined by Jawaharlal Nehru. Its main features — commitment to planning and the adoption of a mixed economy with a dominant role for the public sector — had their roots in India's socio-political ethos. But, having regard to the kind of environment in which the industrialisation effort was launched and the shortages that impeded it, the path chosen could well have been chalked out on purely pragmatic considerations.

Long before Independence, the low level of industrialisation had been identified as the major cause of India's economic backwardness and the poverty of the people. Top Indian industrialists, economists and political leaders had formulated a 15-year plan for rapid industrial advance in order to double the national income. With this prior consensus in favour of planning, the Planning Commission was set up by Prime Minister Jawaharlal Nehru under his own chairmanship, as an expert non-political body to draw up five-year plans for India's economic development.

The first constraint which the planners faced, in their attempts to set up investment in industry and agriculture, transport and mining as well as in education and health, was the shortage of capital. With the low per-capita income of the people, barely enough for sustenance, the level of voluntary savings was miserably low. The state had to mobilise savings through taxation and borrowings. These resources were used for public sector investments in the infrastructure, in power and railways, as well as in some key industries, which called for heavy investments of a magnitude which could not be readily raised by private parties. At the same time, to help the private sector fulfil the targets assigned by the planners, financial institutions were created to provide long-term loans and support equity issues.

Steps had also to be taken to ensure that private investments conformed to plan priorities. Left to itself, private investment might well have gravitated towards catering to the luxuries of the rich, who constituted a small minority of the population but accounted for a high proportion of the purchasing power in the country, while inadequacy of investment in key sectors created bottlenecks in the economy. The instrument of industrial licensing was devised to canalise investments into different industries, in accordance with the

A shimmer of colour in a modern textile mill. In three decades cotton cloth production tripled.

Below left: Indo-British collaboration — the Durgapur steel plant in West Bengal.
Below right: There is a drive for self-reliance in vital agro-inputs, such as fertiliser. The gasifiers shown in this picture of a coal-based fertiliser plant were fabricated in India.
Bottom left: Dramatically silhouetted against the night sky, this fertiliser plant is one of many in the country that aid India's agriculture.

Bottom right: Another agro-input, tractors, here seen being assembled at a plant near Delhi.

plans. Fiscal incentives were also used for this purpose.

Apart from the paucity of capital, the absence of a widespread culture of entrepreneurship had hampered the growth of industries in the past. No doubt, there had been many outstanding examples of far-sighted, risky investments by Indian entrepreneurs even in the days of the Raj. An outstanding example of this kind was the establishment of an integrated steel plant by Jamshedji Tata even before World War I. But, such instances were rare. In general, those who had any savings to invest opted for safe instruments like government securities. Those who took to business preferred trade to industry, particularly as the government of the day did not have any well-conceived programme of protection to infant industries. Much of the private investment before Independence had been British — whether in the infrastructure, like railways and power, or in plantations like indigo and tea, or in the mining of coal and metallic ores, or in manufacturing industries like jute, engineering, cotton textiles, soap and the like.

Encouraged by the example and profitability of British investors, some of the wealthier Indian families turned their attention from trade to industry, particularly after the government had set up a Tariff Board to give limited protection to industries which promised to become viable in the long run. During World War II, when imports were at a very low ebb — while both domestic demand and export demand from civilian as well as military sources were running high — many new factories sprang up in different parts of the country. Still, entrepreneurship for a country of India's size was grossly inadequate, and fear of competition not only from imports but also from big domestic manufacturers, inhibited the growth of smaller enterprises.

Against this background, the state, while setting up the really big units in the public sector, took steps to foster entrepreneurship among smaller investors by selecting certain industries in which they would be sheltered from competition by large-scale producers. In addition, some of the traditional industries, which did not make use of power, were given fiscal incentives to hold their own against the products of modern technology, largely with a view to sustain and generate employment in the hinterland, in places far removed from the congested metropolitan port towns.

Inevitably, after Independence, there had to be a reassessment of the role of private foreign capital in India. There was a brief period of hesitation and uncertainty, in which British investors felt that with the transfer of power, they might no longer be welcome. However, Prime Minister Nehru lost no time in assuring the foreign investment already in the country that it would receive fair non-discriminatory treatment; future investments were to be regulated according to national needs, to be encouraged in industries on a selective basis, but not allowed in purely trading ventures. The role of foreign investment in India's industrialisation in the last three decades has been profoundly influenced by the foreign exchange situation of the country and the way it has changed from time to time.

To start with, India had huge sterling balances in London accumulated during World War II, which made it possible to permit free import of plant and machinery for industrialisation. But, in less than a decade, the sterling reserves had dwindled to a dangerously low level and emerged as the major hurdle in the way of rapid industrialisation. A two-pronged strategy was evolved to deal with this situation. India embarked on a conscious effort to mobilise exter-

nal resources by way of long-term credits, soft loans and grants, from institutions like the World Bank and IDA as well as from friendly governments. Further, in order to ease the foreign exchange constraint on industrial growth, high priority was given to machine building industries, so that the plant and equipment for India's expanding industries, like textiles, cement, paper, sugar, fertilisers and steel, as well as for power generation and transmission, could become available from indigenous sources.

With old historical ties, British co-operation in both these areas was of the highest significance. Among the countries providing official assistance to India, Britain always ranked high and often occupied the highest place. In the programme of developing capital goods industries, British manufacturers who had, in the past, been the main suppliers of machinery to India, played a major role. In the public sector industries, which were financed with the help of official credits, they participated as consultants and suppliers of technology and equipment, as in the steel plant at Durgapur and the Heavy Electricals plant at Bhopal. For creation of capacity to meet the machinery requirements of textiles, cement and other private sector industries, British capital came in as direct investment in the equity of the companies concerned.

In general, with the shortage of foreign exchange, private foreign investment proposals were assessed largely in terms of their impact on the country's balance of payments. It was recognised that at the time it came, foreign capital had a favourable impact on the balance of payments; it financed the import of capital goods for setting up the industry. But, over the years, there would be a continuing liability to make outward remittances which would constitute a net drain, *unless* a substantial proportion of what was produced was earmarked for export, or else helped cut down imports, which were being allowed at the time. All too often, private foreign capital wanted to set up domestic manufacture of things which were no longer being imported, either because they were considered to be not so essential, or because their indigenous production in an adequate measure had already been established. Such investment was not encouraged. Also, partly to limit the volume of outward remittances and partly on some wider policy considerations, there was a strong preference for an Indian majority in joint ventures; exceptions were made in favour of industries with strong export prospects, or where the technology that came with the investment, was of a particularly high order.

India's policy of encouraging private foreign investment on a selective basis was, in many countries, interpreted as a negative attitude towards it. Domestic concern over the possible impact of multi-nationals penetrating the Indian economy, frequently voiced in Parliament, further strengthened this impression. In Britain, there was a much clearer understanding of India's policy. Slowly, British investment in areas where India did not welcome foreign investment began to fade out, the shares being sold to Indian nationals. At the same time, in other sectors, British investment continued to expand at a pace which enabled it to retain its leadership over the inflow from other countries.

While the basic features of India's industrial policy, as enunciated by Nehru in 1956, remained unaltered, concern over the ebb and flow of the country's foreign exchange reserves and the emerging trends in foreign trade, necessitated changes in industrial priorities. In the mid-sixties, dependence on massive imports of foodgrains came

17

to be identified as one of the major factors affecting India's balance of payments adversely. In consequence, emphasis shifted from machinery manufacture to industries which helped agriculture, like fertilisers, tractors, pesticides, and pumping sets.

And then even while there was jubilation over the success of the green revolution, the hike in the price of oil began to create new pressures on India's foreign exchange reserves. Internationally, India began to be classified among the "most seriously affected countries" when the impact of the oil price hike began to be assessed.

Yet, throughout the 70s, India's foreign exchange reserves continued to improve. India's newly established industries had begun to contribute significantly to the country's foreign exchange earnings. Indian industrialists as well as some public sector agencies started setting up projects in other developing countries, using Indian machinery, equipment and technology. India's traditional exports like tea and jute manufactures, handloom cloth and hand-knitted carpets were of course there, but non-traditional products accounted for 21 per cent of the total export earnings in 1979-80 as against four per cent in 1960-61.

Yet another major earner of foreign exchange in the 70s was India's skilled manpower. Of scientific and technical personnel, India has the largest number, except for the USA and USSR. Indians working in jobs calling for the highest levels of technology, such as exploration of outer space as well as in simple construction work, were sending remittances in sufficient volume to off-set the impact of the enhancement in oil prices.

As the 70s drew to a close, India could look back with some satisfaction on three decades of industrial development. The growth record was not spectacular. But, con-

sidering that a number of wars on India's borders had led to resources being periodically diverted from development to defence, and inflationary pressures generated by droughts and crop failures had necessitated the adoption of tight fiscal and monetary measures which had slowed down investment, the overall performance could be judged to be satisfactory.

What was even more encouraging was that the rate of savings had been stepped up to well over 20 per cent — as high as the figure in many prosperous developed countries. The steady uptrend in foreign exchange reserves signified an easing of the foreign exchange constraint and made it possible for a larger number of key industrial raw materials to be placed on the Open General Licence.

Unfortunately, the oil price increases at the end of the 70s have once again tipped the scale, causing a drain on India's foreign exchange reserves. To tide over the immediate balance of payments difficulties, India has successfully negotiated for the largest ever loan from the International Monetary Fund. In the long run, the newly discovered reserves of oil should, in the mid-80s, result in a sizeable decrease in the volume of oil imports.

One can, therefore, say that India is poised for an accelerated rate of growth in the 80s. Much of the resources needed for the purpose can be generated and mobilised within the country. But external co-operation will also be needed. While external finance has accounted for well below 10 per cent of the totality of resources deployed in India's developmental plans, its contribution has been qualitatively most significant. Britain's co-operation in India's industrial progress is likely to be strengthened in the 80s.

MUSIC: CARNATIC AND HINDUSTANI– THE TWO PHASES

V K Narayana Menon

Carnatic music is the music created, performed and heard all over south India, just as Hindustani music can be equated with the music of the north. The fusion of Aryan and Dravidian elements and the cultural pattern it set gave to the music of the south a consciousness of its own within the broad framework of the Indian concepts.

That the music of India is the product of an ancient and sophisticated tradition is now common knowledge. Neither age nor a sophisticated past necessarily makes the current phase of a tradition a distinguished one. What makes the current phase meaningful is the continuity of the tradition. Few major traditions of music have had such an unbroken history of growth and development. Take for instance, the Vedic period, coeval with the High Civilisation of Egypt. Vedic texts are still recited in India, not just mechanically as something from the past, but with an awareness of its relevance to us today, as a living force. I am told that in Egypt, no Egyptian, priest or layman, knows of the prayers spoken in Pharaonic temples. This is not just the linear continuity of an unchanging tradition. It means a continuum of growth and refinement in which intuition and reason meet. It represents the distilled essence of many phases of knowledge and wisdom, renewing itself all the time and revitalising itself in the process, interlinking feelings and experiences of all kinds.

There is a popular misconception that this represents with all its sophistication, an unchanging way of life and thought. This is nonsense. It really represents four millennia of struggle and growth during which dynasties rose, declined and fell; religious faiths were accepted, absorbed and set aside; various schools of philosophy provided intellectual speculation of the highest sophistication to the mind; architecture and sculpture, music and the dance flourished in abundant measure. There have been, and there still are, islands of orthodoxy and primitive narrow concepts; and there have been periods of war and pestilence, despair alternating with triumph. But through it all runs a thread of continuity with a recognisable identity.

In the course of a speech given in Bombay in 1980, Mrs Indira Gandhi said: "Aren't all aspects of life...interlinked? Neither life nor an individual can be divided into compartments. Each part opens out to the other, and many overlap." In the Indian context we see this at all levels. A French visitor to India said: "(India) arouses in me, in a quite metaphysical manner, a profound current of religiosity. The manner in which these people embody their myths, their rites, their religion in dance, music, rhythm, colours, perfume, and involve their body in it, in a kind of solemn and vigorous exuberance, gives me the idea of a sort of mutual dialectical exaltation between matter and mind. Here, the body is lived intellectually, and the spirit physically."

An ancient tradition like this creates a sense of spiritual and physical well-being. It constitutes a renewal of the past in the present, a way of recalling the origins — whether mythical or historical — of the community of man. Current studies, as Professor Kwabena N'ketia has pointed out, have demonstrated that a careful analysis of sound... can reveal cultural patterns, social values, national identities. Music, particularly the highly developed systems of ancient civilisations, has interdisciplinary values built into it. Included in interdisciplinary emanations are "creative expressions in such movement, sound, in verbal and visual media iden-

A black stone Krishna playing the flute, Chola period, south India.

21

Musical instruments used in Carnatic and Hindustani music.
1. EK-TARA (or Khamak or Gopichand) - 20th century, Bengal (top left); MELLER EKTARA - late 17th century, Telengana, Andhra Pradesh (top right); DO-TARA - 1925 Punjab (bottom left); and SARANGI-LIKE INSTRUMENT - 19th century, Kalimpong, West Bengal (bottom right).
2. (clockwise from top): PANCHGHANTA (five bells) -16th century, Maharashtra; WAIST DRUM - Darjeeling, Bengal; CYMBALS; BELLS -18th century, Bundelkhand, Madhya Pradesh; GHUNGRU - 20th century, Madhya Pradesh; KARTAL - 18th century, Saurashtra, Gujarat; and JHEEKA - 20th century, Madhya Pradesh.
3. KHOL - 20th century, Bengal (left); and DHOL -circa 1800, Chingleput, Tamil Nadu (right).
4. SANTOOR - 18th century instrument belonging to a family of renowned santoor players from Kashmir.
5. SAROD
6. SARASWATI VEENA -19th century, Utter Pradesh.
7. (clockwise from left): SHEHNAI - circa 1800, Kalimpong, Bengal; NAGASWARAM - circa 1800, Chingleput, Tamil Nadu; NAGAPHANI - 17th century, Gujarat; KHANGLING - 19th century, Kalimpong, Bengal; NAYA TODI - 20th century, Bastar, Madhya Pradesh; and SILVER FLUTE - 18th century, north India.
8. DAKSHINAVARTA SANKHA - right sided conch shell with clockwise spiral, south India.

Photos courtesy of Namaste -the Welcomgroup Magazine.

2

3

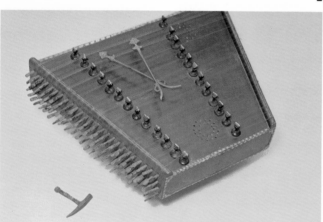

4

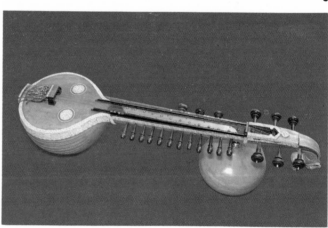

5

6

7

8

tified with individuals, social groups and communities sharing common beliefs and common values."

The early concepts of music gave it a special, a unique character, and a power greater than we credit it with today. In Greek, *mousike* was used for all the arts of the Nine Muses. Musical education, for the Greeks, included the study of mathematics and of astronomy, of literature, and of the other arts. Music was valued as an important element in the formation of character. Relatively little attention was paid to such things as aesthetics. Our own concept of music was not dissimilar. And it is best illustrated by the well-known story of the king who wanted to study sculpture:

A king asked a great sage to teach him how to make sculptures of the gods. The sage replied, "Someone who does not know the laws of painting can never understand the laws of sculpture." "Then," said the king, "be so kind as to teach me the laws of painting." The sage replied. "It is difficult to understand the laws of painting without understanding the technique of dancing." "Then?" "This is difficult to understand without a thorough knowledge of the principles of instrumental music." "Please teach me the principles of instrumental music." "But," said the sage, "these cannot be learnt without a deep understanding of the art of vocal music." The king bowed in acceptance. "If vocal music is the source and goal of all the arts, please then reveal to me the laws of vocal music."

This story is the classic illustration of the unity of the arts and the central position occupied by music. Wasn't it Pater who said that all the arts aspire to the condition of music?

The word *sangita* meant more than music in the narrow sense we understand it today. It implied a close relationship to the dance and to the theatre. The line of demarcation between music and dance, dance and drama, ritual and art was a thin one. Every traditional dramatic performance had something of the character of what we would today describe as dance-drama. Every *nata* had to be, and in fact was, an actor, dancer and *musician* like in *Koodiyattam* even today.

Well before the second millennium BC, that is, even before the advent of the Aryans, India had a high civilisation of its own, usually and popularly described as Dravidian. We have evidence of an even earlier state of culture than the Dravidian. What we now call the classical civilisation of India is a fusion of Dravidian and Aryan culture, a fusion which took centuries to achieve and which was by no means a smooth or easy one. To start with, the advent of the Aryans "meant a severe cultural decline, which lasted for many centuries. Only when Aryan culture was fertilised by the indigenous culture did it begin to advance to form the classical civilisation of India." Culturally speaking, it was like "the victory of the conquered over the conquerors."

The inter-action of the symbolic and representative, of the abstract and the explicit in language and thought, of Aryan affecting Dravidian modes of expression and vice-versa, are seen again and again in the music that has come into being as a result of this fusion. The *Dattilam* and the *Natya Shastra* treat Indian music as one entity. Definitions, concepts, descriptions are applicable both to the North and the South.

But within the framework of this fusion and the cultural pattern it set, there are quite discernible colourations which give Southern creativity, particularly in literature and music, a consciousness of its own. Language must have played a significant role in this context. Words and music have a special relationship, particularly in music which is vocal in character. Words affect the melodic line, even the rhythmic structures. The inflections of a language leave their imprint on melody and rhythm, on style and phrasing. We know of the immense richness of Tamil classics, dating back to the pre-Christian era, of the many epics, "anthologies" of lyrics, long poems, of the wealth and beauty of Sangham literature, all of which represent the consciousness of a community independent of the mainstream of the Aryan cultural pattern, and fully aware of the difference.

The Dravidian sphere of influence, as early as the third century BC, stretched right across the Deccan from east to west and down to Kanyakumari and spilling into Sri Lanka. There was the Andhra Empire in the north, the powerful Pandyan Kingdom to the south. Trade flourished. So did the arts. There is evidence of a high level of poetry, drama and music. This is the area which nurtured Carnatic music and gave it sustenance. The colourful interaction of poetry and music was important and meaningful. Cross-references are significant. Even a work like *Tolkappiyam (circa* second century BC), one of the oldest classics, which is really a grammar of Tamil, has references to music which give us valuable information of the state of the art. Other classics, which use Tamil phraseology, describe instruments, melodies, musical theory and practices. The Sangham literature is full of it.

In the middle of it all, stand out one or two works which give us clear and detailed pictures of contemporary dancing and music. *Silappadikaram* by Ilango Adigal is a moving story, an epic or a "romance" whatever we prefer to call it, in verse interspersed with prose.

It was composed towards the end of the second century AD or the beginning of the third century. Ilango was a Jain and the brother of King Shenguttuvan of the Cera dynasty who ruled over the western coast of southern India. One of the key characters in the story is the beautiful courtesan Madhavi, a fine musician and dancer, and in Ilango's descriptions of her performances we get a clear picture of music and dancing as practised in his day:

"Madhavi's music teacher was an expert performer on the harp and the flute. He could vocalise and could draw from the drums well-rounded sounds, mellow and deep. He could adapt the music to the dance, and understood which style best suited each technique of expression. He had a profound knowledge of the subtle intricacies of the classical melodies, yet he could invent new variations. He taught the various styles of dance and of music, and brought out the most subtle shades of the composer's intentions....

"The young drummer who accompanies Madhavi...was familiar with all the types of dance, musical notation and singing. He knew prosody, modes and rhythms, the blend of beats and counterbeats, and the defects that may arise from their contrast. He was well-acquainted with popular tunes, and he could firmly establish the required rhythm patterns on his drum, using an artful double-stroke to mark important beats. He intertwined his rhythmic fantasies with the plucking of the lute, the lament of the flute, and the soft accents of the songs. He controlled the voice of his drum so that the more delicate instruments could be heard, though, at proper times, he would drown out all music under a deafening thunder of brilliant strokes.

"The flute player of the group was also a scholar who knew all the rules of diction and the way hard consonants are softened to please the ear. He knew four kinds of thrills, possessed the science of modes and adjusted his pitch to the deep sound of the *malavu* timbal. He took care that the drums be tuned to the fifth note of the flutes. He artfully followed the singers, improvising new variations within the bounds of modal forms, and showed his art of melody by setting off each note so that it might be clearly distinguished.

"Then there was the harp master who played a 14 stringed instrument. To establish the mode *(palai)*, he first plucked the two central strings which gave the tonic *(kural)* and the octave *(taram)*. From these, he tuned the third *(kaikkilai)*, then the low strings from the octave and the high strings from the tonic. After tuning the sixth *(vilari)*, he played all the 14 strings, showing all the notes of the mode from the low fourth *(ulai)* to the high third *(kaikkilai)*. The sequences that form the modes appeared in succession. Starting from the third, the scale of the mode *(palai)* known as *Padumalai* was obtained. From the second *(tuttam)*, he started the *Shevali* mode, from seventh *(taram)* the *Kodi* mode, from the sixth *(vilari)* the *Vilari* mode, and from the fifth *(ili)* the *Mershem* mode. Thus the various groups of intervals were arranged. On the harp, the low sounds are to the left. It is the opposite with flutes. A good harp player is able to bend low and high tones with medium ones in a manner pleasing to hear..."

Madhavi herself was an accomplished performer on the "harp":

"Madhavi then carefully followed the eight rules of perfect music: the tuning of the instrument *(pannal)*, the caress of the strings to indicate the mode *(parivattani)*, the exact pitch of each note *(araidal)*, the duration of the pauses *(taivaral)*, the grave adagio *(shelavri)*, the easy blend of the words of the song *(vilaivattu)*, the sentiment *(kaivul)* and the elegant design of the vocalisation *(kurumpokku)*.

"Her fingers, wandering on the strings with plectra carved in emeralds, evoked a buzzing swarm of bees when she practised the eight ways of touching instruments: the isolated pluck *(vardal)*, the caress *(vadittal)*, the hard stroke to bring out the resonance *(undal)*, the presentation of a theme *(uruttal)*, the pull of the string to reach the note from above *(teruttal)*, the chords *(allal)* and arpeggois *(pattadai)*."

These passages are clear, lucid statements on music, musical instruments, styles of playing, subtleties of tuning, finesse in performance that the academic scholarly treatises hardly ever provide. I doubt if there is any literature which describes musical theory and practice with such consummate skill, in language so clear, so meaningful, so communicative as passages in the *Silappadikaram* written about 1,700 years ago, and what is unique, of such relevance to us even today.

In the straight and narrow path of Indian musical history, most historians of music take the *Natya Shastra*, the *Brhaddeshi* and the *Sangita Ratnakara* as the most important landmarks till the mediaeval period, as in fact they are. From the *Natya Shastra* to the *Brhaddeshi* is a jump of several centuries. The *Natya Shastra* deals with *jati*-s, but makes no mention of *raga*-s. The *Brhaddeshi* does. Now we are in the ninth century. What do we know of the intervening period? Relatively little. Most of the texts paid lip-service to the *Natya Shastra*. Few, if any, dared question the authority of Bharata or deviate from the monumental *Natya Shastra*. There are, however, links between the *Natya*

Shastra and *Brhaddeshi*, and vital and meaningful links. One is the *Naradiya-Shiksha (circa* fifth century AD). The other; the Kudumiyamalai Inscriptions *(circa* seventh century AD).

The Kudumiyamalai Inscriptions are on a flat rocky surface in the old native state of Pudukkottai in Tamil Nadu. The inscriptions are spread over an area of approximately 16 square metres. They describe seven *grama-raga*-s which are the link between the *jati*-s of the *Natya Shastra* and the *raga*-s of the *Brhaddeshi*.

This inscription is important because it shows that even in the extreme south of India, as late as the seventh century, musical concepts were a shared heritage. It must be remembered that the Kudumiyamalai Inscriptions were probably the result of the enthusiasm of Mahendra Varma Pallava who was a key figure in the cultural achievements of the Pallavas — another example of Dravidian creativity co-existing with the mainstream of the national tradition. The *Manasollasa* or *Abhilasartha Chintamani* by Someshvara is really an encyclopaedia, though he is also credited with the authorship of a book on music, *Sangita-Ratnavali*, which we cannot trace today. Prince Someshvara was a scion of the Chalukya dynasty and the encyclopaedia which was completed about 1131 AD has two chapters devoted to music. Incidentally, Someshvara was important enough to be referred to as an authority by Sarangadeva in *Sangita Ratnakara*. What is interesting to us is that among the *raga*-s he describes are *Karnata-Varati* which could well be an indication of the "colouration" of these *raga*-s as Carnatic, and the first use of the term Carnatic for music of the South.

And so we come to perhaps the most important work on music in the mediaeval period — Sarangadeva's *Sangita Ratnakara*. Sarangadeva was a Kashmiri. His father immigrated to the South and worked at Devagiri. Sarangadeva was a scholar with a passion for music. Living and working in the South (1210-1247 AD), it is inevitable that his work, while aware of the Northern and the Southern currents, formulates the basis of Carnatic music. The *Sangita Ratnakara* can be described as the first source book for Carnatic music as we understand it today.

In the action and interaction of musical theories and practices, as expounded and practised from Kashmir and Nepal to Kanyakumari, we see two streams emerging even from as early as the seventh century. The line of development of Hindustani music (apart from the *Natya Shastra* and the *Brhaddeshi* which should be considered as part of the common heritage) would seem via the *Sangita Makarand* (seventh to ninth century), the *Sangita-Ratnamala (circa* ninth to 11th century), the *Abhilashartha Chintamani* (12th century AD), the *Ragarnava* (early 14th century), the *Raga Sagara (circa* 14th century); and from then on, the path is clear. The story of Carnatic music would seem to develop along the *Sangita Ratnakara* (13th century), the *Sangita Sara* of Vidyaranya *(circa* 1330 AD), the *Raga Tarangini* of Lochana Kavi *(circa* 1375 AD), the *Swaramela-Kalanidhi* of Ramamatya *(circa* 1550 AD), the *Ragavivodha* of Somanatha (1609 AD), the *Sangita Sudha* of Govinda Dikshita *(circa* 1614-1640 AD), the *Chaturdandi Prakashika* of Venkatamakhin, the *Sangita Saramrita* of Tulaji *(circa* 1770 AD).

The study of the development of music, of practically all musical systems that we know of, is based on the treatises, the books *about* the music, that have come down to us. They represent codifications of the knowledge we have about the music up to the period of writing. India is particularly rich in such works. In fact, the early literature on Indian music is sizeable enough to make a small library of its own.

It is only in recent times that we have begun the study of music in terms of the works of major creative figures in any system. Notation and documentation have made it possible for us to understand and reconstruct the works of masters reasonably accurately. By notation I do not mean staff notation as used in Western music today, but the many ways by which the shapes of melodies and rhythms have been preserved accurately for posterity in the advanced systems of music in East Asia, West Asia and countries like India. The popular misconception that Indian music has no notation and that Indian music cannot be written down is something that is being perpetuated by "musicologists" with insufficient knowledge of music or musical history, Eastern or Western. Few people realise that even staff notation as we know it today was not complete in all its details till the 18th century.

By the 15th century, Carnatic music had "composers" in the sense we understand the word today, of whose works we have reasonably clear and accurate records. Many of them should be described as vaggeyakara-s — composers of songs who were responsible both for the sahitya, the words and the music. Others have composed varna-s which are in the nature of etudes, studies of raga-s, tana varna-s and pada varna-s — concert pieces and dance pieces. There are other forms — tillana-s, jatiswaram-s, swarajati-s, ballad operas, music for dancing, Harikatha-s. These are finished compositions, not just skeletal melodies on which a great singer or instrumentalist could improvise. They are compositions with definite forms, in raga-s and tala-s appropriate to the mood and the character of the works. They can be studied, analysed, taught, written down and published in book form, using Indian notation. The notation is complete and accurate enough for musicians to be able to study the piece for performance purposes. The entire available works of composers like Thyagaraja, Dikshitar, Syama Sastri, Swati Tirunal are available in Indian notation in any music shop in the South.

This is an aspect of Carnatic music which is important and there is no exact equivalent of this in Hindustani music. One of the earliest and most important of such composers is Annamacharya (1424-1503) who can be described as the father of the kriti with its pallavianupallavi-charanam form.

About half a century after Annamacharya was born, Carnatic music saw the birth of Purandaradasa (1480-1564), one of its greatest creative and innovative figures. He is known as the Pitamaha of Carnatic music because, apart from being a great composer, he also put the teaching of music on a consistent and scientific basis.

The 17th century is the century of Kshetragna. The pada, the Carnatic form that has been immortalised in both song and dance, is the great gift of Kshetragna to us. There were others like Arunachala Kavi (1731-1778); Panchimirium Adiappier, the composer of the great Viriboni Varna; Pallavi Gopalier, the creator of the classic Kalyani and Todi Ata tala varna-s.

And so we come towards the end of the 18th century, the beginning of an era which saw the full flowering of the Carnatic spirit in the works of Syama Sastri, Thyagaraja and Dikshitar.

Syama Sastri (1763-1827) was the oldest. Relatively few of his works have come down to us — about 50 only, which in-

clude a few swarajati-s, which are rare examples of this genre. As for his other works, rarely do we come across a marriage of words and music so truly and subtly matched.

Thyagaraja (1767-1847) occupies a unique position in Carnatic music. Few, if any, in the history of music seem to have been able to transmute into a musical language with such effect, the simplicity of faith, the ecstasy of a prayer granted and, above all, a feeling of the imminence of God.

If Syama Sastri was the most lyrical of the trinity, with a penchant for subtleties of laya, rhythm, and Thyagaraja the most abundant of the three, with the widest range of passion and invention, then Muthuswami Dikshitar (1775-1835) was the intellectual, the grammarian, and yet, in musical taste, showing much catholicity.

Let us now examine some of the more identifiable characteristics of Carnatic music. First of all, the classification of raga-s. As far as Carnatic music is concerned, the Chaturdandi Prakashika (circa 1660 AD) of Venkatamakhi is the basis of its current classification. The work was an attempt to classify the entire repertoire of Carnatic raga-s known in Venkatamakhi's time on a rational and scientific basis. It is Venkatamakhi's formulation of the Melakarta scheme that gives it a very special position in the development of Carnatic music.

There have been debates about the melakarta formulation ever since it came into being. Is a mela a raga?* Is it just the skeletal aspect of a raga? Is it a dehumanised raga without any hint of the swarupa, the bhava, that makes a scale into a raga? The debate will go on. Venkatamakhi himself said of the melakarta system. "... I have designed it as a honeycomb cabinet to provide a niche for all raga-s past, present and future..." Suffice to say that Venkatamakhi was the chief architect of a formulation which gave Carnatic music a framework for its raga classification.

Next, the organisation and the classification of tala-s. There are seven basic tala-s — Eka, Roopaka, Triputa, Matya, Jhampa, Ata, Dhruva. The component parts of all these tala-s are Anudruta, Druta and Laghu. Anudruta stands for a beat; Laghu for a beat + finger counts; and Druta for a beat and a rest (khali in Hindustani terminology).

There is another aspect of tala which is very important in Carnatic music — kala pramana. Kala pramana implies two things. One is the choice of the correct tempo for every piece. The other is the maintenance of a strict tempo for the duration of the piece whether a short kriti or a long complex pallavi. There is no room for the kind of accelerando that we get in Hindustani music, particularly instrumental music, which has its own charm.

The classification of our raga-s, and the organisation of our tala-s, show both the likeness of the two systems and their points of divergence. There are, however, other concepts which are shared, but not necessarily stressed or used in the same way. Take for instance, the terms raga-s and ragini-s. The word ragini does not appear in Brihaddeshi. Carnatic music knows what the terms imply, but does not deal with them with any conviction. Or again, take the time

*Over 200 years after the creation of the Chaturdandi Prakashika, Maha Vaidynatha Ayyar composed a ragamalika covering the 72 melakarto-s. And in our own time the Veena virtuoso, Shri S Balachander has performed and recorded the entire 72 melakarta-s treating them as full-fledged raga-s.

theory. Matanga does not say anything about this. Neither does Sarangadeva. But the convention has caught on in the North and is respected, but not in Carnatic music. One gets the impression that Carnatic music, on the whole, is concerned more with rational and tested concepts. Is it because the tradition has had a more homogeneous growth? Perhaps, if the North has gone often by intuition and philosophic speculation, there are historical and sociological reasons for it. To my Southern mind, Carnatic music has a restrained, and in some respects an intellectual character in comparison with Hindustani music today, which is more secular and hence, emotional.

In the final analysis, however, Carnatic and Hindustani music would appear like two facets of the truth of Indian music. The further we travel back in time, the closer the two systems seem to get; the more we go forward, the greater would seem the differentiation in styles. We have to search for values inherent in the two streams of growth and development right through recorded history so as to establish meaningful links between the two. Sarangadeva (13th century) was a Kashmiri who went down South and made his home there. The *Sangita Ratnakara* thus would seem to take in a whole range of known and tested evidence and concepts in music in his day. Kallinatha (15th century) lived in Vijayanagar. Ramamatya (16th century) also lived in Vijayanagar for some years. Pundarika Vitthala, Somanatha, Ahobala all lived and worked in areas that can be described as the northern fringes of areas where Carnatic music was prevalent.

They had a kind of "bi-lingual", "bi-musical" background and what they had to say has a special significance for us. These names are not *nom de plumes* of people about whom we know little, but real people of whose life and career and interests we have authentic knowledge. What they had to say are thus reasonably accurate accounts of the practices current in their time. We have here opportunities to compare and contrast. This is the kind of exploration which we should launch so as to understand why particular concepts and attitudes should develop as they did, why there are meaningful divergences which make sense in particular situations. Theories are only the truths which came out of practices, not the other way round.

Today, sad as it may seem, even a trained Hindustani musician is often lost when listening to Carnatic music and vice-versa. It is true that he can be put on the right path to appreciation easily and quickly. But there is hesitancy, slight distrust, misconception, even a slight superiority complex on either side.

There is an old saying: "The great heart in another peoples' music rarely beats in unison with our own." There is a basic truth here but when we think of India, North and South, and how much we have in common — concepts, myths, symbols — and above all, a heightened meaningful interdependence, I wonder if our minor reservations and gentle distrust are not the result of narrow-minded contentment and, quite often, the inertia of deep rooted habits.

As I said earlier, Hindustani and Carnatic music are only two facets of the truth that is Indian music. If we accept this, we can not only see our two systems in their true perspective, but help us improve our sensibilities, our perceptions, and widen our horizons.

27

FOLK AND CLASSICAL DANCES

Kapila Vatsyayan

For untold centuries India, with its vast variety of ethnic groups, races and cultural groups, has been a veritable treasure house of dance and music.

The contemporary Indian classical dance forms which are governed by elaborate technique and stylised systems of both pure movement and "mime" have had their origins in the dances of the common people. This many-hued garden of dances has not only survived as a vestige of the past, but continues to have the inner vigour and vitality to influence and shape more sophisticated and self-conscious art forms. Thus, the folk and classical forms in India are not mutually exclusive: they are in continual dialogue. The classical forms occasionally provide the thematic content and gravity to folk forms: the folk forms provide the freshness, strength and buoyancy to modern forms

There is not a region, a valley or mountain, a sea-coast or a plain, which does not have its characteristic folk dances and songs. From Kashmir in the north to Kanya Kumari in the south, from Saurashtra and Maharashtra in the west to Manipur and Assam in the east, each region, district and community has its particular folk music and dance. Roughly speaking, depending on the level of social and cultural development, these dances can be grouped under the three categories of tribal, village folk community and traditional ritual dances

The themes of the dances are simple but not naive; sometimes they revolve around the daily tasks on the field of sowing and reaping the harvest, of pounding rice, of weaving textiles, of catching birds and insects: at others they celebrate victory in war or success in a hunt: and at yet others it is the abstract movement of an actual ritual performed to propitiate the gods, or dances which may have a magical import. Finally there are the community dances for all seasons and festivals when men and women dance for sheer joy to celebrate spring, the rains, autumn and winter. Men and women and children all dance; there is no cleavage between performers and audience: everyone is a participator, a creator. There is no entertainer, only entertainment.

Nature has silently and unobtrusively fashioned the movements of the dance, as it has the lives of the people who live in continual communion with it. The Himalayan mountainous ranges extend over a large area in India; all the dances of the mountains have something in common, whether they come from Kashmir, Himachal Pradesh or Uttar Pradesh or Darjeeling. The bend of the knees, the long swaying movements, the inter-twined arms recreate the undulating ranges of the Himalayas. The agitated movements and abrupt changes of posture in the otherwise flowing lyrical movements of the eastern region, particularly Assam and Manipur, speak of sudden storm and uprooting of trees. The tense and watchful and carefully choreographed attitudes in the dancing of the Nagas of NEFA (North East Frontier Agency), Meghalaya, Manipur and Assam denote the unknown perils of the jungle. The dances of the fishermen of Saurashtra suggest the roaring waves of the sea while the folk dances of the plains present a different picture of colour and rhythm by contrast.

Folk dances of particular regions of India have both a regional autonomy and features which are common to other regions of India — while the ecology, environment and agricultural functions give a distinctiveness; legend, myth, literature unite them to other parts. The dances have survived through many centuries of Indian history and have pro-

Friezes from the temple at Chidambaram in Tamil Nadu, south India, top left and far left, bear testimony to the link with antiquity.
Left: Angami Naga dancers.

Below left: The Wangala dance from Meghalaya, north-east India.
Centre left: A dance of the Mathuris of Adilabad in Andhra Pradesh. They claim descent from the line of the Rajput king, Prithviraj Chauhan.
Bottom left: Famous for their vigour and vivacity are the dances of the Ho's from Bihar.
Below right: The Bamboo dance from Mizoram, in the extreme east of India.
Centre right: The virile agricultural dance from Punjab, the Bhangra - full of vigour and vitality, it includes some highly complex acrobatic movements.
Bottom right: Against the backdrop of a temple, a Bharatanatyam dance in the "matsya" (fish) pose. Its sophistication and stylisation make Bharatanatyam a unique form of art-dance.

vided a continuity to the Indian tradition which is not stagnant, as it is constantly adapting itself to new conditions and assimilating influences. Pliability and flexibility is of essence: scope for self-expression, improvisation, is the secret of its survival.

As has been mentioned above, all these dances in their staggering multiplicity can be divided into the dances of the tribal rural communities of India. A tribal belt runs through all parts of India, be it the Himalayas from the north to the east; or the plains and marshlands or the sea-coasts. All these varied groups comprising many racial and ethnic strands ranging from the Austric to the Mongoloid, from the Aryans to the Dravidians, are people who represent the pre-agricultural state of civilisation. While most of them have taken to agriculture and tool cultivation today, their dances and music continue to recall the functions of hunting, fishing, food gathering and animal husbandry. A whole group amongst these several hundred tribes is known by the generic term Nagas. They constitute the Zeliangs, the Maos, the Tankhuls, the Ao's, the Mizos, the Dagles, the Garos and many others. Their dances revolve around the "hunt" and its many ceremonies and rituals.

Some of these are closely related to similar dances in Thailand, Burma, Philippines and other parts of Asia. One amongst these is of special relevance as a Pan-Asian dance. In India, it is performed largely by the Mizos and is called the Bamboo dance. Perhaps, originally the dance was performed as part of the death ceremonies; today it is purely secular. Here, four long bamboo poles are placed across one another. The square thus formed is opened and closed with the beat of the drums by men who sit near the ends of the poles. The dancer hops on one foot outside the cross when it is closed and inside when it is open. The dance becomes more intricate when two or more persons dance together to the bamboo pole clapping and the fast tempo of the accompanying drum. This requires practice. Today the dance is very popular in the whole region and is being practised in schools and colleges.

In deep contrast to these dances of men and women dancing in straight erect postures with nothing but drumming or vocal music as accompaniment, are the dances of the tribes of the plains and the marshlands. The richest amongst these are the dances of the Ho's and Oraons of Bihar, the Marias of Bastar in Madhya Pradesh and the Santhals of Bengal. Kaksar is a typical festival dance performed by the Abhujmarias before reaping a harvest. First the deity is worshipped and then the dance is performed. The men appear fairly attired with a belt of bells around their waists: so do the women, in short brief saris, but richly bejewelled. The dance provides the occasion for choosing life partners: the marriage or marriages which so emerge are enthusiastically celebrated. The rhythms are complex, the choreographical patterns varied. The bell-belts of the men dancers and the jewels of the women add to the variety of rhythmical patterns of the dance. The instruments used are *dhol* (cylindrical drum), *timiki* (bowl-shaped percussion instruments) and *bansuri* (a kind of flute).

Close to lush marshlands of Madhya Pradesh and yet very different, are the tribes of Bihar. Amongst these the Ho's and Oraons are rightly famous for their vigour and vivacity. Dance and rhythm runs through the veins of the Oraons of Bihar. Men and women vie with each other in creating choreographical patterns of extreme complexity and intricacy. Jadur and Karma dancers of the Oraons celebrate a series of festivals, which start in March, April and end in June. All these dances are essentially harvest dances meant as a prayer for the betterment of the crop. These dances are also an abstraction of the everyday agricultural operations of the people. The dancers are usually graceful and the dances have a very well defined structure. To just a few notes at close intervals, the melody is sung and danced in slow tempo. Men and women form separate rows, interlocking patterns of the arms and the legs are intricate, and gradually the tempo builds to a frenzied climax. The musical instruments consist of *nagara* (bowl-shaped drum), *kartal* (clappers) and *khetchka* (wooden clappers). The leader holds a staff of peacock feathers and the drummers (medal players) join the dance at various points.

Migrations from one part of India to another were common in India. One such migration seems to have taken place hundreds of years ago of a group of people from north India to Andhra Pradesh in the south. The Mathuris claim their descent from the line of the northern Raja Prithvisingh Chauhan. Today they are settled mostly in the Adilabad district of the Deccan. They celebrate festivals through dances, chiefly Holi (the spring festival) and festivals revolving around the life of God Krishna. The Mathuris dance two favourite numbers, the Lengi Ka Natch and Lingi. The musical instruments mainly consist of drums and *jhanjs* (the brass plates) which create a clanging sound.

From the northern Himalayas region come many dances which belong to the village communities. Himachal and northern Uttar Pradesh is the home of many interesting and colourful dances. Two popular favourites come from Jaunsar Bavar in Uttar Pradesh. The festival of lights called Diwali is celebrated throughout India at the end of autumn. On a dark night lights are lit and presents are exchanged. This is also the time for the home-coming of married women. The dance begins with semi-circular formations: it breaks into single files of men and women: the song which accompanies is usually set as questions and answers. With gliding movements, graceful knee dips, the dance progresses, until one or two amongst the women proceed to the centre to rotate discs on their fingers or sometimes pitchers full of water turned upside down over their heads. So perfect is the balance that not a drop of water trickles out of the pitchers.

The musical instruments resemble those used by the dancers of Himachal Pradesh, comprising *narshingha* (a large trumpet), brass bells, barrel-shaped percussion instruments and bowl-shaped drums.

In the Punjab, a virile agricultural dance called the Bhangra is popular and is closely linked with the ritual importance which is given to wheat. After the wheat crop is sown, the young men gather together in an open field under the light of the full moon in answer to the beat of the drum. The dancers begin to move in a circle, so that as many newcomers who wish to join can do so without breaking its continuity. The circle goes on widening until a large open circle is formed with the drummer as the leader. The leader, with a large drum hung in front, stands in the centre and plays the *dholak* (drum) with sticks. The dancers first begin with a slow rhythm, with an abrupt jerky movement of the shoulders and a hop-step: this is followed by many vigorous movements of the whole body and the raising of both hands to the shoulder or above the head level. After the circle has been well established and the tempo of the dance has accelerated, the two main dancers dance within the ring in a

Below: Orissi evolved from the dances of the temples of Orissa. The sculptures of the Nat Mandap (Hall of Dance) at the Sun Temple in Konarak evoke the beauty of this dance.
Bottom left: The Rasa dance, lyrical, graceful, from Manipur. The classical repertoire revolves largely round the theme of the god Krishna, Radha, and the gopis (milkmaids).

Bottom right: Sankirtanas, another classical dance from Manipur. Performed generally by men, it has intricate rhythmic patterns and calls for vigourous masculine technique.

kind of duet. This is followed by pairs emerging from different sections of the circle, dancing in the central area and returning to their respective places in the circle. The pair of dancers can execute many variations, ranging from graceful to virile movements, circles, pirouettes, jump and extensions of legs, jumps and leaps. A skilled Bhangra dancer may even perform some highly complex acrobatic movement with the torso touching the floor, through a spinal back-bend or letting another dancer stand on his shoulders, while he dances on his knees. Since there are no rigorous rules of the Bhangra, it leaves an overwhelming impression of fresh spontaneous vigour and vitality. Its movements are nevertheless characteristic of the masculinity of the Punjabi and cannot be mistaken for anything else.

Further north in Kashmir, the occasions of the dance are many. Men, women lie in the lap of snow-clad mountains throughout winter, spring brings new life and a reawakening. Rouf is a typical dance of the women at springtime with across interlocked separate rows made, and each singing a different line of the song, almost as a question and answer. The steps are light moving backwards and forwards with slight swings and sways. The composition is charming for its simplicity and spontaneity.

This is but a sampling of the vast store-house of tribal and folk-dances of the Indian subcontinent. From these have emerged the varied classical traditions of Indian music and dance

Five dance styles are known as classical or art-dance on account of a sophisticated degree of stylisation. The history of these forms cannot be traced backwards beyond two hundred, sometimes three hundred years, when considered from the point of view of their present format. Nevertheless, each has a link with antiquity, with the literature, sculptural and musical traditions of the ancient and medieval period of India and the particular region. They all adhere to the principles ennunciated by Bharata, namely of the division of dance into *nrtta* (pure or abstract dance), *nrtya* (dance with mime), of *tandava* and *lasya* of stylised presentation *(natayadharmi)*. However, the technique of movement is distinctive, with a definite stylisation. Each follows a different set of rules for the articulation of movement. Musical accompaniment invariably comprises a vocalist; a drummer either on the double barrelled drum (called *mridanga, madalam, pakhavaj)* or the two drums *(tabla)*; a cymbal player who recites the neumonics; there is usually one more instrumentalist of string instruments, bowed or plucked. *Bharatanatyam* developed in south India in its present form about two hundred years ago. While its poses are reminiscent of sculpture of the 10th century onwards, the thematic and musical content was given to it by musicians of the Tanjore courts of the 18th - 19th centuries. It is essentially a solo dance and has close affinities with the traditional dance-drama form called Bhagvata Mela performed only by men, and folk operettas called Kuruvanji's performed only by women; nonetheless, its chiselled sophistication and stylisation make it a unique form of art-dance. A body of technique is developed from the fundamental position of the out-turned thighs, the flexed knees and out-turned feet close together, all akin to a demiplie foot contacts, of the whole foot, toe, heel. Toe-heel combinations are all utilised but with this basic stance. Exceptions are limited to two or three sequences with an erect posture. The torso is used as one unit, without being broken up into upper chest and lower waist. Straight lines, diagonals, triangles are basic

motifs for executing movements and in floor choreography. Compositions of Carnatic music provide the repertory. The recital begins with a number which is danced to abstract neumonics called Allarippu. It is followed by another number of pure dance performed to the musical composition *Jatisvaram*. Notes of the melodic line set to a tala are interpreted through the dancer's movements. A number called *Shabdam* introduces mime for the first time: *Varnam* comes next. This is easily the most difficult, intricate and challenging number. The dancer follows closely the streamlining of the musical composition comprising three phases of the *pallavi, anupallavi* and *charanam.* Each line is interpreted in mime prefixed and suffixed by passages of pure dance performed to neumonics and the melodic line. The third phase *Charanam* works up to a crescendo where the melodic line is sung by the vocalist in its solfa passages first and then followed by the singing of the words of the poetic line on the same melodic line. The dancer interprets both. The recital concludes with the *Tillana*, also a pure dance number. In between there are lyrical compositions called *padams* to which mime *(nrtya)* is performed.

Orissi is a close parallel of Bharatanatyam. It developed from the musical play *(Sangita, Nataka)* and the dances of gymnasiums known as the *akharas.* Sculptural evidence relating to the dance goes to the second century BC. From the 12th century onwards there are inscriptions/manuscripts and other records which speak of the prevalence of dance styles of ritual dances of temples and entertainments of the village squares. A 12th century poetic work called *Gita Govinda* has dominated the poetic and musical content of the dance style. The dance was performed by women called *maharis* in the temple of Jagannath; later, men dressed as women, called *gotipuas,* performed these dances in the courtyard of the temple. The present Orissi as a solo form evolved out of all these. It has been revived during the last two decades. Its technique is built round a basic motif in which the human body takes the thrice deflected *(tribhanga)* position of Indian sculpture. The lower limbs are in a demiplie, the upper torso is broken into two units of the lower waist and upper chest, which move in counter opposition

The repertoire comprises numbers which are built on pure dance *(nritta)* design recalling sculptural poses of the Orissan temples: the poses are strung together within several meterical cycles *(talas)* and dances performed to poetry ranging from the invocations to Genesa sung to the verses of the *Gita Govinda*: Oriya poetry is equally popular.

The unit of movement in Orissi is the *arasa* as distinct from the *adavu* of Bharatanatyam.

The dancer has scope to improvise within the *tala* and melodic line framework in the pure dance patterns and the freedom to interpret the poetic-line in a variety of ways to evoke a single mood.

Manipuri is a lyrical dance form from the eastern region of India. Although many forms of ritual, magical, community and religious dances were known to Manipur before the advent of Vaishnava faith in the 18th century, the dances known as the *Rasa* dances evolved only as a result of the interaction of the Vaishnava cult and the several highly developed forms of ritual and religious dances which were prevalent in the area. The origin of the Rasa dances is attributed to the vision of a king. Be that as it may, five different types of ballets, with a well-conceived structuring of *corps de ballet*, solo *pas de deux* revolving round the theme of Radha-

Below: Kathakali, the dance from Kerala, is strongly dramatic, with epic mythological themes. The large skirted costumes and elaborate make up are part of the grandeur of Kathakali. Bottom row: Kathakali has a highly-evolved vocabulary of hand gestures and eye movements, through which the dancer can express a mood, an action, a deed. Here, the dancer-actor conveys (from left): The hood of the snake, Embrace, Like a lotus, A tiger.

Krishna and the Gopis (milkmaids) comprise the large part of the classical repertoire. The second group of the classical dances is known as the *Sankirtanas*, performed generally by men with typical Manipur drums called *pung* or cymbals *(kartals)* or clapping. A large variety of intricate rhythmic patterns are played on the drum and the cymbals. The *Nata Sankirtana* often preceeds the *Rasa*.

In technique, Manipuri is quite different from Bharatanatyam and Orissi. Feet are in front, not out-turned, knees are relaxed, slightly bent forward but not flexed sideways; there is no out-turned position of the thighs. The torso is held in relaxation with the upper chest and waist moving in opposition. The whole body is turned into an imaginery figure of eight or akin to the English letter "S". The arms move as a unit, with no sharp angles through elbow bendings and erect straight lines of Bharatanatyam. The fingers of the hands also move in circles, semi-circles, curves, folding, unfolding gradually. The primary unit of movement is known as the *Chali* or the *pareng* on which the dance is built. The *Sankirtanas* follow a more vigorous masculine technique with jumps and elevations but no leg extensions.

The ritual dances of Manipur are a group apart: the most significant amongst these are the Maiba and Maibee dances of the priests and priestesses before village deities. They often culminate in trances: Lai Haroba is a long ritual spread over many days; the ritual pattern is rigorous and different sections all fall into a dexterous pattern of floor choreography, physical movement performed to a repetitive melody on a bowed instrument called the *pana*. The main dances are Khamba Thoibi, supposedly counterparts of Siva and Parvati. Like Bharatanatyam, Orissi, Manipuri can also be broken up into pure dance pattern — sections and mime. The latter is also lyrical, subtle and, unlike Bharatanatyam, Orissi, there is no dramatic extrovert expression. The comparative placidity of the face, the movements of the fingers are reminiscent of Southeast Asian styles, particularly Balinese and Thai.

Kathak, from north India, is an urban sophisticated style full of virtuosity and intricate craftsmanship. Commonly identified with the court traditions of the later Nawabs of northern India, it is really an amalgam of several folk traditions, the traditional dance-drama forms prevalent in the temples of Mathura and Brindavan known as the *Krishna and Radha lilas*, and the sophisitication of court tradition.

Its origins are old, its present format new, attributed to the genius of Nawab Wajid Ali Shah and the hereditary musician dancer, Pt Thakar Prasadji. The contemporary repertoire was evolved by a few families of traditional dancers, during the last hundred years.

In technique, Kathak is two-dimensional, always following a vertical line, with no breaks and deflections. The *footwork* is the most important part of the dancers' training, where she or he is taught innumerable rhythmic patterns with varying emphasis so that the 100 odd ankle bells can produce a fantastic range of sound and rhythm. Straight walks, gliding movements, fast piroeuttes, changing tempos and meterical patterns constitute the beauty and dexterity of the style.

As in other dance styles, the performer begins with an invocation, either to a god or the chief patron in the audience. The invocation and entry *(amad and salaam)* is followed by an exposition of slow delicate movements of the eyebrows, eyes, lateral neck and shoulders. This is followed by the presentation of phrases of rhythmic patterns known as the *tukras* and *toras*. Time-cycles can be repeated adding complexity to the presentation. Piroeuttes arranged in groups of three, six, nine, twelve, etc, normally mark the finale. The pure dance sections *(nrtta)* are followed by short interpretative pieces performed to a repetitive melodic line. The mime *(abhinaya)* is performed to lyrics of Hindi and Brajbhasa well known to villagers and townspeople alike. The dancer has freedom to improvise, in the pure dance sections: it is common to have a healthy competition with the percussionists: in the mime *(abhinaya)* portions, again the range of improvisation on the poetic line is the test of a good dancer.

Accompaniment comprises a vocalist, a drummer either on the *pakhavaj* (a double-barrelled drum) or *tablas*, (a pair of drums); an instrumentalist who plays the repetitive melodic line known as the *nagina*: other instruments can be added for embellishment.

Kathakali from Kerala is classical dance drama — it is quite different from the forms described above. Unlike the other four, it is dramatic rather than narrative in character. Different roles are taken by different characters: the dancers are all men or were so, till recently. It takes epic mythological themes as its content, and portrays them through an elaborate dramatic spectacle which is characterised by an other-worldly quality, a supernatural grandeur, a stylised large-size costume to give the impression of enlarging human proportions, and a mask-like make-up on the face which is governed by a complex symbolism of colour, line and design.

Character types, such as heroes, anti-heroes, villains, demons, sages, kings, all have a prescribed make-up and costume governed by the principles of co-relating basic green with good, red with valour and ferocity, black with evil, primitiveness; white with purity, and so on. Combinations of these colours suggest the exact character type and his particular mood in the play.

Within the framework of drama with dramatic *personae*, Kathakali is dance-drama and not drama, because the actors do not speak their lines. The dramatic story is carried forward through a highly evolved vocabulary of body movements, hand gestures and eye and eye-ball movements. The vocalist recites, narrates, sings the lines of the dramatic piece; the actor on the stage portrays the meaning through this elaborate language where he has freedom to improvise and interpret the dramatic line. While, therefore, he follows the broad framework of the written dramatic script which is being sung, he makes departures and deviations freely like the dancer of any other style. Also like the dances of the other styles, the mime *(abhinaya)* is interspersed with pure dance sequences *(nrtta)*.

During the last hundred years many poets have written Kathakali plays, which is as much a literary genre as a theatrical spectacle. In technique Kathakali follows the basic motif on a rectangular position reminiscent of a full *grandplie* with the important difference that the weight of the body rests on the outer soles of the feet, and not on the flat feet. The floor patterns also follow the rectangular motif. The pure dance sequences comprise units called the *Kala Samas*, akin to the *adavu* of Bharatanatyam, the *arasa* of Orissi, the *tukra* of *Kathak*, the *Chali* and *parenga* of Manipuri. In mime *(abhinaya)*, Kathakali depends more than any other dance style on the elaborate language of hand gestures which has been developed to the highest degree of finesse and subtlety.

While Kathakali is the most developed and sophisticated of the dance-drama forms in India, there are many others which follow the same principles with varying techniques. The *Yaksagana* of Mysore is a close second: the *Bhamakalapam* is a distant cousin. There are others.

Understandably, the confrontation of the comparatively dramatic styles such as Manipuri, Kathakali, and folk forms with Western influences produced a new form of dance in the 20th century which has been loosely termed as Modern dance. Uday Shankar, its founder, had met and danced with Anna Pavlova, when he was himself unacquainted with the Indian tradition. Later he returned to India to create, to recreate, revive and to break away from the set norms of the tradition. While he borrowed freely and successfully from all styles, what he created was his own, unrestricted to any traditional mannerism, unbound to the meterical cycle and the word-mime relationship. Contemporary themes, labour and machinery, the daily rhythm of life were chosen in addition to myth and legend. Unlike traditional schools, dance was composed first, music accompanied. It did not govern. Gradually a whole school grew up as the Uday Shankar School of Dance. Most modern choreographers belong to this school: the most talented amongst these was Shanti Bardhan (died 1952), the creator of two remarkable ballets called *Ramayana* and *Panchatantra*. In each, while the theme was old, the conception and treatment was totally new. In one the format is that of a puppet play presented by humans, in the other typical movements of birds and animals.

These developments did not leave the traditional dancers unaffected. Without departing from the norms of the particular stylisation, dance-dramas (sometimes called ballets in India) have been created in practically all styles including Bharatanatyam, Manipuri, Kathak, Kuchipudi and Orissi. The themes continue to be rooted in the tradition for the most part. But there are refreshing departures and innovations.

Kathakali — dance drama in pantomime, using a rich variety of facial make-up and headgear from Kerala, South India.

Our proudest possession — your smile.

We try hard to earn your smiles.

From the moment you enter our wide-bodied palaces in the sky you'll know you are in for a rare and pleasurable experience.

Sari-clad hostesses welcome you with the Namaste — a gesture that says: my guest is as my god. They minister to your every whim. Ply you with exclusive delicacies — a choice of Indian and Continental cuisine.

Even the decor — exotic, richly patterned, captivating — and the soul-stirring strains of an Indian raga, evoke a mood of Oriental splendour and luxury.

Air-India has flown many million miles across the skies for almost 50 years now. But our greatest reward is the smile on your face.

AIR-INDIA

Indian hospitality across five continents.

6949

The way to look at international banking services is through BCC

The Bank of Credit and Commerce International was born international — a fact which has certainly helped its growth. The BCC Group now has offices in 46 countries. Capital funds stand at over US$291 million and total assets exceed US$5,300 million. Whatever international banking services you need, a talk with your local BCC manager could be very useful. Speed, efficiency and your convenience are what count at BCC. Contact us at any of our offices — there are 45 in the United Kingdom alone — or get in touch at the following address:

 BANK OF CREDIT AND COMMERCE INTERNATIONAL

CLASSICAL PAINTING AND SCULPTURE

Calambur Sivaramamurti

The highest expression of form in art is through sculpture in the round according to Indian canons. *Chitra* is the term for sculpture in the round, while carving in relief, high or low, is styled *ardhachitra*; and painting, which is a semblance of sculpture, with the third dimension or depth expressed by the technique of light and shade, *vartana*, is *chitrabhasa*, literally meaning semblance of sculpture. *Chitra* is also the word for wonder. That which fills the mind with wonder at the clever manner of execution, especially by a faithful portrait, called technically *viddhachitra*, or by a clever expression of a figure of speech like paranomasia in art or a suggested idea beyond the apparent meaning on the surface as it is normally understood, till further scrutiny reveals a subtle, deeper, and nobler connotation, is *chitra: chittam chitriyate yasmat tasmachchitram idam viduh.* The connoisseur Kshemendra mentions the illusion of depths and heights on an even surface where none exist but those created by the special knowledge and technique of the masters: *atathyanyapi tathyani darsayanti vichakshanah, same nimnonnataniva chitrakarmavido janah, Kavyamimamsa.* Art can also sublimate a theme. Anything found deficient or detracting from the value of a chosen theme could be bettered or ennobled in a picture: *yad yat sadhu na chitre syatkriyate tat tad anyatha, Abhijnanasakuntalam.*

The earliest examples of sculpture in India go back to proto-historic times, the Harappan period in the third millennium BC. The renowned dancing girl from Mohenjo-daro is an image in metal which is world famous. This one, not unlike the princess Malavika, with one hand on her hip and the other hanging free towards one side in an elegant stance described eloquently by the great poet of India,

Kalidasa, is even excelled by such simple and tiny miniature metal images of exquisite form and delicacy of moulding like the buffalo sniffing its snout and swishing its tail in the most natural way and by the tiny spaniel with fur so elegantly modelled as to reveal the sculptor's meticulous study of form in so early an age. All these are in the amazing *cire perdue* or lost wax method known and practised nearly 5,000 years ago. Carving in stone and moulding in clay are equally well represented by elegant examples in both classical and folk styles of that early age.

For quite a long time there is a gap of a period unrepresented by sculptural examples, creating a dark age, which comes to an end by the fourth century BC, when there appear again sculptures of exquisite charm. The Mauryan period with Asoka's craftsmen at work, has examples of such highly sophisticated technique, realistic charm and perfection of study of the anatomy of human, animal and bird that there should have been a long tradition behind it, running into centuries. The highly sophisticated art of Asoka could not have appeared suddenly on the horizon. The two heads, one of a petrician with elegant turban and trimmed moustache, and the other of a plebeian with sturdy and coarse features, glaring eyes and snubby nose, long and unkempt moustache freely flowing down the chin, show the sculptor as a keen observer of life. The anatomy and form of the animal has been so well studied in the magnificent row of elephants on the facade of the Lomas Rishi cave in the Barabar hills. Both the sturdy bull and the stately lion from Rampurva, the quartette lion composition from Sarnath and all the crowning figures of the capitals of the Asoka pillars from different places like Lauriya Nandangarh, Sarnath, Sankisa and other places really make us wonder how

Below: Stone slab showing a stupa from Amaravati Satavahana, second century Madras Museum.
Bottom left: Chowrie-bearer from Didarganj. Maurya, third century BC. Patna Museum. (Photo courtesy of Jean-Louis Nou).
Bottom row, second from left: Kanishka from Mathura Kushan, early second century. Mathura Museum.
Bottom row, third from left: Kubera, god of wealth from Maholi. Kushan, third century Mathura Museum.
Bottom right: Yakshi carrying wine and mangos from Bhutesar. Kushan, second century. Mathura Museum.

exquisite is the art of the court sculptors of Asoka. The elephant at Dhauli cut in the rock seems to emerge with life infused in it. The figure of the elephant, a mere outline incised with the chisel, shows the vigour of drawing of the Mauryan sculptor, skilled in *rekha*, excellent line drawing — *rekha-rekham prasamsantyacharyah, Chitrasutra*. The *chauri*-bearer from Didarganj is a monolith with mirror-like polish so elegantly carved by the Mauryan sculptor that makes one wonder how advanced was the technique and study of the craftsman of the period.

Sunga sculpture of the second century BC is represented adequately by the remains of the carved rail and *torana* gateway that once adorned the *stupa* at Bharhut in central India. These early carvings show the glory of the civilisation of ancient India covering every aspect of life in the town and village, in the palace and cottage, on the hill and dale, garden and forest, of the nobleman and peasant, animals, reptiles, and birds both natural and creations of fancy, *ihamrigas*. Nothing is left out. Even the godlings that were in worship at that time in the form of Yakshas, Yakshis, Devatas, Kinnaras and so forth are sculpturally portrayed in their earliest form. We have here, for example, Sudharma, the heavenly palace of Indra, and dancing heavenly nymphs *apsaras* with specific labels describing them as Misrakesi *apsara*, Ghritachi *apsara* and so forth. There is Sudarsana Yakshi, Chulakoka and the lord of the Yakshas Kubera styled in the label *kupiro yakho*. Mother goddess Sri is mentioned as a *devata* in the label *Siri ma devata*. In a medallion illustrating an episode from the lip of the Master there is Maya dreaming of the descent of the Bodhisattva as a celestial elephant to enter her womb. This is labelled *bhagavato ukranti,* ie "the descent of the lord." Another large medallion on an upright of the rail illustrates the presentation of Jetavana monastery to Buddha by the merchant prince Anathapindada, the fabulous price paid for acquiring the land by spreading gold all over the surface shown as vividly in the carving as explained clearly in the label.

The special cell for the Master in the monastery is labelled *gandhakuti.* The visit of King Ajatasatru of Magadha and Prasenajit of Kosala are two famous episodes from the Master's life represented at Bharhut. The *jatakas* or the stories of the previous lives of Buddha when by an exemplary character the Master qualified himself to ultimately become the enlightened one, are naively narrated; those chosen are the most telling, the *Chhaddanta*, the *Mahakapi*, the *Miga* and so forth where even the animals could behave so nobly as to invite men to emulate their ethical heights.

Contemporary rulers of the Sungas in the Deccan were the Satavahanas whose earliest phase of art has given us the famous panels of Surya and Indra in the Bhaja cave of the second century BC in western India, the former in his earliest simple iconographic aspect in a car yoked to four horses chasing the demon of darkness and the latter riding his stately elephant in a stroll in his Nandana garden of celestial trees, both turbaned and garlanded. The magnificent eastern *torana* gateway of the Sanchi *stupa* was delicately carved by the ivory carvers of Vidisa who were equally at home in carving in stone, as recorded in an inscription on it. An inscription equally informs us of an early Satakarni who had this created. The beautiful carvings in the Karla and Kondana caves are also the result of Satavahana patronage. The famous panel from Jaggayapeta showing the universal emperor Mandhata causing a rain of

gold and the early Siva form against the *linga* from Gudimallam showing him as a sacrificer *yajamana* in a synchretic Agni-Rudra form are among the earliest Satavahana sculptures from this eastern territory on the banks of the River Krishna.

The most magnificent phase of Satavahana art is seen in the exquisitely rendered carving on the rail from Amaravati of 150 AD, portions of which were saved by Colonel Cohen Mackenzie and others who dug, later making them available in the Madras and British Museums like the remains of the Bharhut rail saved by General Cunningham and transported to the Indian Museum at Calcutta. The medallion depicting the subjugation of the elephant Nalagiri by Buddha in synoptic mode, the famous animal earlier rushing through the streets of Rajagriha creating terror by its havoc and later kneeling in peace at the feet of the Master, both the moods mirrored in the citizens in frightened disorder and reassured calm and devotion, is a real masterpiece. The devotion of the four damsels bowing to Buddha's feet symbolising the seated Master is another fine example of the sculptor's excellence of workmanship.

The Ikshvakus who succeeded the Satavahanas were equally enthusiastic in their patronage of art, and among their masterpieces are favourite themes like Mandhata fallen from the luminous celestial sphere to which he points and admonishes his subjects to curb their desires and benefit by the lesson of his fall. The ephemeral nature of physical charms is tellingly narrated in the theme of Nanda and Sundari.

The Kushanas, who ruled in the north as contemporaries of the Satavahanas in the first two centuries of the Christian era had a large empire that extended from the northwestern area of Gandhara to nearly the borders of Bihar with one mode of sculpture (Gandhara) in their western and another the indigenous Mathura school in their eastern part. The Gandhara school is mainly determined by Greco-Roman norms and is an Indian theme expressed in foreign technique and spirit. Some of the themes are also foreign like Hercules and the lion on Bacchanalian revelry. Ascetic Buddha reduced to skin and bone as a theme does not occur outside Gandhara art.

The Mathura school of Kushana art is most pleasing as a worthy companion of Satavahana art in the south. There are nymphs and damsels in different attitudes of sheer delight, one talking to a parrot as her eyes twinkle, clad in transparent apparel revealing the charm of her form, decked in a simple single strand of pearl necklace, tinkling waist zone, jingling anklets, another with a bunch of green mangos suggestive of spring in one hand and a wine jar with cup in the other, a third emerging from her bath wrapping a garment around her thighs. A carving showing a damsel carrying a platter of food in one hand and a water jug in the other is a river sprite suggesting the bounteous river-mothered area watered and nurtured by the perennial flow of the stream. The rippling stream and the anthropomorphic forms of the river goddess are significant in the early Gupta carving of the Varaha panel at Udayagiri in Bhilsa. The carving of Sri Lakshmi, standing on a brimming pitcher, with lotuses suggesting the abundance of breast milk, sustaining children on the lap like the children of the soil by abundant water, both water and milk connoted by the word *payas*, her pearly teeth exposed by her lips parted in a smile indicating her joy already hinted by the spread tail of the peacock dancing in joy as decoration on her armlets,

is a masterpiece of Kushana art. The sleepy eyes of Kubera with rotund belly and care-free attitude suggest the lord of opulence seated at ease. The portrait of the famous Kushan monarch Kanishka, with the head lost but with inscription mentioning him by name intact, is most interesting for comparison with his portrait on his coins.

In the Chandragupta cave at Vidisa, there are early Gupta sculptures carved in the rock representing Vishnu with the *Srivatsa* mark prominent on his chest with the *vanamala,* garland of sweet smelling wild flowers and typical short crown on his head; Ganesa with the early natural head of the elephant without a crown nor even the beginnings of it; Mahishamardani killing the buffalo demon in the earliest conceptual tradition of late Kushana. In another cave, the lintel of the entrance graphically portrays the churning of the milky ocean by Devas and Asuras. The most distinctive rhapsody in stone seen here is probably the representation in the Varaha cave of the therianthropomorphic form of Vishnu as Varaha raising the earth from the ocean. The ocean is multiplied into four massive rippling waters with four princely figures for the four seas personified carrying gem-filled vessels, as the ocean is Ratnakara or the receptacle of rare gems like the *Kaustubha.* The rivers Ganga and Yamuna personified in human form stand on their respective vehicles, the crocodile and tortoise, and carry each a pitcher of water, to show the flow of the rivers into the ocean, with specific stress on their commingling at Prayaga Sangama in Allahabad.

The most glorious picture of this is given by India's prince of poets, Kalidasa. Like sapphires interspersed with pearls, white lilies with blooming lotuses, the waves of dark Yamuna are set against the white wavelets of Ganga. While the nether-world is suggested by Nagaraja at the feet of Varaha, the Rishis in a row at the level of the rivers and oceans recall the terrestrial region, with Devas above signifying the celestial sphere. This monumental carving is indeed a great masterpiece. The Seshasayi Vishnu here in another cave, though early, is a little rugged, while the same theme treated half a century later at Deogarh is magnificent and one of the three great panels of the Vishnu temple there. The personified weapons are dynamic in their action against the demons Madhu and Kaitabha. The Nara-Narayana panel at Deogarh is another great masterpiece showing the atmosphere of peace in an ascetic's grove where even the opposites like the lion and the deer co-exist in amity and friendliness, *maitri.* Their asceticism is highlighted by Urvasi, the most beautiful of the nymphs, created from the thigh of Narayana, putting to shame the celestial dancers who had come to disturb the penance of the great saints, Nara-Narayana. The third and perhaps the most important panel here is Vishnu going to the rescue of the Gajendra, the mighty elephant caught in the coils of an aquatic monster which he destroys with his flaming disc *chakra.* One of the most magnificent sculptures of the Gupta period is the Ekamukhalinga from Khoh now in the Allahabad Museum. Buddha turning the wheel of the law at Sarnath is the most beautiful representation of the theme and vies with the world-famous seated Buddha flanked by Bodhisattvas, a monumental sculpture from Chendi Mendut in Indonesia. The story of Rama and Krishna has been narrated in panels at Deogarh. Among the Gupta terracottas, Seshasayi and Ganesa from Bhitargaon and Vishnu with personified weapons and Nagini from Rajgir are famous. Metal images of the period are represented by such magnificent master-

pieces as Buddha in the Rockefeller collection, Brahma with four heads but with only a single pair of arms, deer-skinclad from the Karachi Museum and the famous Buddha from Sultanganj now in Birmingham Museum.

Corresponding to the Gupta of the north are their contemporaries, the Vakatakas, from the Deccan. They have given wonderful examples of art. The sculpture from Parel near Bombay represents a unique form of Siva with his dwarf ganas playing their instruments, illustrating the Indian orchestra. The magnificent panels in the Ramesvara cave in Ellora, Parvati in penance, Parvati playing dice and beaming in her triumph over Siva, Siva dancing in *lalita* with the seven mothers and Ganesa, and the large and impressive panels in the Elephanta cave representing themes like Siva as Gangadhara receiving the Ganga as a triple stream on his head, Siva destroying the demon of darkness Andhaka, Ardhanarisvara in hermaphrodite form, as bridegroom Kalyanasundara wedding Haimavati, as dancer Nataraja and as ascetic Yogesvara. A rare collection of Buddhist bronzes, one of them inscribed, is a unique collection of metal work of the Vakataka age. Siva as a dwarf vamana from Mansar near Nagpur is a recent find, a unique sculpture.

Though there are just a few examples to represent the Vardhana phase of the sixth-seventh century AD, nevertheless it was a great period of art during the time of Prabhakara Vardhana and Harsha. The sculpture of a feminine bust wearing a diaphanous tunic from Gwalior is a beautiful one.

A number of beautiful sculptures of rare aesthetic value, like for instance, the nymph from the Gwalior Museum wearing an apparel with variegated patterns worked on it illustrate the Gurjara Pratihara school. Another example is the famous Visvarupa from Kanauj. There is a rare sculpture of Manmatha with his consorts, Rati and Priti, his favoured season spring suggested by mango blossoms. Yet another example is a loving *Nayaka* as Dakshina equally accommodating towards his several *Nayikas* and such others from Abaneri. There are both Maitraka and Gurjara Pratihara sculptures of great charm representing such themes as Visvarupa Vishnu, Skandamata, Kaumari, Varahi, Indrani and other mothers, Siva dancing with the mothers and so forth. This art has been further developed by the Chalukyas whose sculptures, though many of them are damaged, still reveal the charm of the monuments of Somnatha and Modhera.

From Kashmir, the earlier sculpture of the Karkota period is scarce, though of the later dynasty of the Utpalas, there are such magnificent panels as Manmatha with his consort and his parrot, and portraits like Avantivarman with his queen proceeding to worship the deity of the temple Avantiswami among the remains of his famous Vishnu temple, the construction of which and of his liberal patronage, poet Kalhana has made a mention in his *Rajatarangini.* Kashmir is famous for its metal images including a magnificent Vaikuntha form of Vishnu of the ninth-tenth century AD now in the National Museum, an inscribed Svachchhanda Bhairavi, a Devi, Mabishamardini and Narasimha, all from Chamba.

Under the Palas of eastern India, the art flourished immensely. Nalanda became a centre of art as of learning and some of the most beautiful icons representing the Buddhist pantheon come from Nalanda, like Jambhala, Tara, Buddha standing and also Brahmanical figures like Vishnu with

*Below left: Buddha head
Gupta period.
Mathura Museum.
Below centre: Vrishaka
Gurjara Pratihara,
ninth century.
Gwalior Museum. (Photo
courtesy of Jean-Louis Nou).
Centre left: Penance of Arjuna
Pallava, mid-seventh century
Mahabalipuram.
Bottom left: Seshasayi Vishnu
Pallava, seventh century
Mahabalipuram.*

*Below right: Rati on a swan,
Nayak, 17th century.
Menakshi temple.
Madurai.
(Photo courtesy of Jean-Louis
Nou).*

weapons personified, Surya, Sankarshana. Another famous centre of metalwork is Kurkihar, illustrated by the famous descent of Buddha from heaven by the jewelled ladder flanked by Indra and Mahabrahma, Buddha turning the wheel of the law, Parnasabari, Ushnisheyijaya and so forth. Stone sculpture is as interesting and there are such examples as Vishnu with consorts, Surya, Matsya, Varaha, Kalyana-sundara, Nartesvara dancing on bull, Khasarpana, Tara, Prajnaparamita, Manjusri, Manjuvara and so forth.

The Eastern Gangas who ruled Orissa have given exquisite temples of which quite a large number cluster around Bhubanesvar. One of their earliest temples is Parasuramasvara, of the seventh century AD. Muktesvara, a dream of the sculptor realised, is a miniature temple of delicate workmanship with all the architectural features graphically portrayed, including the *torana* gateway, the tank, the *jagamohan mandapa* leading on to the *deul* shrine. The Naginis here carrying objects of worship like a conch of water, a garland of flowers, a crown and necklace, incense in incense burner and so forth is a remarkable group, and is excelled only by the charming pierced windows with tell-tale illustrations of stories from fables like the wise monkey and the crocodile carved on them. The *torana* is exquisite and the presence of the stepped water tank makes the temple idyllic.

Another magnificent temple is *Rajarani*. There are several beautiful sculptures here all around, including nymphs preparing themselves for dance by applying anklets to their feet, teaching the peacock to dance, holding the bough laden with blossoms to gather flowers and so forth.

The most astounding temple monument of the Gangas is the one for the solar deity at Konarak which is literally a monumental chariot on several wheels drawn by seven horses. The monumental sculptures of the running elephant and horse here, once seen, are never forgotten. Similarly, the monumental group of musicians on the *jagamohan*, one playing the pipe, another sounding the drum, a third clanging the cymbals and so forth. Every inch of the wheel, nay, every inch of the wall of the temple is decorated with different patterns of flower and foliage, animals and birds, *nayikas* and *nayakas*.

The sculpture from the Chedi area in Bundelkhand recalling the nuances of both Paramara in Malwa, and Chandella, the border territory of the Chedis, has the most magnificent *torana* gateway in Gurgi.

Chandella sculpture itself is most concentrated in Khajuraho, where the temples dating from the 10th to the 12th century have a wealth of sculpture representing gorgeous royal processions, rare iconographic forms and erotic scenes illustrating many of the *ratibandhas* of the *Kamasutra*. Some of the rather longish human figures here, particularly feminine, like those of Burne-Jones of the pre-Raphaelite school, are indeed very charming and conform to the *satya* type described in the *Chitrasutra*. The *abhisarika nayika*, the girl inflamed by love braving her journey to the place of tryst even at midnight as she hesitatingly proceeds to meet her lover, is indeed a most suggestive stroke of the sculptor. Undoubtedly, the most beautiful Paramara sculpture is the inscribed Sarasvati of Bhoja in the British Museum and Siva dancing in the centre of the niche of the *sukanasa* projection of the Udayesvara temple at Udaipur.

In the south the great Pallava king Mahendravarman, who was at once a sculptor, painter, poet, musician, engineer all in one, created for the first time rock-cut temples with his Mandagapattu cave temple proclaiming in verse his achievement as the curious minded king, *vichitrachitta*. Among his several simple massive cave temples the most famous undoubtedly is the one at Tiruchirapalli, where a well-known Gangadhara Siva is a striking example of Mahendravarman's time. His son Narasimhavarman, who was a great warrior and patron of art has made Mahabalipuram, the harbour of the Pallavas, who had a great navy, immortal through his famous monuments. They include the five *rathas* with their beautiful sculptures like Ardhanarisvara and Harihara, Gangadhara and Kaliya Krishna, the famous Govardhanagiridhara, Krishna lifting the mountain to save the cowherds and milkmaids from a week-long torrential rain — a long and impressive scene in the Govardhana cave — the never to be forgotten, almost unparalleled, monolithic composition of Arjuna's penance where the suggestive idea of the nether world, terrestrial world, and celestial is suggested by making Ganga flow in all the three regions, the glory of asceticism, extolled in the figures of the *rishikumaras* or the young hermits, Siva's grace, as he presents Arjuna his unfailing weapon Pasupata, is all a tribute of the sculptor to the glory of Pallava art. The Kailasa temple at Kanchipuram with its precious sculptured decoration is a gem of Pallava art.

The Cholas, who continued the tradition, have magnificent early temples at Kodumbalur, Srinivasanallur and other important places in their realm, but the most striking examples of Chola architecture and sculpture is from the huge temples built by the father and son, emperors Rajaraja and Rajendra, at Tanjavur and Gangaikondacholapuram. The Bhikshatana and Kalantaka images at Tanjavur compel attention as do similarly the Nataraja and Chandesanugrahamurti at Gangaikondacholapuram. While Nataraja here is accompanied by Karaikkalammaiyar, the saintly woman sounding the cymbals and famous all over Southeast Asia, particularly at Bantei Srei, Chandesanugraha Siva is suggestively represented as crowning the remarkable royal victor over Southeast Asia and almost the whole of India, and his grateful acceptance of the garland wound round his head by the Lord himself placing himself almost in the position of the devotee Chandesa.

The Western Chalukyas, of whom Mangalesa must be remembered for his magnificent cave temple at Badami with lovely monolithic panels of Vishnu seated on Sesha, Narasimha, Trivikrama and so forth, and Vikramaditya for his masterly temple at Virupaksha built with the help of his art-minded queen Lokamahadevi at Pattadakal, have contributed in no small measure to the glory of the Deccani art. Vikramaditya the great patron appreciated the beautiful Pallava temple built by Rajasimha at Kanchipuram with the help of his art-minded queen Rangapataka, and literally imported almost the selfsame sculptors from the south to beautify his realm with temples like Virupaksha resembling the Kailasa as can be seen visually and understood through the inscriptions mentioning the *sthapati,* the sculptor-architect brought over by him to build, simulating the architecture at Kanchipuram.

The Rashtrakutas who succeeded the Chalukyas were great builders in their own right and the most magnificent rock-cut temple in south India, the Kailasa, has remained a wonder of creative art. A Rashtrakuta inscription mentions the imaginary conversation between celestials in the sky admiring the Kailasa temple at Ellora and wondering whether the sculptor could repeat his performance with such success.

Below left:
Candesanugrahamurti
Chola, 11th century.
Gangaikondacholapuram.
Centre left: Shiva dancing
Hoysala, 12th century
Hoysalesvara temple, Halebid.
Bottom left: Mandapa of
Srizaugam temple.
Vijayanagar, 17th century.
Below right: Bronze group
from the Chola period.
Tanjavur Art Gallery.

Here some of the sculptures like Ravana shaking Kailasa, Rati and Manmatha, the triple stream of Ganga, Yamuna and Sarasvati and so forth are unrivalled.

The Hoysalas continued the tradition of the later western Chalukyas; and Hoysala Vishnuvardhana's greatest contribution are the charming embellished temples with exquisite sculptures in Belur and Halebid besides others. His wife Santala helped him in this patronage of art and devotion to his faith.

The Vijayanagara period of art in south India is indeed a great phase where the Chalukyan and Chola traditions are almost combined. Among Vijayanagara monarchs, Krishnadevaraya, the great emperor flanked by his queens as depicted in metal at Tirupati, will ever be remembered as the builder of several temples including the famous ones for Vithala and Krishna at Hampi, his capital. One of the great and imposing *gopuras* at Chidambaram has a fine portrait of Krishnadevaraya in stone. The most exquisite Vijayanagara temple with sculpture worthy of it is the famous one for Jalakanthesvara within the fort, itself a lovely one, in Vellore. It is of the 16th century; and the hunting scenes with prancing horses and equestrians fighting tigers and boars as motifs on pillars of the *mandapa* pillared halls in Vellore are famous. There are similar ones in Srirangam. The cat running after doves carved in stone, but quite misleading, by appearing almost live ones by the skill of the sculptor who executed them, is indeed an interesting motif on the roof of the *mandapa* against the *kapotapali* or the roofline with dove-cots for the doves.

The huge monolithic sculptures like Rati on parrot, the gypsy *kuratti*, the marriage of Siva and so forth from Madurai that arrest attention displaying the charm of 17th century art is practically the swan song of south Indian art, nay, Indian art. Yet, the *sthapati* in south India lives on and the traditional art continues though much shorn of its original vitality.

The bronzes of the Pallavas are famous and among them the most important are perhaps Tripurantaka with a single pair of arms in the Sarabhai collection, a gem of metalwork, and Vishapaharana Siva swallowing deadly poison to save the three worlds from dire calamity. The eight-armed Nataraja from Nallur, Somaskanda from Tiruvalangadu are equally noteworthy.

Among the Chola ones, the beautiful bride Parvati now in the Sarabhai collection, Nataraja from Tiruvarangulam in the National Museum, Vrishbhantika and Devi from the Tanjavur Art Gallery, Ardhanarisvara from Tiruvengadu, are all exquisite. The Chola period was the most prolific in the creation of metal images in hundreds and thousands.

Portrait sculpture of the Vijayanagara period in metal can have no better examples than Krishnadevaraya and queens, Achyutaraya and some others which have become as famous as historical relics as objects of art.

Ivory carving of the Nayaka period has given us beautiful examples of Tirumala Nayaka with his queens, a theme that is repeated in stone as well as in metal.

Painting in India has as great an antiquity as sculpture itself and the earliest at Ajanta in caves IX and X go back to the second century BC. In fact, they are the only extant examples to illustrate any school of that date. While some early paintings from Central Asia like Buddha with symbols all over his body from Balawaste is an illustration of late Kushana, of about the third-fourth century, there are Gupta paintings from Bagh which are the only surviving ones for that period. Contemporary painting in the Deccan is Vakataka and is richly represented at Ajanta in caves I and II, XVI and XVII. Among these paintings one can never forget the flying celestials, the close embrace of the lovers on the neck, the dying princess, the touching story of Visvantara, the dance scene from Mahajanaka Jataka, and so forth. Here the six limbs of painting — *chitra shadanga* — perfection of line in delineating form, similitude in portrayal, depiction of iridescence and glow in charm of beauty, patterns of form and proportions, manipulation of colours are all magnificently illustrated, *rupabheda, pramana, bhava, lavanya, sadrisya* and *varnikabhanga*.

Seventh century paintings of the Pallavas are seen in fragments in the Kailasanatha temple at Kanchipuram and in Panamalai, while fragments of early western Chalukyan are noticed in the Vaishnava cave at Badami of the end of the sixth century. Rashtrakuta painting has survived in Ellora both in the mid-eighth century Kailasa temple and in the Jaina one of the ninth century at the farthest end.

The magnificent Chola series of paintings in the Brihadisvara temple illustrating the fight of Siva with the Tipuras, the almost invincible demons, lords of the dreaded castles of iron, gold and silver, the story of Sundaramurti, the celestial dancers, Siva watching the dance, Rajaraja and his spiritual *guru*, are all masterpieces of art of 1000 AD.

Hoysala painting is represented by a rare collection of illustrated palm leaf manuscripts. They are indeed so delicate and charming and so colourful that they form a class of their own. The Tirthankaras, Yakshas and Yakshis, Srutadevi the goddess of learning, portraits of Vishnuvardhana and Santala, are all colourfully represented on large palm leaves constituting the important test *Dhavala*.

Vijayanagara painting is illustrated by a magnificent series at Hampi of the 15th century AD wherein the spiritual preceptor Vidyaranya is shown moving in a palanquin in a procession. There are other scenes from the *Puranas* like Bhikshatana and Mohini effectively portrayed here as well as in Chidambaram. In the Virupaksha temple here, there is Tripurantaka, Madanantaka, the marriage of Arjuna and other themes effectively painted.

At Lepakshi the Vijayanagara painter has a revelry of colour and form in a large number of panels illustrating various themes detailing the iconography of Siva.

The Nayaka phase is illustrated not only by Bhikshatana and Mohini at Chidambaram but also by several paintings of the Siva series from the Kapardisvara temple at Tiruvalanjuli, the Tyagaraja temple at Tiruvalur and a fine Jaina series from Tirupattikunram near Kanchipuram. In this last the story of the juvenile sports *balalilas* of Krishna as the cousin of Neminatha is effectively depicted.

In Kerala, the Chera paintings from Tirunandikkarai constitute an important landmark though it is the late ones of the 17th-18th centuries from Mattancheri palace, Padmanabhapuram palace, the temples like Tiruvanjikulam, Ettumanur and others that give effective and adequate examples showing a colourful galaxy of over-decorated form developed from the norm of the late Chalukyas and Hoysalas. In the north, Pala painting has wonderful examples on the palm leaf manuscripts of the 11th-12th centuries AD. In western India, a peculiar stylisation which starts even about the 15th century by the depiction of the further eye a little away from its normal situation and other similar noticeable features mark the school of painting on paper illustrating the Jaina manu-

THIS PAGE
Below left: Camels in combat
Moghul, 17th century
National Museum, Delhi.
(Photo courtesy of Jean–Louis
Nou).
Below right: Krishna and
Radha.
Kangra School.
18th century.
Patiala Museum.
(Photo courtesy of Jean–Louis
Nou).
Bottom left: Mural from the

Mattancheri Palace.
Kerala.
Bottom right: Flying celestials
Cave painting, Ajanta
Vakataka period.
(Photo courtesy of Jean–Louis
Nou).

OPPOSITE PAGE
Left: Painting of the Pallava
period, seventh century
Kailasanatha temple
Kanchipuram.
Top right: Paintings from the

ceiling of Mandapa
Sivakamasundari, Chidam-
baram
Vijayanagara period, 15th
century.
Bottom right: Painting from
Rameswara temple.
Kapardisvara.
Nayak period.

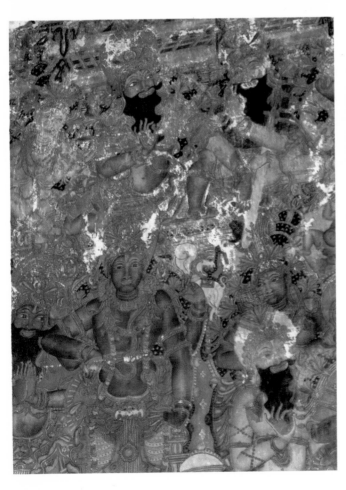

scripts like the *Kalpasutra, Kalakacharyakatha* and so forth.

The Mewar and Malwa schools represent the earlier phase of the Rajasthani mode of which of somewhat later date are other schools like Kota, Bundi, Jodhpur, Jaipur and others which bear influence from the Moghul school which was the great school of the court under the emperors and flourished mostly during the time of Humayun, Akbar and Jehangir. There is a rare delicacy, a predilection of portraits and special finesse in the Moghul paintings where birds, animals, trees have also been wonderfully rendered and lovingly represented. Akbar specially loved these themes, and encouraged artists both Hindu and Moslem in his court to an extent that makes Moghul art a great and living tradition.

In the Pahari hills miniatures were produced with great enthusiasm, each school with its own hallmark of beauty like the delicately painted Kangra, the colourful Basohli that could add clipped wings of butterflies to add brilliance to its colour, Chamba, with large and wonder-filled eyes, and the pleasing school of Kishangarh with eyes peculiarly curved and longish and the figures themselves elongated, specially distinguished from the rest. The themes are delightful in

landscapes and colourful depiction of seasons and months, juvenile sports of Krishna, *Ramayana, Bhagavata, Puranas* and so forth, all full of devotion, love and valour.

The Company school which had its hey-day during the early rule of the British East India Company, especially in Bengal and Patna, almost goes along with the *Pata* paintings continuing a long tradition of the *Yamapata* and other long scrolls illustrating Puranic themes and the fruits of sin and merit depicted in the *Yamapata* and continued in almost modern *Pata* paintings of Bengal.

In the south and in the Deccan flourished the Maratha school with a little modelling in a paste of sawdust on a wooden frame covered with cloth and with semi-precious stones set on colourfully painted figures popularly styled as the Tanjavur school, with its allied school, the Mysore, and the Maratha version from the Deccan, the Paithan school. Such paintings also hail from Andhra Pradesh, from places like Kalahasti, Tirupati, Guddapah, Kurnool and so forth. These have given birth to the tradition of painting on cloth of which examples of Kalamkari and Andhra Pradesh are famous.

1. *Husain mural in ceramic tile, Indraprastha Building, New Delhi.*
2. *Artist: Satish Gujral Murals for Shastri Bhawan, New Delhi.*
3. *Artist: Tyelo Mahta "Human Landscape" 1976 Photo courtesy of National Gallery of Modern Art, New Delhi.*
4. *Artist: Akbar Padamsee "Orange Nude" 1960 Photo courtesy of National Gallery of Modern Art, New Delhi.*
5. *Artist: A Ramachandran "Nuclear Ragini" Photo courtesy of National Gallery of Modern Art, New Delhi.*

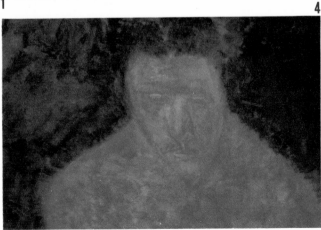

1

2

3

4

5

CONTEMPORARY PAINTING AND SCULPTURE

Richard Bartholomew

Like the vision of the Himalayas, magnificent in mystique and manifest moods, Indian painting and sculpture of the past make their presence felt, physically and imaginatively, to the Indian artist practising today. He may make a pilgrimage to the vast regions to worship or to trek and explore, enjoying a vacation, a respite from modern urban life. Or he may accept it as a part of nature, the greater environment which conditions climate and which affects the weather. But he knows it is there, permanent, prominent and for ever pristine. It is a source of inspiration and a challenge, a stretch of horizon indicating where the gods live and where the rivers that nourish the land have their origin. His relationship with his cultural past, his access to and his experience of the poetic schools of miniature painting, the sensuous temple sculpture, grand architecture as embodied in mosques and temples is precisely this.

The contemporary Indian artist lives in the world of today, in the India of now with her antecedent cultural history acting as the climate, as it were, for the weather of modern changes — the presence of the cinema, television, the computer, atomic research, aviation, heavy industries, etc, linking India not only with the past and its heritage but also which affects the weather. But he knows it is there, permaning which shapes the life of the individual.

It must be remembered, therefore, that India, a country with a glorious art heritage of 5,000 years which influenced the whole of Asia, and which in turn was influenced by the impact of Greco-Roman art, schools of Persian painting and British colonial rule and its academic art schools, is still a developing country in the widest term.

Art history is significant for the practising artist: but sensitivity and sensibility are more important. The former, for all its significance, is "history", subject to interpretation. The latter is the very stuff of which art is made. The two interact and fuse at points of intimate and profound contacts: as when M F Husain, now India's pre-eminent painter, experienced Indian temple sculpture in the collection of the Rashtrapati Bhavan Museum for the first time in 1948 — an encounter with the manifestation of the human physique presented as sensuous form embodying the rhythm of life. This sentient sculpture with its flow of line, dynamism of movement and its presence determined and shaped Husain's draughtmanship, his grasp of the vital figure, the quintessential human image.

Similarly, after years of painting in oils in the European academic tradition — derivative of Impressionistic styles — Jamini Roy in the early 1930s encountered the folk idiom of rural painting in Bengal, discovered its vitality and its contemporaneousness and based his characteristic and expressive work on its methodology.

Around the same time Amrita Sher-Gill, another pioneer of modern painting in India, who was trained superbly in Paris in the European manner, identified herself with the Indian villager and the country folk. Her early paintings reflected the sadness and the insularity of simple hill people in colour and delineation which were austere but dramatic. In the middle period she depicted village scenes of the Punjab — a girl on a swing, an old story-teller — with a palette which was more vivid, warm and reminiscent of the colour schemes of the miniatures. Finally, under the spell of miniature painting of the Kangra school, which she analysed carefully and studied, Amrita created and projected what was in fact a remarkable blend of tradition and

6. Artist: F N Souza
"Landscape in Grey"
Photo courtesy of National
Gallery of Modern Art, New
Delhi.
7. Artist: M F Husain
"Farmer's Family"
Photo courtesy of National
Gallery of Modern Art, New
Delhi.
8. Artist: G R Santosh
Untitled

Photo courtesy of National
Gallery of Modern Art, New
Delhi.
9. Artist: Bikash Bhattacharya
"The Totem"
Photo courtesy of Lalit Kala
Akademi.
10. Artist: Jeram Patel
"Contours"
Photo courtesy of National
Gallery of Modern Art, New
Delhi.

7

8

6

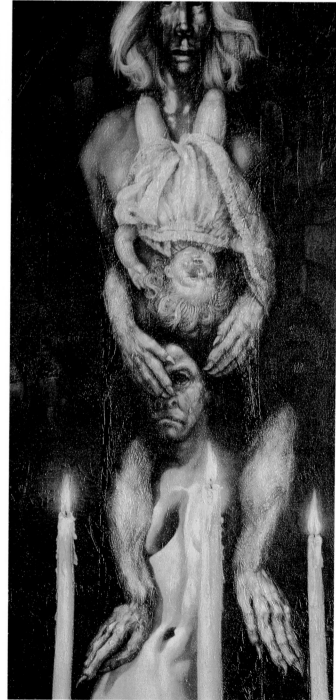

9

10

modern practice — a poetic mode in which the soft landscape set off the legendary figures, the atmosphere of the one relating to the mood and mystery of the other.

More recently from the 1960s onwards a whole school of painters from the south of India — led by the late K C S Paniker — have derived inspiration from Kalamkari paintings, astrological charts, wood carvings and iconographic imagery prevalent in the south. Ranging from the pictographic, their work, which combines fantasy, calligraphy and dramatic draughtsmanship manifests itself at its best as "revelatory" painting — a psychic happening, or an ideographic animation of image and aural colour.

Colour, of course, is the Indian painter's province of specialisation, his prime motif in expression. The Indian environment and its social milieu are resplendent in colour, as we can see from a monsoon sunset or from Indian fabrics and textiles. The miniatures of all schools of Indian painting — Basholi, Guler, Kangra, Krishangarh, Bundi, Kotah — testify to its profuse and variegated use, for creating planes and perspectives, symbolising the mood, depicting nature's glory, creating pictorial movement. It is not so much the organisation of line as the organic concept of colour which makes the Indian miniature a homogenous and integrated visual proposition. We are made not only to see colour but to envisage it as well.

With this tradition and concept to inspire them some modern Indian painters such as Biren De and G R Santosh in the 1960s made colour the vehicle and theme of their paintings. They presented iridescent colour-symbols and the mystique of the procreative forces as symbolic forms charged with colour energy and spectral aura. Even though indirectly related to the transcendental and metaphysical concepts of *tantra*, a philosophy of ultimate self-realisation, their practice is in a sense an extension of the Indian sensibility and its belief in vision.

It would appear from these brief accounts of developmental trends that only contemporary Indian painting flowered from the 1930s in India and that the contact with tradition was confined to one form of expression. Indian art without Indian sculpture would be like a literature which is rich in lyric poetry but deficient in drama. Though less obvious as an extension of the Indian's sensibility, sculpture, which was more pronouncedly dissociated from society during colonial rule, did find fresh roots after a stifling period of post-Victorian sterility and stagnation. Humanistic in all its periods, but essentially romantic in essence, Indian art, particularly Indian sculpture, is a manifestation of the spirit and the belief in the good life. While the ingredients of Indian painting include symbolism and poetic allusion, Indian sculpture embodies the immanent spirit and its outward manifestation.

This element of the spirit, revealed as form and embodied in man, in the anatomy of men and women as depicted in Indian sculpture, portrays rhythm, bodily grace and movement. The physiques of the gods, goddesses, kings, sages, saints and attendent personages embody inspiration as breath, filling the body with an outwardly generative force which lifts it from the mundane plane of performance and action to one of resolution and poise. The body is not idealised physically but further humanised and harmonised and structured as a sensuous presence.

This basic Indian philosophy of sculpture animates the late Ram Kinkar Baij's two magnificent creations in concrete in Santiniketan — the "Santhal Family" (1938) and "To the Mill" (1956). The forward thrust, the centrifugal movement, the buoyance and lively lilt of the figures, active when seen from all sides, proclaim a genius who not only understood his subject and identified himself with it, but who also succeeded in making such a common-place material as concrete subservient to his needs. Ram Kinkar is without doubt a giant among contemporary Indian sculptors. He followed no trends, was not influenced by contemporary movements and styles prevalent abroad, or by commercial considerations in India. He worked on his own almost in isolation in Santiniketan, insular and creatively unique.

These notes, intended to provide a survey of the mid-century awakening in contemporary Indian art, have left out two diametrically opposed forces that shaped the development. The Bengal School of painting, a revivalist movement, led by Abanindranath Tagore and Nandalal Bose in Santiniketan, was inspired by the cave paintings in Ajanta and the Moghul miniatures. However, rendered in a decadent and archaic style and over-burdened with literary subject matter, the movement, though it found many patriotic adherents, had little vitality and contemporary relevance. It subsisted for three decades, almost giving up the ghost only by the 1950s. In pictorial terms it was much too sentimental and effete.

Much more effective and fecund was the Progressive Artists' Group which Francis Newton Souza formed in 1947 in Bombay and which spearheaded the modern movement. Besides Souza, amongst others Raza and Husain were associated with the group. The objectives of the group was to jettison the baggage of "traditional" sentiment, strengthen the vocabulary of painting by addressing the spectator directly in the idiom of modern art. There was to be no East or West in art, only art imbued with sensitivity and sensibility. In terms of art history the past had its relevance but the present possibilities of expressionism, surrealism and abstract art were to be the perimeters of the contemporary vision. This view might not have been expressed so manifestly but in effect the movement opened up avenues which led to modernism in Indian painting. This is relevant, as in a specific sense a lot of "contemporary" Indian art is imitatively traditional. There are pockets of miniature painters in Jaipur, and Udaipur, and Nadhwara. The folk and the tribal artist still practise art which is indigenous, and timeless, in theme and treatment echoing forms which have primitive and tribal origins, as in Bastar, in Madhya Pradesh, in Warli, in Maharashtra, or at Madhubani, in Bihar.

But the Himilayas stand, in nature and in art. The factors described and enumerated earlier function. The work illustrated in this essay provides a representative cross-section of significant art produced during the past half century with emphasis on the last two decades.

The work primarily falls into three categories. First there is what appears to be figural art in which the human form is rendered in its essentials, as a point of focus: but implications and nuances differ from artist to artist as the image is more of a symbol of life and humanity — a dream motif, a reminiscence, an esoteric ritual — than a depiction of people in definite human situations. (No Indian artist, not even those who subscribe to what has come to be understood as socially committed art — Gulam Sheikh, Vivan Sundaram, Nalini Malani, Gieve Patel, Sudhir Patwardhan, Bhupen Khakkar — presents a life situation as positive

11. *Artist: Aspita Singh*
"Drawing"
Photo courtesy of Lalit Kala Akademi.
12. *Artist: V S Gaitonde Untitled*
Photo courtesy of National Gallery of Modern Art, New Delhi.
13. *Artist: Ram Kuman Untitled*
Photo courtesy of National Gallery of Modern Art, New Delhi.

14. *Artist: Biren De*
"August 1971"
Photo courtesy of National Gallery of Modern Art, New Delhi.
15. *Artist: S H Raza*
"Painting 1976"
Photo courtesy of National Gallery of Modern Art, New Delhi.

12

11

13

14   15

16

17

18B

18C

18A

19

from the complex rhythm of trees and from natural formations. For example, she combines found stone pieces slightly carved with metal off-shoots. Prodosh Das Gupta creates variations on the germinal and universal egg-form. His figurative sculptures of the past are memory embodied images inspired by the kind of breath decribed earlier.

As one can see from these broad categories the contemporary Indian artist is concerned primarily with interpreting nature — the nature of man, for instance, expressing itself in manifestations of the dream, as in Husain's "Farmer's Family," Tyeb Mehta's "Human Landscape," Ramachandran's "Nuclear Ragini" and Anupam Sud's "Composition." Or with the mystery of nature in man and woman, locked in embrace, the one merging with the other, generating a cycle of energy in supreme bliss and repeating in themselves the history of man in a timeless moment which is both real and transcendental embodying the past and the future. This is the theme of Santosh's paintings of the past 10 years.

The Indian artist is also concerned with nature as the phenomenal environment. Francis Souza's bleak British landscape, powerfully suggested and delineated, is a contrast in its form of expression to Raza's "Painting 1976" in which the Indian environment is interpreted symbolically in four panels, top and bottom, left, depicting daytime, top right, evening, and bottom right, night. That this quasi-abstract portrayal of nature's moods and cycle — in terms of colour and its emotive implications — is based on an innately intuitive approach can be seen from the bands of colour placed horizontally on top of the central square composed of four sections. Significantly, this composite band repeats the luminiscent colour scheme of Biren De's "August 71" in which a glowing jewel symbol is encased in an aura comprising concentric bands ranging from green, blue, mauve, orange, red to yellow. This concentric compression — the aura — encloses an intensely white jewel-like iridescence.

Between the dream as an automatic psychic process in which imagination formulates itself in sleep, and reverie and reminiscence, which are day-time experiences referring to past and future, there is another manifestation of the spirit, memory, a reservoir that stores time-experiences as latent feeling which can be evoked. The landscape of memory is the subject of painters like Ram Kumar and V S Gaitonde. Nature as the phenomenal environment — the mountains, the sea, mist, cloud, sunshine and the perspectives of the landscape — when recalled as experience gets reflected as forms of feeling. It would appear that the planes of time get interlocked with the multiple perspectives of the landscape in Ram Kumar's paintings. There is sweep of variegated masses, structures in the painting referring abstractly to landscape elements, which suggest movement in time and space. The atmosphere which characterised many landscapes is transmuted into a complex but tangible mood. Wordsworth's definition of poetry "the overflow of powerful feelings recollected in tranquility" applies aptly to Ram Kumar's formulation of the remembered landscape.

In Gaitonde's work, quieter, more delicate, and more introspective, the theme of the sea, the surf, the play of light and the sea's mystique itself, is orchestrated as music heard within the mind and expressed as a score or an organic fabric, a fine lace-work of melodic motifs.

Contemporary Indian art is modern in its forms of expression. It is Indian in its mode of expression because it embodies, in this place and time, as I have defined, a specific sensibility.

social comment. Their so-called narrative paintings depict a story, or an incident or event but obliquely, by analogy, even allegory and through romanticisation).

Second, there are paintings dealing with the themes of cosmic and generative energy rendered symbolically.

Third, there are paintings which are ostensibly abstract but which relate to nature and the landscape.

Contemporary Indian sculpture has developed in about the same direction. Janakiram makes primarily iconic sculptures in beaten metal, welding in details. Nagji Patel's stone carvings are phallic in structure and in form. Latika Katt's recent series of "growth" sculptures derive inspiration

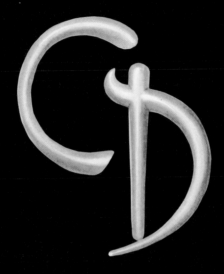

The Symbol
of the best Shirts
in India

Charagh Din
THE SHIRT PEOPLE

64, Wodehouse Road, Colaba, Bombay

For years we've hoste

Now we're giving India to the worl

The tradition of Indian hospitality is timeless. And today it's nowhere more evident than in the ITDC experience. With an accommodation chain that's the largest in India — ranging from 5-star hotels and beach resorts to travellers lodges. Plus a country-wide tourist transport network and an entertainment division. Each embodying the impeccable service and warm hospitality that typifies the unique Indian experience.

Now we're carrying this experience abroad. Backed by an expertise in tourism that compares with the best, we have already secured a number of international assignments. The hotel project at Dokan and Mosul in Iraq, Limassol in Cyprus and the Mayur Restaurant in Prague. Each created in contemporary style,

Ashok Hotel, New Delhi, India   Lotus Ashok, Limassol, Cyprus

e *world in India.*

yet with the unmistakable Indian spirit.

For years the world has been our guest in India. Today we're ready to host the world, anywhere across the globe.

...ha Mahal Palace Hotel, Mysore, India   Mosul Hotel Project, Iraq

For information
contact Air India offices anywhere in the world,
or write to:

Divisional Manager (Marketing)

India Tourism Development Corporation
Jeevan Vihar, 3 Sansad Marg
New Delhi-110001 India

Tel 310923   Telex 031-2831
Cables TOURISM NEW DELHI

 **The Ashok Group**

India's host to the world

India Tourism Development Corporation

CAS-423

Behind every pair of good jeans
there is a famous label

AViS
JEANS
THE TOUGH ONES

THE SEARCH FOR ENERGY

Maheshwar Dayal

Energy plays a fundamental role in economic and social development. In fact, there is a direct correlation between the level of economic development and the consumption of energy, and in developing countries the standard of living is found to rise with increase in the per capita consumption of energy. The need for large increases in energy production and consumption was realised in the early stages of India's planned development, and major efforts have been made in this direction with considerable success. The growth in the energy production and consumption — both commercial and non-commercial — has more than tripled over the last three decades.

The energy scene in India today is based on a large variety of sources, ranging from heat energy obtained by burning agricultural and animal wastes to electricity obtained from nuclear fuels. Besides energy from fuels, significant amounts of energy are obtained from the use of draught animal power. The most important commercial energy sources are coal, lignite, oil and hydro electricity, supplemented to a small but increasing extent by nuclear energy. Firewood, agricultural waste and animal waste are the important non-commercial sources.

Coal is the most abundant resource of commercial energy in India today. It is used as an important energy source in practically all sectors of the economy except agriculture. The production of all grades of coal in 1980-81 was 114 million tonnes. The total estimated reserves (proven, inferred and indicated) of coal up to a depth of 600 metres and in seam thicknesses of up to 1.2 m amount to about 85,000 million tonnes (1978). The distribution of coal is, however, uneven, with mines being located in just a few states (particularly West Bengal, Bihar and Andhra Pradesh). Coal thus has to be transported over long distances to meet the demands of industry, powerhouses and the domestic sector. The estimated demand for coal at the end of the sixth plan (1984-85) is 168 million tonnes.

Lignite is found in the states of Tamil Nadu, Gujarat and Rajasthan. In 1976-77, a production of about 4 million tonnes was achieved (mostly in Tamil Nadu); this, however, for various reasons, had decreased to 2.9 million tonnes by 1979-80. However, as a result of various schemes being launched in the sixth plan, the production of lignite is expected to increase to 8 million tonnes by 1984-85.

Oil is used for a variety of purposes in all sectors of the economy. Besides being a source of energy, oil is also an important raw material for the production of petro-chemicals and fertilisers. Over 80 per cent of the total oil used as an energy source is consumed in two sectors — transport and household. Another sector which is showing a continuously rising demand is agriculture, where oil is used to run tractors and irrigation pumps. The total oil consumption in 1978-79 was about 28 million tonnes, of which about 15.7 per cent was for non-energy uses. It must be emphasised that the use of oil in India is restricted almost entirely to vital needs of development. About 40 per cent of the crude oil requirement is met through indigenous production; the balance of the requirement of crude oil and petroleum products is being met through imports, which have been absorbing over two-thirds of the country's earnings of foreign exchange. As on January 1, 1980, the net recoverable reserves of oil in the definite category were about 360 million tonnes and of gas about 250 billion cubic metres. The production target for domestic oil, both on land and offshore for 1984-85 is 21.6 million tonnes, while

Much research is now going into the development of renewable sources of energy: A biogas plant, below left; and using biogas to operate a refrigerator, below right, a kiln, bottom left, a small cooker, centre right, and a still, bottom right, are among the various practical applications of solar power.

the demand may reach a level of 45.5 million tonnes.

The total installed power generating capacity in India which was only 2,300 MW in 1950, increased to about 31,000 MW by March 1980. During this period, the per capita annual consumption of electricity increased from 18 kWh to 130 kWh. The total electricity generation in 1979-80 amounted to 112 TWh and in 1980-81 to 121 TWh (provisional). The installed capacity for hydroelectric power generation increased from 560 MW in 1950-51 to about 11,791 MW at the end of 1980-81. The total hydroelectric potential in the country is presently estimated at about 75,400 MW at 60 per cent load factor. Only about 11 per cent of this potential has been developed so far. Efforts are being made in the Sixth Plan to develop the hydroelectric potential to a level of about 16,150 MW. However, a substantial portion of the unexploited potential lies in sub-Himalayan regions of northern and north-eastern India which, due to terrain and distance from load centres, present technical and practical problems for harnessing and transmitting the power. Exploitation of the potential in low head sources and canal drops appears to be increasingly attractive.

Large as the commercial energy resources of India appear, the reserves are small in per capita terms compared to many other countries. While India has reserves of 176 tonnes of coal per person, the USA has 13,488 tonnes, the USSR 22,066 tonnes and China 1,168 tonnes. The proven reserves of oil are only 0.55 tonnes per capita as against 34.83 tonnes in the USSR, 16.32 tonnes in the USA and 2.86 tonnes in China. Interestingly, low per capita resources of fossil fuels are a feature of developing countries in South and Southeast Asia, Latin America and Africa.

Firewood is the most important non-commercial fuel in India. It is obtained from forests, privately owned plantations, wood lots and from trees on roadsides and on the banks of rivers and canals. About 23 per cent of the total area of the country is covered by forests. The wood from forests meets a variety of industrial demands besides fuel requirements. The available information about firewood resources is somewhat inadequate. It would, however, appear that firewood accounts for about two-thirds of the total energy contribution from non-commercial sources in rural households, and about 40 per cent in urban households. The total consumption of firewood in 1975-76 has been estimated at 133 million tonnes. It is becoming increasingly scarce, and in many parts of the country it has ceased to be non-commercial in the strict sense. The competition for land-use for agricultural, industrial and housing activity will lead to additional constraints on fuel wood production. This may particularly affect the rural population.

The amount of agricultural wastes available as a source of energy depends on the extent of agricultural production and varies with different crops. Few reliable studies are available on the quantity of vegetable matter produced with each crop. The working group on energy policy estimated that about 203 million tonnes of agricultural wastes might have become available in the country in 1975-76, of which the actual consumption as fuel might be about 40 million tonnes. About 73 million tonnes of animal dung are also estimated to have been consumed in 1975-76, almost all of it in the household sector.

As already mentioned, draught animal power is a significant source of energy, particularly in the rural areas. There are roughly 80 million work animals, of which 70 million are bullocks; the rest are buffaloes, horses and camels. In addition, there are donkeys, mules and elephants. Though no specific data is available, each animal is estimated to generate 0.373 kW on average. There are about 15 million animal-drawn carts in the country, 75 per cent of which operate in rural areas. The total freight carried by the carts has been estimated at 3,120 million ton-kilometres in rural areas and 11,700 million ton-kilometres in urban areas per year.

It will be seen from the above that great progress has been made in the production of energy, and the types of energy being produced, as compared with the position three decades ago. This has been brought about by considerable efforts in the field of research, development and application of technology. Thus in 1947, the relatively small amount of commercial energy consumption was largely provided by coal and hydroelectricity; a very small amount of oil, mostly imported, was used. One of the earliest areas of development in this field was an expanded programme of exploration and drilling for oil. This involved R&D in all the associated fields of basic as well as applied sciences, including geophysics, geology, mathematics, mechanical and chemical engineering disciplines. A major result has been the growing location of oil fields in India both onshore and offshore, so that today India is producing more than 40 per cent from its own fields inspite of an increasing overall consumption of oil which has risen from just 8 million tonnes a year in 1953-54 to about 30 million tonnes in 1978-79.

A special feature of the growth in oil technology has been the offshore developments which have also involved inputs of R&D in the areas of marine science and technology. The growing indigenous production of oil helped in the expansion of certain oil-based products which were necessary for economic development in the late fifties and sixties.

Early analysis of the energy situation in India also led to the conclusion that recourse will have to be made to non-conventional sources such as nuclear energy, to supplement the conventional resources, in increasing fashion. For this purpose, R&D started in the mid-fifties on establishing an integrated base for nuclear energy development, and atomic research reactors as well as associated technologies to deal with the needs of the complete nuclear fuel cycle were developed. By the early sixties, an analysis of the regional distribution of energy resources indicated the economic viability of introducing nuclear power in areas far from the coalfields, and hence nuclear power installation work was also started. The first nuclear power station at Tarapur went into production in 1969 and has by now already earned well above its investment cost from large-scale sales of electricity on a regular commercial basis to the power networks of Maharashtra and Gujarat in western India. Another atomic power unit at Rajasthan has also been operating for some years now and work on additional units is proceeding. Thus, to the conventional resources of energy, nuclear resources have also been providing a modest supplement.

Inspite of the considerable growth in the quantum and range of energy production, the level of energy consumption remains low as compared with the total population of the country. The per capita consumption of commercial sources of energy is only about 178 kilogrammes of coal equivalent as compared to average values of two to six thousand for the industrially developed countries. This is a measure of the very large population base of the country; nonetheless, it signifies the need for much greater production as well as

Practical applications of solar power further include a crop dryer, below left, together with a solar-powered hut, below right, and brewery, centre right.
Bottom left: An up-to-date windmill design.
Bottom right: A photovoltaic pump in use in the fields.

greater efficiency in the utilisation of energy. For this purpose, apart from industrial scale production, a great deal of research and development has been initiated, for the application of modern science and technology in the field of energy. The programme has been based and is evolving with due regard to the indigenous sources of energy and the escalating demands of a large and growing population.

Thus coal is the most important source of commercial energy and since India has large reserves of coal, this is likely to continue to be the main source in the next decade or so. Research and development in this sector has been well established and a number of organisations are doing extensive work in this field. Schemes in progress relate largely to the improvement of mining practices so as to increase the recovery of coal and protect the resources from fire hazards and collapse of mines. Work is also being initiated for the development of mining technologies so as to develop larger and deeper mines to meet the greatly expanded requirements for coal in the next several years. Considerable work has been done in the field of coal beneficiation. This is essential in order to treat the ash and waste material in coal and render it more useful. A number of washeries have also been set up and are in regular production. The R&D schemes in the field of beneficiation also cover areas of agglomeration of coal, more efficient recovery from washeries, utilisation of rejects from beneficiation plants, froth flotation, oil agglomeration and chemical demineralisation. From the point of view of supplying coal-based smokeless fuels, low temperature carbonisation techniques have been developed, and work is being done to bring this to the stage of wider commercialisation. R&D efforts in coal combustion, particularly to improve the efficiency of burning of low grade coals which are plentiful in India, are extremely important. In this connection, work is under way at several research centres on fluidised bed combustion. A 10 tonnes per hour experimental fluidised bed boiler has been developed and tested, and work is underway to upscale this. Fluidised bed processes have been developed which offer promise of expansion to enable utilisation on a commercial scale.

With the ever-increasing prices of oil, technologies for the gasification and liquefaction of coal are becoming increasingly interesting from an economic point of view. Work is being pursued on both these aspects in India by the different coal research institutes. Processes for gasification and liquefaction have been developed and upscaling for commercial exploitation is being investigated.

An important new development in India in R&D related to coal is magneto-hydro-dynamics (MHD). Work in this area is being co-ordinated by the commission for additional sources of energy through an integrated programme. An experimental coal-based MHD unit (5-15 thermal MW) is already under construction. This could be a promising method of significantly expanding the efficiency of utilisation of our coal reserves. In other industrialised countries, attention so far on MHD has been largely based on use of natural gas as the feedstock. Development of coal-based MHD plant shows promise of raising the overall efficiencies of coal utilisation for power from 35-40 per cent to as much as 60-65 per cent. The techno-economic viability of these plants will be calculated as work on the experimental unit proceeds and its operational experience accumulates

In the area of oil, a number of research and development institutes have been set up and have been accumulating valuable experience. These include the Institute for Petroleum Exploration, Indian Institute of Petroleum, Indian Oil Company (R&D centre) Institute for Reservoir Studies etc. The Institute for Petroleum Exploration has been carrying out basic and applied research to support the exploration programme, and assist in understanding the environment of reservoir studies including sedimentary processes and delta formation, oil generation, production and reservoir problems. Work has also been proceeding on indigenous development of equipment required for oil exploration and also development of sophisticated techniques for resolving geological, geophysical and reservoir problems. The Institute for Reservoir Studies is providing R&D inputs necessary to develop methods of secondary and tertiary recovery technologies in order to maximise the yield from oil reservoirs.

In order to meet the needs for the various oil products that are required by industry, agriculture and transportation, a major development that has taken place in India is the setting up of a number of refineries. This has helped to cut down the need for importing refined products which are much more costly, to just 10 per cent of the total consumption of oil and its products. The import requirements at present are therefore almost all in the form of crude oil and the refining is almost entirely done in India. R&D in the oil sector thus has also increasingly included R&D in the refining technologies. In view of the fact that the demand for middle distillates is large in India, accounting for 54.1 per cent of the total consumption of oil and oil products, process technologies to upgrade heavier fractions such as LSHS to distillates products is being worked out. A scheme for establishing secondary processing facilities is already in progress in a number of refineries.

In the area of hydro energy, research and development is being done in all the areas of hydro engineering including civil engineering, hydraulics and power equipment. This is a field in which there has been long engineering experience in India, and we have been happy to receive increasing numbers of students, research workers and trainees from other developing countries. Among the new developments being worked on are lower cost civil structures, different soil conditions and development of micro-hydel and low-head schemes and equipment.

Considerably more R&D needs to be done in these conventional energy areas of coal, oil and hydro. The areas of special research interest have been identified, and include low-temperature carbonisation, gasification, liquefaction and transport of coal, enhanced recoveries for oil and reduced power system losses.

Turning now to non-conventional sources of energy, reference has already been made to development in the field of nuclear energy. Research and development has enabled the country to possess the capability for the full range of operations required in the nuclear fuel cycle, from mining of nuclear fuels, processing and manufacture of fuel elements for reactors, reactor construction and operation, and reprocessing of the used fuels. Work is also proceeding on fast breeder technologies and a fast breeder test reactor which will also produce power on a demonstration basis is under construction. Studies are in progress regarding the feasibility of using thorium of which vast deposits exist in India. Fusion is also being investigated

It is realised, however, that increasing attention needs to be given now to the renewable sources of energy. For this

Conventional sources of energy include hydroelectric power, such as the hydro power stations at the Gandhisagar dam, top right, and the Khaper Khera power station, below left. Efforts are being made to develop hydroelectric potential.
Below right: The thermal power station at Bokharo.
Centre left: Non-conventional sources are being tapped in the search for new forms of energy. The Bhabha Atomic Research Centre, with the reactor "Apsara" on the left, led to the development of atomic power.
Centre right: The Rajasthan atomic power plant.
Firewood is the most important non-commercial fuel in India, but is becoming increasingly scarce due to the stripping of forests.
Afforestation projects, such as the teak forest of Assam, bottom left, and the bamboo plantations in Meghalaya, bottom right, help restore the ecological balance.
Colour photography by Satish Sharma. B/W photos courtesy of Press Information Bureau, Government of India, and Indian Council of Agricultural Research.

purpose, important efforts have been undertaken in India particularly in the field of solar energy, biomass and wind. Although 40 per cent or more of the total energy used in India in fact already comes from such sources, the manner of their use is traditional and inefficient, leading to loss of potential energy and deforestation. The challenge now is to develop modern methods of using these sources so that the efficiency of energy conversion is greatly enhanced, and energies used in a concentrated way to provide mechanical and electrical power, and liquid fuels. This would enable the growth of intensified economic activity in the rural as well as urban areas which could increase purchasing power and standards of living. Research and development has been carried out for some years, but has been recently intensified, towards meeting these objectives. This is now being done as a co-ordinated national effort under a newly created commission for additional sources of energy which has been given executive and financial powers for the development of new and renewable sources of energy. Several renewable energy systems and devices have now been brought to the stage of commercial utilisation or are on the threshold of such production.

Biogas   Based on cattle waste, biogas is one such area in which India has made pioneering advances. Almost 100,000 such units of the family type are in operation in different parts of the country, and in the current five-year plan it is intended to build 400,000 such units. Large community/institution type plants are also being increased. Recent R&D has led to significant results in diversifying the feed possibilities for biogas plants, increasing efficiency and reducing costs. Plants based on water hyacinth and various agricultural/vegetable wastes have been developed. The gas has been used for cooking and lighting; engines for using the gas to produce mechanical power and also to generate electricity are now in commerical production. The utilisation of these engines is being expanded. Biogas-generated mechanical and electric power appears to be economically competitive in large areas of the country not covered by the transmission network, as generation by this method involves less investment than that in conventional power plus transmission in several areas, while the running costs are small and offset by the value of the residue which is very good fertiliser.

Solar thermal   In the solar thermal systems, water heating units are already in commerical production. These have been applied for domestic, institutional and industrial units for low and medium temperature heat requirements. Apart from flat plate collectors with or without selective coatings, new types of collector systems such as evacuated tube, glass fibre body, parabolic and parabolid concentrating collectors are under development. Solar drying systems have also been brought to the stage of commercialisation; these include solar timber kilns, solar thermal air heating systems for grain and cash crop drying, milk drying, tobacco curing etc. Solar cookers for individual and group uses are also in commercial production now in some parts of the country, and large scale utilisation is being promoted. Solar stills for conversion of saline and brackish water into potable drinking water (an important requirement in many rural areas of India) have also been developed.

Solar photovoltaics   In the area of solar photovoltaics, in-

digenous manufacture of single crystal silicon solar cells has been developed and is underway. Facilities for production of solar grade silicon have also been established. Work is going on to develop economical methods of producing the raw material and for reducing the cost of solar cell production. Other solar cell materials being studied include cadmium sulphide, polycrystalline and amorphous silicon etc. Photovoltaic systems have also started being used (in a small way as yet) for lighting in community establishments and lighthouses, communication equipment, cathodic protection of oil piplines, offshore platforms providing power for radio and television sets, and pumping water for micro-irrigation and drinking water supply. Several such units have been installed in different parts of the country for demonstration purposes and the number of such units are being steadily increased.

Wind   In regard to wind energy, newly developed windmill pumps have been installed in different parts of the country. Small-size wind electric generators have also been developed.

Fuel wood and biomass   To meet the fuel wood crisis, work is being intensified on energy plantations and on identification of species which can be grown on a short rotation system and on saline and alkaline soils. Work is also underway for the utilisation of biomass and wood wastes and residues.

The production of fuels and chemicals from agricultural residues offers the opportunity to combine improved waste disposal and energy recovery technologies into one process with lesser environmental degradation. Ethanol, a potential chemical feedstock, can be obtained by fermentation of enzymatically hydrolysed cellulosic materials with a conversion efficiency of 97 per cent. Considerable research has been carried out in India on the different bioconversion routes for ethanol production from cellulosic residues. However, other uses for these residues, particularly industrial uses, as also the question of land use for production of ethanol instead of food, would have to be considered.

Likewise, it has been found that it would be more advantageous to use ethanol and methanol as raw materials in the chemical industry rather than as fuels. There is a great need for increasing the production of alcohol for use in the chemical industry in India which is well established and is growing; this could also in some cases contribute to lessening the pressure on petro-based feedstocks which have uses as an energy source. Nevertheless, work is being intensified for the conversion of biomass products which are not being used for other purposes, such as ligno-cellulosic materials, as also wood and agro wastes.

A wide range of energy resources have been developed in India and work is underway for expanding their production as well as developing new techniques and harnessing new resources. In a big country like India with the various requirements of industry and agriculture, of the centralised and decentralised sectors of the economy, and the need for energy in various forms (heat, light, mechanical and electrical power), there is scope for the development of different forms of energy suited to different applications at different locations. The development in all these areas — conventional, non-conventional and renewable sources — offers every hope of meeting the objective of making India self-sufficient in energy.

Natural habitat of the
Kyasanur Forest Disease v
Insets show the monkey t
rodent and the ticks, all
involved in the cycle of th
virus. Ecological change
caused the existence of th
new virus.

Ronald Ross, who made the
discovery that malaria is
transmitted by mosquitoes.

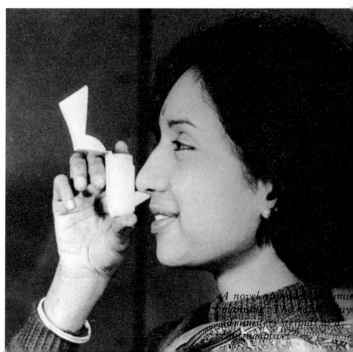

A novel ap
planning
administers steroids
```
```

MEDICINE
AND THE HEALTH
REVOLUTION

V. Ramalingaswamy

India has a rich heritage of medicine dating back to the Vedic times. The classical works of legendary men of medicine — the physician Charka, 1000 BC, the surgeon Sushrut, 600 BC and the clinician *par excellence* Vagbhatta, 600 AD — are well known. The Ayurvedic system of medicine which they founded still flourishes today. Apart from its rich *materia medica*, Ayurveda, meaning literally the science of life, views man as an integrated personality. It recognises the influence of mind over the body and vice-versa, and looks upon health as not merely the absence of disease, but as one of complete mental and physical well-being. Sushrut was credited with amazing surgical skills. Ayurveda presents a holistic approach to man and his problems and is truly, not simply a disease-oriented but a health-oriented system. It emphasises ethical aspects of the art and science of *healing*.

In medieval times, there was a fruitful interaction between Ayurveda and the Unani system of medicine brought into India by the Moghuls and still later, Ayurveda interacted with modern medicine brought into India by the British, French and Portuguese colonisers. As a result of the interaction of Ayurveda and Unani in medieval times, the use of metallic and mineral preparations in the treatment of disease came to be established.

Shortly after Ehrlich, Pasteur and Koch ushered in the golden age of medicine in western Europe around the middle of the last century, medical officers in India working on their own initiative and with limited laboratory facilities were making important contributions to our knowledge of tropical diseases. Thus Lewis discovered trypanosomes and filaria, Vandyke Carter discovered spirilla, leprosy and mycetoma, McNamara discovered cholera and Fayrer worked with snake venoms. A bacteriological laboratory was established in Agra in 1892, and a plague laboratory was set up in Bombay in 1896 which eventually became the Haffkine Institute. A string of Pasteur Institutes began to be established from 1900 onwards. By 1897, Haffkine, who was deputed to work on the plague problem, had evolved a vaccine which was the first to be used on a large scale against this disease and which, with modifications, remains an effective weapon for the prevention of plague even today. In the same year Ronald Ross discovered the transmission of malaria by mosquitoes at Secunderabad and a few years later, Donavan, working in the physiology department of the Madras Medical College, Madras, demonstrated the presence of the parasite now known as *Leishmania donovani* in the spleens of patients suffering from kala-azar. Shortly afterwards, Rogers demonstrated the effectiveness of emetine in the treatment of amoebiasis.

These were truly impressive advances in the study of communicable diseases made in a relatively short period of time. It was against this background that the Indian Research Fund Association, the predecessor of the present Indian Council of Medical Research (ICMR) was established in 1911, two years before the British Medical Research Council was established. The *Indian Journal of Medical Research,* the official organ of the ICMR, has been in continuous publication since 1913, as the main forum for communicating research contributions in the field of medical sciences in India. From its inception, medical research in India began to be addressed to the most important health problems of India, initially to communicable diseases and subsequently to nutrition, maternal and child health, indigenous drugs and more recently to contraceptive technology, non-communicable diseases and health care delivery systems.

At the same time, it was realised that progress was not possible without basic research; and that there could be no development without it. The urgent health problems facing the country were investigated through a deliberate planning process. A network of institutions was established. Research in medical colleges was strengthened. Research units were established to provide continuing support to researchers in the frontier areas of medical science. Regional institutions were encouraged to tackle regional problems, and conditions were created for attracting young and promising workers to a career in research. Projects were supported on the basis of their scientific merit, timeliness and promise, and the pool of talent available in the country was brought to bear upon problems of national importance. An organisation with great flexibility and competence to mount a substantial research effort to meet the health needs of India was thus established.

The net result of this effort has been that substantial gains to national health were made in return for relatively small investments. Life expectancy at birth has increased from around 32 to a little over 50 years in the past 25 years, a phenomenal rate of nearly one year of increase every year. Crude death rates have been declining from a high of 47.2 during 1911 to 1921, to somewhere around 15 at the present time.

The infant mortality rate has also declined since the turn of the century although it is still quite high, ie around 125 per thousand live births at the present time. India adopted family planning as an official policy and as an integral part of socio-economic development, way back in 1952. Stabilising the growth of population was at the centre of planned development. The census of March 1981 revealed that India's population stood at 684 million at that time. The population growth rate for the decade 1971 to 1981 showed for the first time a slight decrease over the rate recorded in the previous decade (1961 to 1971).

Ronald Ross's discovery of the transmission of malaria by the anopheles mosquitoes, followed by the accumulation of a vast amount of information on the biology of malaria transmitting vectors in India, paved the way for the spectacular initial successes achieved in India in the control of malaria which led to the euphoric concept of eradication of malaria. The successes were achieved mainly by interrupting the man-vector contact through residual insecticide spraying of houses and reduction of vector population through anti-larval measures. DDT was highly effective against mosquitoes which rested indoors. The result was that the incidence of malaria in India came down from 75 million cases in 1947 to a little over 100,000 in 1967. Likewise, mortality from malaria came down from 800,000 to zero level during this same period. Today, however, the problems of multiple malaria vector resistance to insecticides, the exophilic behaviour of vectors, drug resistance of the parasite together with factors associated with human ecology and managerial problems, have conspired to bring about a setback to the malaria control programme. An intensive research programme has been mounted in India to overcome these problems and the incidence of malaria is again beginning to go down.

Equally spectacular results were obtained in the initial stages in the control of kala-azar as a fallout or a bonus from the malaria control programme. As mentioned earlier, the causative organism of kala-azar was discovered by Donavan in Madras in 1903. Upendra Brahamchari discovered in 1920 ureastibamine as a specific treatment of kala-azar. Antimony compounds continue to be the mainstay of kala-azar treatment even today

Nearly one quarter of all leprosy patients in the world live in India, ie about three million, about a fifth of whom are infectious. The National Leprosy Control Programme, based upon survey, education and treatment with sulphones, was launched in India nearly 25 years ago and an extensive infrastructure for leprosy control operations has been built in the country. While some progress has been made, new cases continue to be discovered, deformities continue to occur, the drop-out rates are still high and an indefinite number of cases remain undetected and untreated. Added to this is the growing menace of the twin problems of resistance and persistance of lepra bacilli. As we progress through the 1980s, a new sense of hope is being generated for the control of leprosy, and this is in the field of anti-leprosy vaccines. While the World Health Organisation who sponsored studies are using killed leprosy bacilli in the vaccine, Indian researchers are using cross-reactive mycobacteria, either killed or alive, for this purpose. Encouraging responses have been obtained by Indian researchers using the cross-reactive mycobacteria on skin test conversions.

Though the Indian vaccines are presently under trial, Indian researchers, while awaiting the outcome of these studies on primary prevention of leprosy using vaccines, are undertaking studies for the widespread use of combination drug therapy with rifampicin, clofazimine, dapsone and other chemo-therapeutic agents in suitable combinations to bring down the infection load in the community. There is a modest optimism that what was seemingly a situation of despair in the sixties and seventies can now be converted to a situation of hope and promise in the eighties and nineties in the control of leprosy.

Two-hundred and thirty-six million people in India are exposed to the risk of infection with filaria. Ordinarily filarial infection does not kill but produces ill-health and incapacitation. By blocking the lymphatic channels, it produces the ugly condition of elephantiasis. Unplanned urbanisation is changing ecological conditions favourable for the spread of filariasis everywhere. For example, Pondicherry, in south India, is highly endemic for filariasis, with a micro-filaria carrier rate of 17.8 per cent in the general population and a very high density of vectors that transmit filariasis.

The problems of resistance of vectors to insecticides and of behavioural changes in the vectors themselves have tended to outwit man in his search for the control of insect vectors transmitting filaria. The ICMR is implementing a new integrated strategy for the control of filariasis by which immature vectors will be attacked by a judicial use of bio-environmental methods, minor engineering and, in selected instances, by the use of insecticides. People are being involved through a process of education in order to secure their participation actively in the control programme. The control of vectors through biological methods such as the use of micro-organisms that are naturally inimical to the vectors, is the approach that is being used here. Bioregulation of certain vector populations already occurs in nature. No single measure is likely to control the mosquitoes in all situations. It is, therefore, essential to think in terms of integrated control measures. Source reduction is an age-old dictum in vector control which has unfortunately receded to the background in recent years under the euphoria of DDT.

Tuberculosis is an age-old scourge, a leading cause of mortality and morbidity in India today and in many developing countries. Its' treatment has changed over the years from a clinical speciality to a widely applied community health activity. The ICMR's Tuberculosis Research Centre at Madras, which is a superb example of international co-operation in research, in this case involving the British Medical Research Council and the World Health Organisation, discovered in 1959 that ambulatory, domiciliary treatment of tuberculosis is highly effective without the risk of infection for family contacts. These findings constituted a major departure from the traditional sanitorium treatment and offered a new avenue for nation-wide programmes in the control of tuberculosis in developing countries. Domiciliary treatment offered great social advantages without any clinical disadvantages when compared with sanitorium treatment. By this method, the cost of treatment was reduced considerably and it was possible to extend the chemotherapy of tuberculosis into the rural areas and far-flung areas of any country.

Again in 1964, this centre demonstrated that intermittent regimens of treatment can be as effective as daily regimens of treatment, thus making the delivery of drugs over a long period of time much more convenient and under full supervision. Then came, in 1972, the short course regimens which reduced the conventional duration of treatment to approximately one half — about six months or so. The work of the centre has proved to be of immense value not only to developing but also to developed countries. India is attempting to control tuberculosis through the National Tuberculosis Control Programme which consists of early case detection, continued chemotherapy and BCG vaccination.

It is estimated that nearly 1.5 million children die in India each year on account of acute diarrhoeal disease. A simple glucose salt mixture has been shown to be highly effective when given orally in the early stages of the disease in dramatically reducing mortality among children suffering from acute diarrhoeal diseases, including cholera. This treatment is inexpensive and obviates the need for hospital admission, so it can be used even by the rural masses in the remotest corner of the country. Intensive efforts are being made to popularise this simple remedy. Indian scientists have made major contributions to the study of cholera toxins; they discovered the infant rabbit model for the experimental study of cholera and demonstrated dramatic results in reducing mortality from acute diarrhoea in children by the oral glucose-salt-fluid treatment. The most striking example is a recent finding that the delivery of glucose saline oral fluid reduced the death rate from cholera in the state of Manipur in India down to 0.8 per cent, which constitutes a significant landmark in our fight against cholera.

Viruses are of increasing concern in public health. The National Institute of Virology in Pune is a major biomedical resource in this part of the world. It is an international reference centre on arthropod-borne virus diseases. In the course of the 25 years or more of its existence, this institute has discovered 25 viruses which are entirely new to science, which have been registered as new viruses in the International Catalogue of Arthropod-borne Viruses. The discovery of the disease, now widely known as *Kyasanur Forest Disease*

(KFD), is a significant contribution to biomedical science. An indigenous virus, now known as KFD virus, was maintaining itself in the Kyasanur Forest on the eastern slopes of the Western Ghats in Karnataka in an enzootic cycle with ticks mainly parasitic on small and large animals. The virus is entirely new to science and the disease is the only disease in which ticks, monkeys and man are involved. Encroachment by man of forests results in the creation of artificial boundaries between virgin forests and new cultivations, with rodents, insectivores and parasitic arthropods entering into new relationships with man and his domestic animals. Human cases are dead ends of a tangential line of transmission. The disease is characterised by high fatality rates. Partial protection against the disease has been demonstrated by the use of a formalised tissue culture vaccine developed in India.

This institute is also now playing an important role in studies on the epidemiology and control of Japanese encephalitis which has assumed epidemic proportions in the southern and eastern parts of India in recent years.

The regulation of human fertility in the best interests of the mother, child and society and indeed in the best interests of the future of man, is the most crucial issue of our time. There are many gaps in our biological and sociological knowledge relating to human reproduction and fertility regulation. We need safer, more effective and more acceptable agents of contraception.

It is also clear that where motivation is high and infrastructure for delivery of services is adequate, currently available contraceptive methods are effective. Indian scientists are working on broadening the range of choice of methods of contraception. Copper T 200 has been shown to have advantages over Lippes loop; newer, long acting hormonal contraceptives are being investigated. Non-surgical methods of sterilisation which can be readily performed by non-physicians on an out-patient basis are being studied. The potential of prostaglandins for inducing abortion has been established. Two novel approaches — the intra-nasal administration of steroids and the immunological approach to fertility regulation in the female — are being developed by Indian scientists, which hold great promise for the future. A simple, reliable and inexpensive diagnostic kit has been developed by Indian scientists which should facilitate the medical termination of pregnancy at an early stage when the safe vacuum suction method can be applied.

Malnutrition continues to be an important contributory factor to much of the mortality and morbidity especially in mothers, infants and young children. Studies at the National Institute of Nutrition (NIN), Hyderabad, which is the oldest research institute under the ICMR, showed that the diets of children with protein energy malnutrition do not provide sufficient energy, and as a result the entire approach to the control of this form of malnutrition has undergone a radical change not only in India but in other developing countries as well. Scientists at the NIN showed that the nutritional needs of infants can be met effectively from locally available and culturally acceptable low cost foods, against this background the institute has developed a large number of recipes. Home-based technologies in preparing such foods using simple techniques have been demonstrated. In suitable combinations, cereals and legumes can satisfy nutritional requirements of young growing children. Adequate diets can be designed even for small children on the basis of cereals and legumes in accordance

Below: Primary health care. The use of simple technologies and village-based health care agents benefits the community. A worker (right) explains child care to a group of village women.
Bottom: Involving the community. Health workers from within the community can help create a health revolution.

Photos courtesy of Indian Council of Medical Research and Central Health Education Bureau.

with local customs and habits. It has been shown that it is the use of a simple technology and determined human action that holds the key to the improvement of nutrition of children under the age of three.

Nutritional blindness in the form of keratomalacia due to deficiency of vitamin-A in children below the age of five years continues to occur; estimates vary between 15,000 and 40,000 cases of such blindness occurring every year in India. NIN has developed a method by which this form of blindness can be prevented at the community level. The method consists of administration of a massive dose of vitamin-A (200,000 international units) once in six months to children at risk between the ages of one and five years. This method is now part of a national programme for the prevention of blindness. Over 20 million children are being covered under this programme.

Iron deficiency anaemia is one of the most wide-spread conditions in India and other parts of the developing world. It is especially common in pregnant women and pre-school children. This condition contributes significantly to high maternal mortality. The NIN has now developed a method by which common salt can be fortified with iron so that the iron intake of communities would go up substantially. Ferric ortho-phosphate is the compound that is used for fortification, and approximately one milligram of elemental iron is provided daily by this method. Field studies have demonstrated that over a period of 12 to 18 months, the introduction of iron fortified salt in a community results in a significant reduction of anaemia.

Endemic goitre occurs all along the sub-Himalayan mountain ranges of northern India and also in pockets in other parts of the country. The provision of salt fortified with potassium iodate to ensure a regular intake of as small a quantity as 100 micrograms of iodine everyday has been shown to reduce the incidence of goitre to the point of elimination in the Kangra valley. Injection of pregnant women with iodised oil is known to wipe out deaf-mutism and cretinism. Iodised oil can also be given by mouth, and is quite effective. These studies have formed the basis for a national goitre control programme throughout the country.

Lathyrism is due to the consumption of the pea, *Lathyrus sativus*. The toxin in the pea has been identified and it has been shown that the toxin can be removed by simple domestic processing.

It must be added that improvement in community health in developing countries is not merely a question of applying available technologies. There are many situations in the developing world where the existing technologies need to be improved, and new technologies discovered eg oral polio vaccine containing live virus, which has been so effective as a public health measure in Western countries in practically wiping out poliomyelitis. It does not seem to produce as high antibody levels to the three virus types as one would like to see in developing countries, even when the potency of the vaccine is ensured during transit under cold chain conditions. A carefully controlled trial involving 300,000 rural population in Chingleput district in south India, extending over a 10 year period, has revealed that BCG vaccine is not effective against lung tuberculosis. The reasons for this are not entirely clear but further work is going on. There are also problems connected with the dosage and effectiveness of drugs in populations that are chronically undernourished and suffering from endemic parasitic diseases. The interaction of commonly used drugs with contraceptive agents is also a subject of study.

The basic philosophy of medical research policy in India is not only to make medicine more efficient but also to apply the results of research endeavour for the human good. It also aims at maintaining a climate of discovery for the flourishing of indigenous scientific talent.

India is a staunch advocate of the Alma Ata Declaration using the primary health care approach for the achievement of the goal of health for all by the year 2000. To achieve this target, an inter-sectoral approach needs to be adopted and health has to be conceived as a major pathway to development. Experience across the world has shown that major improvements in health are possible by the determined application of known health technologies and at costs that are affordable even by the poor nations of the world, given able leadership, well designed and effectively operated programmes and appropriate forms and techniques of health care delivery along with professional back-up support.

Community-based studies in India have shown, as in other parts of the world, that infant and child mortality rates can be reduced by one-third to one-half or more within one to five years at a cost less than the equivalent of two per cent of the per capita income. The use of simple technologies, village-based health care agents, supportive supervision of their work by the health infrastructure, the use of appropriate mix of interventions to suit local epidemiological situations and the involvement of the community in these activities are the guiding principles. It is possible to bring about a health revolution within a reasonably short period of time. India's sixth five-year plan places major emphasis upon primary health care approach.

In conclusion, reference may be made to India's efforts at increasing its medical manpower to fulfil the needs of primary health care. A vast expansion in the opportunities for medical education has taken place since India attained Independence in 1947. At that time there were only 14 medical colleges, and today there are 106 medical colleges producing 13,000 physicians every year. A little over one-half of these physicians wish to pursue further studies leading to the postgraduate degrees. There have been concomitant developments in the training of paramedical and auxiliary staff. Efforts are being made by India to correct the distortion that had crept into the medical and health manpower structure. Intermediate levels of health workers are being strengthened and community based health workers are being inducted into the system.

Reorientation of medical education, restructuring of auxiliary cadre and introduction of a new type of community based health worker constitute the most important elements of the alternative model of health care which India is pursuing at this time. A joint report was prepared in 1980 by the Indian Council of Medical Research and the Indian Council of Social Science Research. Entitled *Health for all: an alternative strategy* it proposes an alternative health care model strongly rooted in the community and providing effective and suitable health care services with a referral system, integrating preventive and promotive aspects of health with curative aspect, and combining the valuable elements in Indian culture and tradition with the best elements in the Western system.

An impressive part of India's Mogul legacy, the 17th century Red Fort in Delhi.

Kleinwort Benson, merchant bankers, are pleased to be associated with the Festival of India and extend best wishes for its success.

Kleinwort, Benson Limited.

Merchant Bankers

20 Fenchurch Street, London EC3P 3DB
Tel: London 623 8000

AGRICULTURE AND THE ENVIRONMENT

M S Swaminathan

It has been estimated that the first human form might have had its origin about 25 million years ago in Africa. Agriculture or settled cultivation, however, began only about 10,000 years ago. In the long intervening period man satisfied his first hierarchical need through hunting and food gathering. In India we have detailed evidence of agriculture in the Indus valley and other areas which came under the influence of the Harappan culture, dated between 3300 BC to 1750 BC. In the Mesolithic Age, which began about 10000 BC and ended with the beginning of agriculture in the Neolithic Age (7500 to 1710 BC), the people of India were food gatherers. Studies of the food habits of primitive tribes of Madhya Pradesh in the Mesolithic period have shown that rice and millets formed the staple diet of the people. However, these grains were supplemented by roots, leaves and fruits of numerous plants growing in the forests. In fact, famine was never a problem in the past in the tribal areas of Madhya Pradesh since the people were always able to draw their food supplies from over 165 varieties of trees, shrubs and climbers growing naturally in the forests.

The Neolithic agricultural revolution took place in the fertile crescent area of the Middle East. The hilly region embracing Israel, Jordan, Anatolia, Iraq, the Caspian basin and the adjoining Iranian plateau was the region where two of the major cereals of the world — wheat and barley — were domesticated. Today some of this region is affected by desertification. In contrast, some of the areas regarded as hopeless deserts in the beginning of this century, like the Imperial Valley in California, have flourishing agricultural systems today. Human interference with the environment leading to denudation of forests played an important part in

converting fertile lands into desert. Conversely, human action in promoting appropriate plant cover and conserving moisture has made deserts bloom. Thus agriculture is made or destroyed by what happens to the environment.

Although there is no firm evidence, it seems probable that it was women who began cultivating plants while men went out hunting. In the Donipolo Temple at Along in Arunachal Pradesh, there is a portrait of a woman who is believed to be the first to cultivate rice on earth. It is a tribute to the observational and analytical skills of the early domesticators that they could extract from the wild flora and fauna almost all plants and animals of potential use to man. In fact, without the help of tools of analytical chemistry, the early cultivators identified not only crops which give food, fodder, feed, fibre and fertiliser but also plants of medicinal value. Consequently, 20th century man has not been able to introduce any new plant into cultivation except fungi which yield antibiotics.

When man learned to produce food and to store it, he was compelled as well as enabled to live in larger communities. With time and energy released for a whole spectrum of new activities, non-agricultural crafts gained attention. "Agriculture cradled culture" to quote the Prime Minister of India, Mrs Indira Gandhi.

The early cultivators found that a serious obstacle to sustained production is the operation of the law of the diminishing returns of soil fertility. Hence, they introduced practices such as shifting cultivation, organic recycling and the cultivation of a legume which fixes atmospheric nitrogen in the soil for the purpose of restoring and maintaining soil fertility. They also chose strains of crops which were adapted to local conditions. Thus the wheat cultivators

77

Below left: A portrait in the Donipolo Temple at Along in Arunachal Pradesh showing Abo Tani, who first produced rice. When men went out hunting, women started growing plants from seeds gathered from the native vegetation. (Photo courtesy of Dr M S Swaminathan.)

Bottom left: Grains of "Triticum sphaerococcum" found in the Mohenjodaro excavation. (Photo courtesy of H K Gorkha.)

The traditional and the modern: An old lift irrigation method, below right, and the Rajasthan Canal which takes water to the desert areas of the state, bottom right. This is one of the longest man-made canals in desert areas. (Lift irrigation photo courtesy of H K Gorkha; Rajasthan Canal photo courtesy of Dr M S Swaminathan.)

of the Harappan period grew a species of wheat which had a high degree of drought tolerance. This species known as *Triticum sphaerococcum* had dwarf plant stature and spherical grains. Excavations at Mohenjodaro dated at about 1755 BC have yielded grains of this Indian dwarf wheat. It is interesting that more than 3,000 years later, we now have turned once again to dwarf wheats, this time the dwarfing character coming from the Norin wheat developed in Japan.

Thanks to conscious and unconscious selection over the centuries, we have a rich variety of crop species and varieties in India. In fact, in rice alone over 30,000 different strains have been identified. The north-eastern Himalayan region has proved to be a veritable mine of valuable genes in crops like rice, citrus and maize. The wide diversity of soil and climate is reflected in the rich genetic variability present in most crops. Diversity of growing conditions led to the possibility of cultivating tropical, sub-tropical and temperate plants in some parts of the country or the other. A visit to the fruit and vegetable markets in major cities will provide a glimpse of the rich diversity of crops cultivated. Genetic variability both in plants and animals also helped to insulate crops from total damage due to pest epidemics. The mutual inter-dependence of plants, animals and human beings led to the growth of mixed farming systems involving crop-livestock integration. The cow was venerated because it became a reliable companion of the farmer. It provided nutrition, power and fertiliser in addition to skin and hide and bone meal after death.

The decline of the Harappan culture was to a great extent caused by widespread deforestation and gradual desertification of land. This is why in later periods the protection of the integrity and fertility of the land was given considerable importance. For example, in the Magadhan Empire lands could be confiscated from those who did not use them properly. In other words, the right to use land for productive purposes was granted but the right to abuse land was denied.

Irrigation was another field where there was considerable progress from the early days of agriculture. The Grand Anicut across the River Cauvery in south India was built in the second century. Effective methods of conserving rain water were developed. In south India, no village is generally without a temple and no temple without an adjoining tank. Thus storage of rainwater in tanks was invested with religious significance. In spite of all this, striking progress in the domestication of plants and animals, in irrigation and in soil fertility restoration, there were periodic famines caused by the total failure of monsoon rains. During the last quarter of the 19th century a series of famines occurred all over the country. This led to government action in establishing state departments of agriculture to assist farmers in increasing and stabilising crop production.

Before Independence, farming was accorded an inferior status in the hierarchical positions of prestige attached to different professions. Only plantation and commercial crops were invested with some status in terms of educated people being drawn to their cultivation. Consequently, the growth rate in Indian agriculture was only about 0.3 per cent per annum during the period 1900 to 1950. Agricultural stagnation meant rural stagnation and this in turn led to the drain of both brain and resources from the village to the town. The neglect of rural areas was so great that in 1947 most villages did not have even one source of safe drinking water.

Stagnation also meant that no attempts were made to provide any form of commercial energy in support of agricultural occupations. Even today, the farm sector which provides nearly 40 per cent of the export earnings and sustains over 70 per cent of the population, consumes only about 10 per cent of the commercial forms of energy. Thus, the contribution of this sector to our economic well-being is immense, considering the insignificant investment of resources and energy. Whenever agriculture failed due to unfavourable weather, famine conditions prevailed. This is why considerable thought was given in the pre-Independence days to the development of famine codes and scarcity manuals.

During the period 1950 to 1980, the development of the infrastructure necessary for the modernisation of agriculture received high priority. The outmoded land tenure system at last received some attention, resulting in a gradual elimination of the *zamindari* and other intermediary tenures. Impressive progress took place during this period in developing powerful instruments for technology development, technology transfer and technology sustenance. The Indian Council of Agricultural Research, the network of agricultural universities and several associated institutions in the country, provided an effective mechanism for carrying out location-specific research and for developing appropriate technologies to suit different agro-ecological, socio-economic and socio-cultural conditions. Technology transfer mechanisms included the development of extension networks supported by input delivery systems. For sustaining agricultural advance, policy and operational instruments such as the Agricultural Prices Commission and Food Corporation of India were developed.

We can see three distinct trends during the period 1950-80, in terms of programme development. The first major step in promoting accelerated agricultural advance was taken in 1961 when the Intensive Agricultural District Programme (IADP) was initiated. This programme was designed to maximise production in areas endowed with irrigation facilities. Later, the introduction of high yielding varieties of seeds was superimposed over the area approach, since the earlier strains did not respond to higher levels of nutrition and irrigation. Through this step the missing link in the package programme (IADP), namely genetic strains which can respond well to the rest of the package, was provided. The area approach was also structured to meet specific ecological conditions like drought-prone, hill and desert areas. The area and crop-centred approaches, however, were found to be inadequate for the purpose of enabling the economically handicapped sections of farmers to take to new technology. It is this lacuna which was attempted to be remedied through the introduction of special programmes for small and marginal farmers, agricultural labour and tribal people. Thus, gradually, an individual farmer-cum-a-specific area model of programme development was born.

Infrastructure development during the period 1950-80 has been particularly impressive in the fields of agricultural research and education, irrigation, fertiliser production and in the storage and distribution of grains. Credit systems for the rural poor were also improved. As a result of the various steps taken during this period, the growth rate in agriculture rose to about 2.8 per cent per annum, thus keeping slightly above the growth rate in population. Also, land use patterns which were predominantly based on the home needs of the farming family tended to shift towards market needs.

Below left: Women threshing paddy in Kerala with their feet. (Photo courtesy of H K Gorkha.)

Centre left: Harvest from the sea. A trawler hauls up the catch; alongside is a traditional country craft for sardine fishing. (Photo courtesy of Indian Council of Agricultural Research.)

Bottom left: Because of a rich variability in growing condi-

tions, India produces a wide range of tropical, subtropical and temperate fruits and vegetables. (Photo courtesy of H K Gorkha.)

Below right: Intercrop of tapioca in a coconut garden.

Bottom right: Crop-fish mixed farming. The perimeter canal of the paddy field harbours fish. (Photo courtesy Indian Council of Agricultural Research.)

Fifty years ago, Mahatma Gandhi pointed out that the divorce between intellect and labour has been the bane of Indian agriculture. In other words, his recipe for agrarian and rural prosperity was: "Marry brain and brawn in rural professions." This is what started happening after India became independent. Consequently, the progress made by India in agricultural production during the last 30 years has been described as a miracle by many experts. However, as the Prime Minister of India, Mrs Indira Gandhi, pointed out in her Frank McDouggal Lecture delivered at the Food & Agriculture Organisation of the United Nations in Rome on November 9, 1981, there is no miracle or short-cut in agricultural progress. If in the Punjab there was a dramatic increase in production during the last 15 years, it is because the state already had four of the major substrate requirements for the rapid adoption and diffusion of new technology. These are: owner cultivation, land consolidation, rural electrification and rural communication.

The tasks ahead, however, are indeed challenging. The present population is more than 700 million and it is expected to exceed 1,000 million at the beginning of the 21st century. In addition to this large human population, a majority of whom depend on agriculture not only for food but also for employment and income, we have one-seventh of the world's entire cattle population living only on one-fiftieth of the world's land surface area. The animals also have to be provided with food. How can this be done in such a way that the environmental assets are conserved and protected? This will call for a systems approach to farming.

I would like to briefly refer to some of the major farming systems in India since these differ entirely from the temperate systems of land management.

(a) Multiple cropping systems in irrigated areas: various two, three and even four-crop sequences are now being followed. In promoting multiple-cropping systems, attention should be paid to ensuring that grain and fodder legumes find a place in the rotation, for improvement of human nutrition and soil fertility. Also crops having the same pests and diseases should not be grown in succession. Introduction of grain and fodder legumes in the rotation will improve human nutrition as well as soil fertility. A mung-bean-rice-wheat rotation is a good method of combining cereals and legumes in north-west India. Short-duration varieties of pigeonpea (Cajanus cajan) have made pigeonpea-wheat rotation possible. A jute-rice-wheat rotation is becoming popular in parts of Assam and West Bengal in India as well as in Bangladesh.

The introduction of relative insensitivity to photoperiod and temperature through breeding has been responsible for the development of "period fixed" rather than "season bound" varieties. For purposes of breeding varieties for multiple-cropping, per-day yield has to be used as a selection criterion in segregating generations. Also, other factors such as seed dormancy will need attention, since if a crop ripens before the monsoon rains have ceased, the grain will sprout if there is rainfall at harvest time.

(b) Rain-fed farming: production possibilities in high-rainfall areas, are similar to those in irrigated areas. However, in the unirrigated semi-arid areas commonly referred to as dry-farming areas, considerable production risks exist. Grain legumes, sorghum, millets, cotton and oilseed crops are mostly grown in such areas. A wide variety of fruit trees can also be grown. Research thrusts in semi-arid areas should lay stress on water and soil conservation

and land use planning based on precipitation, evapotanspiration and the moisture holding capacity of the soil. At the organisational level, watershed management and the introduction of varabandhi or rotational distribution of water saved in farm ponds will be necessary. Contingency plans should be developed and introduced so as to minimise the risk of total crop loss during aberrant weather. Seed and fertiliser reserves will have to be built so as to make the adoption of alternative cropping strategies and compensatory programmes in irrigated areas possible. It is also necessary to find more profitable crops for some of the semi-arid areas. There are many under-exploited plants with potential economic value.

(c) Mixed cropping and intercropping: various crop combinations are used by farmers, particularly in unirrigated areas, but not all are scientifically sound. Therefore, intercropping systems based on complementarity between the companion crops have to be developed. Among the major components of complementarity are: (i) efficient interception of sunlight; (ii) ability to tap nutrients and moisture from different depths of the soil profile; (iii) non-overlapping susceptibility to pests and diseases; (iv) introduction of legumes to promote biological N-fixation and increase protein availability.

(d) Multi-level or three-dimensional cropping: in garden lands where a wide variety of plantation crops, fruit trees, coconut, oil palm and other tree crops are grown, it is possible to design a crop canopy in which the vertical space is utilised more efficiently. Plant architects will have to take into account the effective use of both horizontal and vertical spaces when breeding varieties for use in three-dimensional crop canopies. Efficiency in such a cropping system will again be based on the extent of the complementarity generated among crops in the system. For example, studies have shown that coconut, cocoa and pineapple form a good combination from the point of view of efficient interception of sunlight and extraction of nutrients and moisture from different soil depths. Studies of the root system of companion crops are of particular importance. The introduction of grain and fodder legumes in these three-dimensional crop canopies will provide opportunities for animal husbandry. A careful study of all the major garden land cropping systems based on the extent of symbiosis and synergy among the system components will be useful in developing specifications which plant breeders can use in developing ideotypes (ie conceptual plant types) for efficient performance in three-dimensional crop canopies.

(e) Kitchen gardening and home fish gardening: kitchen gardening can be one of the most efficient systems of farming from the point of view of solar and cultural energy conversion. Vegetables rich in beta carotene and iron need to be developed and popularised. If planned intelligently and scientifically, backyard gardens, roof gardens and other methods of growing vegetables and fruits in whatever space is available around mud huts as well as brick houses can make a substantial contribution to improved nutrition. Where ponds are available in large numbers, home fish gardening can be an excellent method of supplementing income and source of food.

(f) Forestry and agro-forestry: the importance of improving the productivity of forest canopies cannot be over-emphasised. Agro-forestry has been defined as a sustainable management system for land which increases overall production, combines agricultural crops, tree crops, forest

plants and/or animals simultaneously or sequentially. Sylvi-pastoral, sylvi-horticulture, sylvi-agriculture and other combined land-use systems can help to meet the food, feed, fuel and fertiliser needs of people in many hilly regions. Plant breeders have yet to give attention to breeding varieties suitable for such systems of sylviculture. Shrubs and trees suitable for raising energy plantations in villages need to be identified and popularised.

(g) Mixed farming: mixed farming systems may involve (i) crop-livestock; (ii) crop-fish, and (iii) crop-livestock-fish production programmes. In Kerala and eastern India, fishing in rice fields is common. The minimal use of pesticides will be important in order to avoid problems of fish mortality and transfer of toxic residues through the food chain. This will involve maximum use of genetic resistance and the development of integrated pest-management systems in crops like rice and jute.

(h) Sea farming: there are considerable opportunities for the spread of scientific sea farming practices involving an appropriate blend of capture and culture fisheries. The rate of growth of oysters, mussels, prawns, lobsters, eels and a wide variety of marine plants and animals is high in tropical seas. If along with such integrated sea farming practices, the cultivation of suitable economic trees like casuarina, cashewnut and coconut can be popularised along the coast, thriving coastal agriculture-cum-mariculture systems can be developed. In addition to improving income and nutrition, such farming systems can help to arrest coastal erosion.

The sixth five year plan of India (1980-85) lays considerable stress on land and water use based on principles of ecology, economics, employment generation and energy conservation. Ecological security is the foundation upon which alone enduring food and water security systems can be developed.

Food production in India has increased from about 50 million tonnes in 1950 to about 135 million tonnes in 1981. Thus the progress made in food production during the last 30 years has been more than that achieved during the preceding 10,000 years. It is not only in food grain production that progress has been striking. Fruit and vegetable production now exceeds 50 million tonnes annually. The production of cotton, jute, sugarcane and a wide variety of industrial and commercial crops has been equally striking. Milk production will go up from 30 million tonnes in 1979-80 to 38 million tonnes in 1984-85. Fish production is likely to increase from 2.3 million tonnes in 1979 to 3.5 million tonnes in 1985.

The supreme consideration underlying all this development is human happiness and welfare. This is why India has introduced impact on employment as an essential component of technology development. Today, thousands of tribal and illiterate women produce hand pollinated seeds of hybrid cotton. India is the only country in the world which has introduced hybrid cotton into commercial cultivation.

In 1949, Jawaharlal Nehru said, "Everything else can wait but not agriculture." This statement is as valid today as it was over 30 years ago. Agriculture being essentially a solar energy harvesting enterprise is the most important source of renewable wealth in the world. Advances in space exploration have shown that we have to depend only on mother earth for food. Green plants by virtue of their ability to capture and use solar energy will continue to feed us, provided we do not undermine the renewable base of agriculture.

CRAFTSMEN AND THE CREATIVE PROCESS

Pupul Jayakar

"A purple coloured bird, mighty, heroic, ancient, having no nest"

Rig Veda

Insights into the ancient craft traditions of India reveal the anonymous nature of creation, direct perception skill and discipline as integral to the creative act, form as born of right relationship of matter to space and energy. The Chandogya Upanishad speaks of this abiding place of creation as — "That space here within the heart, that is the full, the non-active." Space where all the senses abide undifferentiated; where in the flowering of the senses simultaneously, the barriers of the within and the without, the seer and the sense object, dissolve. From this arises the supreme insight of the creator craftsman, who sees with a listening eye, sees unending space and the tiny seed; sees into the within of things. And so creates.

In India however diverse the forms and multiple the objects produced by craftsmen for the use of people in cities, in villages or for primitive man living in tribal society, the root of the creative process has always been the artisan tradition. To explore the roots of this tradition and to assess its place in the aesthetic and social life of the country it is necessary to examine the norms that have moulded the vision of the Indian craftsman and dictated his vocabulary.

The pattern craft traditions in India were to take and which were to survive for 5,000 years appear mature and firmly established in the cities of the Indus valley. Craftsmen in these cities had discovered the use of the wheel and control of fire: this had transformed his methods of transport and the tools with which he moulded his clay pots. He had learnt to cast and forge metals. Man had discovered geometry and the sacred nature of the abstract, and had evolved simple tools for the measurement of angles: this enabled him to build with precision and accuracy.

A vast number of amulets and seals have been discovered at the Indus valley cities, miniature carvings in clay, faience, metal and semi-precious stones. Possibly used as portable shrines, they acted as holders of power and divinity, drawing the wearer of the amulet within the field of protection and giving him the magical powers depicted on the seals. The sacred form as image and icon is not readily recognisable. Rites and rituals anticipate the gods. The recurrent symbols that were to fertilise the Indian unconscious, appear mature and fully developed on seal and amulet.

In the north lay the oldest road in the world, connecting western China to Syria and eastern Europe. Caravans with merchants, monks, pilgrims and craftsmen, carrying myth, icon and artifact meandered over the vast land spaces of Asia. This road was connected through the Himalayan passes to India. Through the centuries, traders, craftsmen and warriors entered India — to trade or to conquer. With conquest came foreign craftsmen, new design vocabularies and techniques. These in turn absorbed or were absorbed by indigenous craftsmen and their comprehension of form and technique. It was through these passes that Hieun Tsang returned to China, in the seventh century, taking with him six sculptures of the Buddha, which were to be the inspiration for the Buddha image as it developed in China.

Invasions of the nomadic Aryan peoples from the north brought into the ways of thought, into the way of art and vision, into the roots of the social structure in India, new elements and directions. They came, the song-lovers, with their nature hymns, their invocations to Aditya the Sun God, to Vayu the wind, to Usha the dawn maiden; new volumes of sound, new dimensions of language, new relationships with nature, new ponderings were being introduced into the consciousness of the peoples of this country.

Below left: Painted within the body of an elephant, Krishna the magnificent blue god plays the flute, flanked by gopis, girls of the cowherd community.
Wall painting by Ganga Devi, village Rasidpur, Madhubani, Bihar.
Bottom left: Palghat. A pictograph of the goddess of plants. Enclosed within a magical square the goddess is both male and female. Formed of two triangles, the upper triangle is "ghat," the pot as the female, the lower triangle is "pala," the mountain, as male. Jivya Soma, tribal-Ganjad, Thana District Maharasthra. (Photo courtesy of Pupul Jayakar).
Below right: The ten Mahavidyas or goddesses of Tantra. Painting on paper. Bathohi Jha, Tantrik, Village Jitwarpur, Madhubani, Bihar. (Photo courtesy of Batohi Jha
Centre right: A horse-headed human figure, holding a bow and arrow. Painting used in magical rituals. Rajasthan, 19th century.
Bottom right: Cows adoring Krishna the divine cowherd. Fragment of painted cloth from Nathdwara, Rajasthan, 19th century. (Photo courtesy of Pupul Jayakar).

Into the prose culture of the Indus, Gangetic and Narmada valleys, flowed the Sanskrit poetry of the Vedas. Vast volumes of sound chanted with the wind and the rain and thunder.

These Vedic hymns were sung — writing and script were unknown. Sound word and meaning were received and held in the ear. The quality of listening was alive and sustained the quality of vision.

The Aryans were great poets and story lovers. With the epics, the Ramayana and the Mahabharata, and later with the Puranas, the Indian artisan gained access to a fabric of myth and legend, which became the material around which he wove his themes.

Panini, the first of the great grammarians, in the fifth century BC used the word *shilpa* as a generic word to include painters, dancers, musicians, weavers, potters, tailors. Later, the word came to include even acrobats. The word for the artisan was *kari,* a word which became synonymous with skill. From the earliest times, the art traditions in India have known varied directions. Panini mentions *raj shilpins* as the artisans who created crafts for the king and his court, and the *gram shilpins* as village craftsmen. Five types of craftsmen were available to each village — the potter, the blacksmith, the carpenter, the barber and the washerman. In a contemporary Indian village the same five craftsmen supply the skills necessary to sustain the rural economy.

The early beginning of this era saw the inventions of a large number of tools or *yantras.* New functions demanded the development of a new technology with its own producer-consumer relationships. Definite principles of geometry and space perception were laid down for the craftsman, along with highly developed concepts of colour symbology. Indian texts are however silent on tools and their evolution, except for those concerned with tantra and alchemy.

Co-existent with the emergence of new technologies was an intense interest in alchemy and tantra which in turn motivated many new discoveries in metallurgy. *Yantras* or crucibles were evolved to withstand the intense heat, for use in alchemic experiments. Within the laboratory there was an active involvement with colour chemistry. The colours emanating from the flame of the burning of different metals were observed. Copper produced a blue flame, tin a pigeon coloured flame, iron a tawny flame, peacock ore a red flame. These observations of alchemy and tantra became the symbols of the goddess as primeval energy. The investigations of the alchemist into medicinal herbs generated discoveries in the art of dyeing. Many of the ancient processes of dyeing are to be found in the early Ayurvedic pharmacopeas.

We have seen that from the earliest times the Indian mind had probed into problems of vision and into the possibilities of extending the horizons of perception. A few centuries before the beginnings of this era a great flowering in the field of poetry, music, the arts and philosophy had enriched man's sensibilities. His concern with meditation and self-knowledge had revealed vast dimensions of consciousness and had brought to art comprehension of space and stillness, of movement and passivity. This revolution at the roots of the human mind generated a new craft vocabulary. Racial memories and yearnings were given iconic form and attribute, myths and symbols concretised in stone. As in all monumental art it was vision, the direct seeing, listening, feeling that projected the image, later to be followed by complex theories of art, evolved to shape and make permanent the truths revealed to the artisan sage. For no theory precedes and gives birth to great art, but follows it. And so in India too the torrent of visual forms witnessed in the first thousand years of this era were followed by theories of aesthetics to modulate the work of future artisans. As these theories grew fixed and relied less for their sustenance on a living vision, art forms became repetitive mirrors of tradition.

What made an art object was *rupa* or shape, *pramana* or proportion and *varna* or colour. Perfection of form came to be based on certain rules of measurement, of length and breadth. These rules of measurement were applicable not only to architecture and sculpture but to functional objects like textiles, gold ornaments, mule chariots and weapons.

Each *varna* or colour had its rich nuances of emotion and association. Colours reflected the tones of the changing seasons and of the songs evoked by them, the abandon of spring or the joy of the harvesting. But *rupa, pramana* and *varna* when put together did not make an object of art. What brought the object to life was its filling, its permeation with *rasa.*

Rasa was the essence, that fullness of seeing, listening, touching and feeling — that element that permeates, transforms and quickens to life. *Rasa* was the very quality of "seeing", "listening", "feeling". The rising wave of beauty without which the object of perfect proportions and colour remained lifeless. At the core of all the complex theories of art lay the comprehension that creative expression sprang from one source. No art form was the outcome of the operation of a single sense like the eye or the ear. Great art emerged from all the sensory perceptions acting fully and totally as in one stream and not by one sense acting alone. *Chitrasastra,* the art of sculpture and painting, was the first amongst the crafts. Just as rivers poured into the ocean, so all arts were dependant on *chitra.* But knowledge of *chitra* could only come from a knowledge of vocal music, instrumental music and dancing. The starting point then for the serious artist was the study of vocal music. The ear awakening to listening, to sound, to volume, to meaning. The awakening to word miniatures to the *doha* or the poetic couplet, to *raga* and *ragini* musical modes, to mood and emotion. From vocal music there came comprehension of instrumental music. The awakening to space and sound, to movement without known meaning, yet with form and harmony. To the understanding that art is not dependant on word meaning or form meaning, recognisable to the ear and the eye.

From instrumental music emerged dancing. That art in which music was projected into movement and physical form. Dancing that contained sound and movement, poetry and abstraction. To an awakening of the understanding of *mudra,* the symbol as gesture in which is concentrated meaning.

From dancing emerged *chitra,* sculpture and painting, in which sound, movement and meaning were frozen into form. And to the sensitive eye that perceived and the ear that listened was revealed not only colour, form and meaning but the music, the "sound-form", the *dhvani* that lay frozen within it. *Chitra,* in which we have seen is contained the complete vision, within which all the senses operate. For here is meaning and abstraction, colour and dimension, mood and emotion, movement and the freezing of movement, symbol and poetry, space, volume and form.

The craftsman who had deeply understood this was the

Below: Motor car and man with artificial wings flying. The Marwari businessman returning from Calcutta or Bombay brought back stories of strange happenings, which were translated into wall paintings by the painter builder. Shekavati, Rajasthan, 20th century.
Centre: Mural painting of archaic aeroplane showing the Wright brothers. Men and women point to the new machine in amazement. Shekavati, Rajasthan. 20th century.
Bottom: Mural painting of train, with horses and riders clearing the railway track. Painting on wall. Late 19th century Shekavati, Rajasthan.

Below left: Two European women driving a car, one holds the steering wheel. Early 20th century. Painting on a wall of a Marwari Haveli or family home, Shekavati, Rajasthan.
Below right: Mural painting from Shekavati, Rajasthan. Late 19th century.
Bottom left: Head of Buddha, gilded bronze. 14th century, Nepal. (Photo courtesy of Madan Mahatta).

Bottom right: Bronze figure of Mother Goddess holding cup and knife in her two hands. Cast by the lost-wax process by metalsmiths for tribal patrons. 6th century AD, Middle India.

Below left: On a yoni patta, are enshrined a Sivaling protected by the head of a cobra, to the left is Ganesh, to the right five round metal balls, symbolic of the goddess. The schematisation of form and the compactness of conception give the portable miniature shrine, cast in a metal alloy, power and divinity. Punjab hills. 17th century.

Below centre: Terracotta horse, a symbol of the free, heroic spirit — swift, virile, proud. Early 20th century. (Photo courtesy of Pupul Jayakar).

Below right: Chitrakar painter from Puri Orissa. 20th century.

Bottom: Terracotta horses, bulls and guardian figures of earth and field. Ayanar shrine, Tamil Nadu. 19th century.

rasik or the *rasadhari,* the holder of the essence, the *kalakar* capable of mastery of vision and technique.

The classical craft tradition had flowered around the kings and their courts and the temples built by the kings to glorify the gods. Craftsmen who had inherited the technical mastery of tools and materials that was the genius of the peoples of the Indus valley, to this had been fused that awareness of nature and the elements and that quality of comprehending space and sound that were the gifts of the Aryan peoples.

Surcharged with ideological concept, rich in symbol and myth; elegant and sophisticated — the classical stream was responsible for the creation not only of great sculpture and architecture but of objects of daily use that in their concern for beauty of form and in their understanding of functional problems of materials and technology have rarely been equalled.

Within the craft tradition, the artisan community with its *srenis* or guilds had taken shape. Great schools of hereditary craftsmen flourished. The media of learning were formulae in Sanskrit verse and diagrams and sketches. The tradition was the alphabet, the training in the syntax of ornament; in the comprehension of geometry and complex *yantras* structured on the point, the *bindu*; in the discipline of tool and material. The tradition was also the great source to which the craftsmen came for sustenance and contact with the sensibilities and aspirations of the community. Knowledge was communicable from father to son, from master to disciple. The craftsman was both designer and craftsman. The division between the fine arts and crafts had no validity.

Craft objects that emerged within this stream bore resemblance to the forms that preceded them, but the intention was never imitative. With change of patron came change of form and sometimes of technology. In the craft communities that evolved around temples and places of pilgrimage, however, a stability of form, technique and idiom continued. Religious rituals demanded that only the finest without blemish could be offered to the godhead. Craft guilds of weavers, sculptors, *chitrakars* or painters, dyers, goldsmiths flourished. The patrons were the temples and the pilgrims who came to offer and to take back icon and artifact to their distant homes.

Srenis or craft guilds occupied a unique position in the social, economic and religious life of the community — in a way similar to the role of large industrial houses in India today. There is mention of guilds of weavers, grain dealers, donating cloth and grain to the Buddhist monastries of Ajanta and Nasik. Ivory carvers were the donors of the carved railings and gateway that form the pilgrim's path around the main stupa at Sanchi, first century BC. A record exists of silk weavers of Gujarat having built a mighty temple to the Sun at Mandor, Rajasthan, in the seventh century AD.

With the establishment of Moghul rule in India new elements were introduced into the consciousness of the craftsman and into his relationship with his material and tools. For the first time in the history of Indian art, a new function, that of designer, was established dividing the craftsman from his inspiration. In the royal workshops the anonymous nature of the creative act was replaced by individual names of painter and craftsman. In the royal textile workshops with the introduction and assimilation of Islamic influences and an aesthetics that turned to the flowers and fruit of a more temperate climate, a new delicate hued pallete — the green of meadow grass, old rose, pistachio green, *amras* (mango juice) and the mauve of blooming iris replaced the indigenous lac reds, madders, indigos and myrabolams. With these colours a new plant chemistry was introduced to the dyers of India.

Miniatures of the period reveal textiles of an extraordinary beauty and richness of texture and pattern. Heavy gold cloth was often used for end pieces in the finest muslins. As the goldsmith fashioned the beaten sheet of gold and glowing, jewel-like enamels, so the painter, weaver or embroiderer used his skill to bring life to the jewel-like ornaments on the heavy gold end pieces.

A great flowering of craftsmanship was witnessed in the royal workshops. Jewellery, enamelling, jade and marble inlay, ivory carving and other crafts flourished. Objects of sophistication, elegance and beauty were produced, drawing their inspiration from the love the Moghuls had for gardens and for hunting. With this a fundamental change in design vision was inevitable. In the ancient tradition, the integrated approach to all forms of creative expression, the religious nature of craftsmanship and the concern with problems of mass and volume had given to the object produced, depth and dimension. In the Moghul courts the emphasis in design concept shifted from the living form to calligraphy and inlay, to elegance and preciousness. The wedge had been introduced that was to divide craft production from the major arts of sculpture, painting and architecture. Except for isolated centres of south India where the powerful temples and religious *maths* continued to be sources of ancient craft patronage, the major expressions of the artisan tradition declined in the rest of India.

The rural or *desi* craft idiom was based on the vernacular forms of the artisan guild. Inherent in it was a total anonymity of name. Negating the linear movement of history, of progress, of evolution or development, it revolved around a cyclic sense of time in which agricultural magic, ritual, symbol and myth as repositories of the archaic past and the existential present existed simultaneously.

It was an art that was not concerned with imitation. It took new elements that entered into its environment and restated them in the vernacular idiom. Rural art forms were precise and free of the inessential. It was as if the peasant craftsman saw directly into the heart of the object and then expressed the "seeing" with the utmost economy of line.

There has always been a plasticity latent in the craft situation as it operates in rural societies. A plasticity of soft materials, clay, wood, the use of the lost-wax process in casting metal objects and a plasticity of form which is free of the classical imperatives of proportion and attribute. With this there continues a spontaneity, a rapport between the community and the craftsman, a functional, even poetic appreciation of the craftsman's skill.

The potter as the most ancient creator of form, the earthen pot or the icons of the goddess, is also the priest who moulds the clay horses that guard the earth and her shrine. At the festival of the goddess it is the potter-priest who sings the primeval ballads of the goddess, of her ancestry and her exploits.

Primitive metalsmiths in the valleys and heartlands of India have continued through centuries to forge ritual metal objects using the ancient process of hollow and solid casting of metal. Earth, fire, bees-wax and molten metal are used in a transforming alchemy. Taking shape in darkness, the metal images with inner bodies of sacred earth are later hammered or chiselled into final shape. Miniature in size,

Below left: Terracotta figure of woman. Used as ritual offerings of tribals in Gujarat. 20th century. (Photo courtesy of Madan Mahatta).
Below centre: The Mother Goddess, blind, with no eyes, ears, nose or mouth. Terracotta figurine. 20th century.
(Photo courtesy of Madan Mahatta).
Below right: Metal craftsman preparing a wax mould. A

tradition that has created the bronze masterpieces of Indian art. Tanjore 20th century.
Bottom: The story of Jesus and Virgin Mary is retold on cloth in a vernacular idiom. At the centre is the ascension of Mary. The legend in Telegu characters unfolds the story. As drawn by Mr Kailasham and Guruppa Chetty, Sri Kalahasti, Andhra Pradesh. (Photo courtesy of Pupul Jayakar).

Opposite page: Detail from bottom photo showing a) the Anunciation b) The Virgin Mary embracing her mother. Joseph is in the background, c) The angels announce the news of the birth of the holy babe to shepherds. (Photo courtesy of Pupul Jayakar).

the lost-wax process predestines the flow, the weight and the rhythm of the coiled withes, which outline the sacred forms.

Though no woman is a member of the craft guild, it is through her that an archaic peoples culture survives in rites and fertility rituals known as *vratas*. These *vratas* with their varied symbols permeate every stage of the cycle of man's life, north of the Vindhyas, providing the ritual bound base that conditions the life of the Hindu householder. Untouched by the Brahamanical canons which demand discipline and conformity, the *vrata* observances free the craftsman and the woman participator from the inflexible hold of the great tradition. Multi-dimensional in approach, the rituals bring into operation song, dance, the visual arts of picture and image making, magical formulae of incantation and gesture. The demands of sex and fertility, wealth and prosperity, are translated into minutely detailed rites expressed through craft, icon and painting, which give to the vast country a common ritual, symbol and vision.

Colour is life. Expressing itself in the oral ballads of India; in the sun-faded red cloths worn by women as they work in brilliant mustard fields. In the songs and *vrata* rituals that herald the seasons, the fragrance of mango blossoms, and the sound of humming bees. Colour transforms the village hut or the earth with the painting of mystical diagrams, or the imprint of palms of a woman's hand on walls, to ward off evil.

This delight in colour and a living participation in the lives and wild adventures of the gods is visible in the paintings with which, wherever possible, rural people surround themselves. The walls of huts, the street, the shop and the market place become the canvas on which the records of the race, the exploits of god or hero are recorded. But the paintings are transitory and anonymous. They appear on walls, fade, to be whitewashed over and to re-appear with the cyclic movement of the seasons and related ritual.

Five colours are used by women to paint. The black of burnt grain, yellow from turmeric or chunam mixed with the milk of the banyan tree, orange from the wild Palasa flower, red from the Kusum flower and green from the pomegranate rind; a tradition of brewing magical colours from plants that has remained unchanged from the time of the *sarada* Tilak in the 11th century AD.

The gradual decay in design vocabulary and the emergence of hybrid concepts in the main craft centres of India did not at first affect rural vision. Eventually roads, transistors, plastics, infiltrated secluded village societies, shattering their isolation. "Progress" is today gradually changing the village environment and the craftsman's resources of material, form and function. The linear time stream of technology-based societies is inevitably taking over the rural craftsman's cyclic sense of time.

Challenged, the craftsman in city and village responds with ancient pride and skill. Fine craftsmanship is dormant but alive, quickening the craftsman's eye and hand. He responds to right patronage with vitality and magnificence.

At Trichur in Kerala, the Marars, the Chakiars re-enact the legends of the goddess. On a dark night in the light of flickering oil lamps an image of Bhagvati Kali is drawn on the earth with coloured powder. The goddess symbolising the power and the abundance of the earth and nature, its tranquility and its savage ferocity, is portrayed holding a flame in one of her many hands. To the thunderous sound of chanting and drum beats the magician priest dances the destruction of the goddess. With his feet he wipes away her limbs, her eyes, her breasts, her face, till only the form of the fire held in one hand remains. For, there is no ending to primeval female energy; fire is eternal. As the form of the goddess finally disappears into the dust from which she emerged, in the distant darkness, an oil lamp is lit. The fire from the hand of the goddess, symbolically leaps across space, to light the oil lamp, so that her victory over the demon can be re-enacted. The drums reach crescendo. Creation, destruction, the cycle of birth and death, whether in the great tradition, seen in the bronze image of Natesa or in the hands of the village painter in his dust image of Bhadrakali, the eternal dance begins.*

As related to me by Dr Kapila Vatsyayan.

COURTLY LIFE IN MOGHUL INDIA

B N Goswamy

Clearly as some kind of exception to the rest of Indian history, we have a wealth of detail, almost an excess of it, from the Moghul period, at least between 1550 and 1700. These times come vividly alive, for it is possible to sense their temper, feel the texture of their fabric, in different ways. On the one hand there are those familiar, uncommonly rich written records — memoirs, biographies, chronicles, travellers' accounts, histories, administrative manuals. On the other, there is an unusual range of visual "documents": illustrations to celebrated texts and to memoirs and histories, royal albums of painting and calligraphy, countless isolated leaves, even an occasional mosaic or fragment of mural.

From all this material, there are matters that are naturally omitted, and others that are stated with excess; but the intention clearly was to record in them the truth, at least truth as it was perceived by a given group of people. How else would one account for the appointment of all those *waqia-nawises*, "14 zealous, experienced and impartial clerks" of whose duties Abul Fazl tells us in the *Ain-i-Akbari* in such detail:

"Their duty is to write down the orders and the doings of His Majesty and whatever the heads of the departments report; what His Majesty eats and drinks; when he sleeps, and when he rises; the etiquette in the State Hall; the time His Majesty spends in the Harem; when he goes to the general and private assemblies; the nature of hunting-parties; the slaying of animals; when he marches, and when he halts; the acts of His Majesty as the spiritual guide of the nation; vows made to him; his remarks; what presents he makes; the daily and monthly exercises which he imposes on himself; appointments to mansabs; contingents of troops; salaries; jagirs; *irmas* money; *sayurghals* (rent-free lands); the increase or decrease of taxes; contracts; sales, money transfers; peshkash; despatch; the issue of orders; the papers which are signed by His Majesty; the arrival of reports; the minutes thereon; the arrivals of courtiers; their departures; the fixing of periods; the inspection of the guards; battles, victories and peace; obituaries of well-known persons; animal fights, and the bettings on them; the dying of horses; capital punishments; pardons granted by His Majesty; the proceedings of the general assemblies; marriages, births; *chawgan* games; phenomena; the harvests of the year; the reports on events.

Little may have survived of the accounts of each day at the Akbari court, but it is clear that clerks like these continued to be active in the reigns that succeeded. Certainly, in the time of Jahangir (1605-1627), the Englishman, William Hawkins, noted that the emperor "hath writers who by turnes set downe everything in writing which he doth, so that there is nothing passeth in his lifetime which is not noted, no, not so much as his going to the necessary, and how often he lieth with his women, and with whome; and all this is done unto this end, that when he dieth these writings of all his actions and speeches which are worthy to be set downe might be recorded in the chronicles."

Much as the clerks' diaries were first corrected, and then presented to the emperor himself for approval, the works produced in the enormous *karkhanas* of paintings attached to the Akbari court were "weekly laid before His Majesty by the *daroghas* and the clerks; he then confers rewards according to excellence of workmanship, or increases the monthly salaries." The painters had their task cut out for them. "Persian books", Abul Fazl tells us, "both prose and poetry,

Arrival of a white elephant at the court of Akbar. This is an illustration to an unidentified text, circa 1580-85, but it is known from a painting in the "Akbarnama" that a giraffe was presented to him, and rare animals were welcome at Akbar's court. This illustration shows the white elephant as the centre of attraction, heavily bedecked with golden bells, festoons and plumes, caparisoned with a gold-spangled cloth, and standing under a rich canopy.
Bharat Kala Bhavan, Banaras.

were ornamented with pictures, and a very large number of paintings was thus collected. The *Story of Hamzah* was represented in twelve volumes ... The *Chingiznamah*, the *Zafarnamah*, this book (the *Akbarnama*), the *Razmnama*, the *Ramayan*, the *Nal Daman*, the *Kalila Damnah*, the *Iyar-i Danish*, etc, were all illustrated." Along with this, as a part of the records of the realm, were painted a prodigious number of portraits. "His Majesty himself sat for his likeness, and also ordered to have the likenesses taken of all the grandees of the realm. An immense album was thus formed ...."

The painters of Jahangir were, similarly, constantly occupied, recording things and events that reflected imperial taste and interests: a dying man, a turkey-cock newly arrived from Goa, a favourite elephant from the royal stables with his young ones, a feast given to the shaikhs, a picture of the occasion for forming the frontispiece to the *Jahangir Nama*. Everything seemed to come within the painters' ambit, with obvious approval from the emperor himself. They were all busy — Abulhasan, Mansur, Bichitr, Manohar, Govardhan, Bishandas, Hashim — chronicling the reign in their own manner.

At first sight, it might seem as if the documents we have from the Moghul period, the verbal and the visual records, are explicit, and complete in themselves. It is only gradually, however, that one realises that there could be much profit in seeing them closely together. For such is the scale at which things happened, and such the complexities of conventions and relationships, that much can elude one if one is not alert to the various levels at which information is being communicated in these records. Everything seems to be informed by some meaning, and significance could attach to minor details that one would, elsewhere, casually pass over: whether or not a person wears rings in his ears, thus; the direction, right or left, in which a courtier's *jama* is tied; the height and the distance at which a noble stands from the emperor; the manner in which he disposes his hands or holds a sword. The direction of the gaze, the tilt of the head, the objects tied to the belt, could each have a tale to tell, possess a meaning that is all too often lost upon us. Behind appearances in the Moghul times, and *in them*, there are all kinds of subtleties. And one realises that small things serve as openings into things much larger.

To take an example. One may at first have serious problems with taking in paintings of court scenes that appear all too crowded and confused, or to make sense of the many goings-on in a painting, at the centre, off-centre, at the margin. Thus, when a prince takes leave of the emperor, or an ambassador is being presented, all too much seems to be going on, and without any special kind of order. And yet there is a definite kind of order in everything, the Emperor Akbar having introduced it in so clear a manner through his regulations. A longish passage in the *Ain* on how the emperor spent his time, or the strict regulations that governed admission to the imperial court, become unusually interesting, in this context.

"His Majesty generally receives twice in the course of twenty-four hours, when people of all classes can satisfy their eyes and hearts with the light of his countenance. First, after performing the morning devotions, he is visible from outside the awning, to people of all ranks, whether they be given to worldly pursuits, or to a life of solitary contemplation, without any molestation from the mace-bearers. This mode of showing himself is called, in the language of the country,

darshan; and it frequently happens that business is transacted at this time. The second time of his being visible is in the State Hall, whither he generally goes after the first watch of the day. But this assembly is sometimes announced towards the close of day, or at night. He also frequently appears at a window, which opens into the State Hall, for the transaction of business; or he dispenses justice calmly and serenely, or examines into the dispensation of justice, or the merit of officers .... Every officer of government then presents various reports, or explains his several wants, and is instructed by His Majesty how to proceed....

Whenever His Majesty holds court they beat a large drum, the sounds of which are accompanied by Divine praise. In this manner, people of all classes receive notice. His Majesty's sons and grandchildren, the grandees of the Court, and all other men who have admittance, attend to make the *kornish*, and remain standing in their proper places. Learned men of renown and skilful mechanics pay their respects; the daroghas and Bitikchis set forth their several wants;... During the whole time, skilful gladiators and wrestlers from all countries hold themselves in readiness, and singers, male and female, are in waiting. Clever jugglers and funny tumblers also are anxious to exhibit their dexterity and agility."

Again:

"About a watch before daybreak, musicians of all nations are introduced, who recreate the assembly with music and songs, and religious strains; and when four *gharis* are left till morning His Majesty retires to his private apartments.... In, the meantime, at the close of night, soldiers, merchants, peasants, tradespeople, and other professions gather around the palace, patiently waiting to catch a glimpse of His Majesty. Soon after daybreak, they are allowed to make the *kornish*."

If we do not fully understand what the *kornish* as a form of salutation was, Abul Fazl speaks to us in clear terms:

"With the view, then, of promoting this true humility, kings in their wisdom had made regulations for the manner in which people are to show their obedience. Some kings have adopted the bending down of the head. His Majesty has commanded the palm of his right hand to be placed upon the forehead and the head to be bent downwards. This mode of salutation, in the language of the present age, is called *kornish*.... The salutation, called *taslim*, consists in placing the back of the right hand on the ground, and then raising it gently till the person stands erect, when he puts the palm of his hand upon the crown of his head..."

This leads us on to matters of etiquette at the Court:

"When His Majesty seats himself on the throne, all that are present perform the *kornish*, and then remain standing at their places, according to their rank, with their arms crossed, partaking in the light of his imperial countenance....

The eldest prince places himself, when standing, at a distance of one to four yards from the throne, or when sitting, at a distance from two to eight. The second prince stands from one and one-half to six yards from the throne, and in sitting from three to twelve. So also the third; but sometimes he is admitted to a nearer position than the second prince, and at other times both stand together at the same distance. But His Majesty generally places the younger princes affectionately nearer.

Then come the Elect of the highest rank, who are worthy of the spiritual guidance of His Majesty, at a distance of three to fifteen yards, and sitting from five to twenty. After

Below left: Encampment scene, an illustration from the "Babarnama," circa 1598. According to the text, Babar's advance to Qandhar, after having established himself at Kabul, is illustrated here. This scene shows the arrival of Babar at the royal camping ground. The camp life is indicated by a sleeping man with his attendants and camels resting in the foreground; a grocer appears selling cereals to a customer, in the background.
National Museum, New Delhi.
Below right: An imaginary meeting between Jahangir and Shah Abbas of Persia, circa 1618. Symbolic paintings by Jahangir's painters to glorify the king and his court, seem to have been produced in considerable number; and he is often shown with great independent monarchs from other parts of the world in attendance upon him. The scene probably represents one of Jahangir's unfulfilled desires, that Shah Abbas of Persia should submit to him in person. Shah Abbas' likeness was known to the Moghul court from portraits commissioned through the Moghul artist, Bishan Das, who accompanied the Indian Ambassador to Isfahan.
Freer Gallery of Art, Washington DC.

this follow the senior grandees from three and a half yards, and then the other grandees, from ten or twelve and half yards from the throne.

All others stand in the *yasal* (the outer railing). One or two attendants stand nearer than all."

In a less formal setting than that of the durbar with all its gravity, in a scene, for example, of the birth of a prince in the royal household, one may not have success with identifying the chain of activities and the range of persons present within or outside the palace walls except through help, once again, from Abul Fazl who tells us of the organisation of the royal harem:

"His Majesty has made a large enclosure with fine buildings inside, where he reposes. Though there are more than five thousand women, he has given to each a separate apartment. He has also divided them into sections, and keeps them attentive to their duties. Several chaste women have been appointed as *daroghas,* and superintendents over each section, and one has been selected for the duties of writer. Thus, as in the imperial offices, everything is here in proper order....

The inside of the Harem is guarded by sober and active women; the most trustworthy of them are placed about the apartments of His Majesty. Outside the enclosure the eunuchs are placed; and at a proper distance, there is a guard of faithful Rajputs, beyond whom are the porters of the gates. Besides, on all four sides, there are guards of Nobles, *Ahadis,* and other troops, according to their ranks."

Through familiarity with passages like these, one gets to make more sense of what is going on in the paintings of the period. The converse of this process of understanding of one source through the other, at the same time, turns out to be equally fruitful. If the *shamsa* which Abul Fazl mentions among the many ensigns of royalty is not easily comprehended at first, one turns to paintings. Likewise, one takes in through these painted works, the *awrang,* "a throne made of several forms ... inlaid with precious stones;" the *chhatra* or umbrella; the *sayaban,* "of oval form and a yard in length,... its handle like that of the umbrella,... covered with brocade and ornamented with precious stones;" the *kuwarga,* the *naqara,* the *duhul,* the *karna,* the *surna,* the hall". The royal standard, the *alam,* we see carried along with the *qur,* "wrapped up in scarlet cloth bags," the *chhatratogh* is "adorned with the tails of Tibetan yaks;" the *toman togh* is "like the *chhatratogh,* but larger;" the musical instruments in the royal *naqarkhana* are the *kuwarga,* the *nagara,* the *duhul,* the *karna,* the *surna,* the *nafir,* the *sing,* the *sanj.*

All these, at the court, were matters of grave import for the use of royal insignia by lesser persons like the princes or amirs on the borders was tantamount to defiance of imperial authority. No one except the emperor was entitled to the yak-tail flywhisk, the *chamara* or *chauri,* and, as Jahangir notes in the *Tuzuk,* the amirs were told clearly that they should "not sit in the *jhaorakha,*...should not order the royal servants to do *kornish* or prostration, and should not force singers to remain on duty in the manner customary in (royal) durbars, and should not beat drums when they go out...."

It is like this, when information is pieced together from diverse sources, and one takes in the enormity of detail that belongs to this glittering age, that a comprehensible picture begins to emerge. It is a picture of a court with untold riches but also exquisite taste, in which even while emperors and princes fought battles and kept enemies at bay, or struggled with the intricacies of administering a virtual subcontinent, they found the time to describe with remarkable precision the colours in the plumage of a newly arrived bird, to document the discovery of the *itr* of roses ("of such strength in perfume that if one drop be rubbed on the palm of the hand it scents a whole assembly and it appears as if many rosebuds had blossomed at once"), to admire a jewelled dagger, "on its hilt a yellow ruby, exceeding clear and bright, in size equal to half a hen's egg," to measure the marble steps leading to a tank lit by lamps at night, to order men marching through a valley of oleander flower "to put bunches of the flower in their turbans...(so that) a wonderful flower bed was produced," or to put gold nose-rings on choice fish in a pond of crystal-clear water. Here was a court, one senses, where goldsmiths composed verses as religious leaders engaged each other in earnest debate.

This was a court that dazzled, none more than the wide-eyed, all-observing Europeans who were steadily pouring in to see for themselves the fabled "gold of Ind," and, with luck, perhaps to obtain permission to trade with it. Sir Thomas Roe's description of the Emperor Jahangir setting out on one of his routine journeys has something of awe at the spectacle he saw:

"The King descended the stayres with such an acclamation of 'health to the King' as would have out cryed cannons. At the stayres foote, where I mett him, and shuffled to be next, one brought a mighty carp; another a dish of white stuff like starch, into which hee putt his finger, and touched the fish and so rubd it on his forhead, a ceremony used presaging good fortune. Then a nother came and buckled on his sword and buckler, sett all over with great diamonds and rubyes, the belts of gould suteable. A nother hung his quiver with 30 arrowes and his bow in a case, the same that was presented by the Persian ambassador. On his head he wore a rich turbant with a plume of herne tops, not many but long; on one syde hung a ruby unsett, as bigg as a walnutt; on the other syde a diamond as great; in the middle an emralld like a hart, much bigger. His shash was wreathed about with a chayne of great pearle, rubyes, and diamonds drild. About his neck hee carried a chaine of most excellent pearle, three double (so great I never saw); at his elbow, armletts sett with diamonds; and on his wrists three rowes of several sorts. His hands bare, but almost on every finger a ring; his gloves, which were English, stuck under his girdle; his coate of cloth of gould without sleeves upon a fine *semian* as thin as lawne; on his feete a payre of embroidered buskings with pearle, the toes sharp and turning up."

The emperor himself has this note on the *tuladan* occasion, when he was, like his father, weighed against different metals and precious objects which were to be given away in charity among the needy and the poor:

"On Wednesday the 9th of the aforesaid month, the 21st of Shahriwar, after three watches and four gharis, the feast for my solar weighing, which is the commencement of the 38th year of my age, took place. According to custom they got ready the weighing apparatus and the scales in the house of Maryam-zamani (his mother). At the moment appointed blessings were invoked and I sat in the scales. Each suspending rope was held by an elderly person who offered prayers. The first time the weight in gold came to three Hindustani maunds and ten seers. After this I was weighed against several metals, perfumes, and essences, up to twelve weighings, the details of which will be given hereafter.

Below: The Panch Mahal at Fatehpur Sikri, Akbar's short-lived capital.
Bottom left: The Red Fort at Delhi.
Bottom right: The Red Fort at Agra.
Opposite page: The Pearl Mosque, in the Red Fort, Agra.

98

Twice a year I weigh myself against gold and silver and other metals, and against all sorts of silks and cloths, and various grains, etc, once at the beginning of the solar year and once at that of the lunar. The weight of the money of the two weighings I have over to the different treasurers for faqirs and those in want.

When the emperor held the Nauroz festival, to mark the first day of the new year, or the *Khushroz*, the Day of Fancy Bazaars, whether by day or by night, it was, predictably, a spectacle. But even when, as was customary, the emperor went to the house or garden of one of his nobles at his invitation, all was a-glitter. Like when he visited, in the second year of his reign, the house of the great Asaf Khan, along with his ladies, to spend the night there:

"The next day he presented before me his own offerings, of the value of ten lacs of rupees, in jewels and jewelled things, robes, elephants, and horses. Some single rubies and jacinths and some pearls, also silk cloths with some pieces of porcelain from China and Tartary, were accepted, and I made a present of the rest to him. Murtaza Khan from Gujarat sent by way of offering a ring made of a single ruby of good colour, substance, and water, the stone, the socket, and the ring being all of one piece. They weighed 1½ tanks and one surkh, which is equal to one misqal and one surkh. This was sent to me and much approved. Till that day no one had ever heard of such a ring having come to the hands of any sovereign. A single ruby weighing six surkhs or two tanks and 15 surkhs, and of which the value was stated to be £25,000, was also sent. The ring was valued at the same figure."

Honours flowed from the emperor's stirrup, as the chronicler would put it. The occasion when Jahangir conferred a special distinction upon Khurram, the future Shah Jahan, upon his successful campaign in the Deccan, must have been quite special:

"I gave him a mansab of 30,000 personnel and 20,000 horses, and bestowed on him the title of Shah Jahan. An order was given that henceforth they should place a chair in paradise-resembling assemblies near my throne for my son to sit upon. This was a special favour for my son, as it had never been the custom hitherto. A special dress of honour with a gold-embroidered *charqab*, with collar, the end of the sleeves and the skirt decorated with pearls, worth 50,000 rupees, a jewelled sword with a jewelled *pardala* (belt), and a jewelled dagger were bestowed upon him. In his honour I myself came down from the Jharokha and poured over his head a small tray of jewels and a tray of gold coins."

On this very day, the great elephant, Sarnak, came to the emperor's notice, and he records:

"I saw without doubt that what had been heard in its praise and of its beauty was real. It stood all the tests in size, form and beauty. Few elephants are to be seen of such beauty. As it appeared acceptable to me, I myself mounted and took it into my private palace, and scattered a quantity of gold coins on its head."

There was so much of this order that brought to the Moghuls a very special kind of joy: a perfectly calligraphed album-leaf, the hilt of a dagger made from walrus tooth by the Ustads Puran and Kalyan, the fragrance of the *keora* flower, "so penetrating that it does not yield to the odour of musk," watching the mating of a saras pair. But perhaps too much went on at the same time. One sometimes gets the feeling as if in the midst of so much coming and going, of ceaseless rounds of receptions and festivities, of watching deer-fights and capture of elephants, of the near scramble for jewels and precious stones that characterises the reigns of all the six great Moghuls save perhaps the last one, Aurangzeb, there must have been a surfeit of activity, an excess of noise, as it were. But right then, in the records of the courtly life in Moghul India, one suddenly comes upon passages of wonderful quiet that soothe and place things silently in perspective. There are few descriptions, thus, that will match in feeling this meeting between the Hindu recluse, Jadrup, and Jahangir who sought him out once again in Mathura:

"On Monday, the 12th, my desire to see the Gosain Jadrup again increased, and hastening to his hut, without ceremony, I enjoyed his society. Sublime words were spoken between us. God Almighty has granted him an unusual grace, a lofty understanding, an exalted nature, and sharp intellectual powers, with a God-given knowledge and a heart free from the attachments of the world so that, putting behind his back the world and all that is in it, he sits content in the corner of solitude and without wants. He has chosen of worldy goods half a *gaz* of old cotton like a woman's veil, and a piece of earthenware from which to drink water, and in winter and summer and the rainy season lives naked and with his head and feet bare. He has made a hole in which he can turn around with a hundred difficulties and tortures, with a passage such that a suckling could hardly be put through it."

Jadrup's self-denial then prompted the emperor to recall to his mind these verses of Hakim Sanai:

Luqman had a narrow hut,
Like the hollow of a flute or the bosom of a harp.
A noodle put the question to him —
"What is this house — two feet and a span?"
Hotly, and with tears the sage replied —
"Ample for him who has to die."

The image one is left with at the end of a passage like this is of a bejewelled potentate walking through endles marble corridors, to the accompaniment of the cries of heralds reverberating over heads bent in obeisance at every corner, and entering not a royal audience hall but a private chamber where he shuts himself up so as to be able to sit there all by himself, seeking answers.

THE INDIAN EXPERIENCE

René Lecler

The young lady wearing a Copenhagen travel agent's badge sat, quiet and alone, on a bench in the gardens of the Taj Mahal in Agra — and a single tear ran down her face. "Are you all right?" I asked her, "Is there anything wrong?" She looked at me as if coming out of a dream and replied: "No, I am fine... It's just this place. I have read so much about it and yet no one had told me how fantastically beautiful it is. I can't get over it..." I have sympathy for her. I have seen the Taj many times myself and it has never failed to move me.

Going to India is like that — not so much a journey as an experience. I am convinced that the world of tourism is divided into two — those who have been to India and can't wait to get back, and those who have never been and would not dream of going. Size, diversity, beauty, the almost careless flowering of countless cultures make any visit to India a kind of continuous cinerama which leaves you speechless, and everything appears to contribute to your confusion. Take size for instance. It is more than 3,200 kilometers from the snows of Kashmir to the southerly shores of Cape Comorin and more than 2,800 kilometers from sun-baked Gujarat to steamy Bengal where lancers and tigers used to roam. In between live more than 700 million Indians, speaking 14 major languages — some more widespread than European tongues — and more than 250 dialects. Some Indians are a rich mahogany colour, others are as fair as Western Europeans. A few are rich and powerful, most are poor but the land is so fertile that its wealth consistently defies the birthrate. India produces everything from cashew nuts to railway engines and nuclear energy, and when India's star was rising most Europeans still lived in caves. India is magnificent, breathtaking, utterly ex-

hausting and quite unforgettable. One should approach India with one's mind cleared of all prejudices and preconceived notions. Leave these behind and before you can say anything, India will embrace you, look at you, evaluate you, turn you inside out and my guess is that you will never be the same person again.

Don't try to see everything and indeed, as a tourist, don't try to understand India. It would take two lifetimes to do that. Just let India flow over you. In India everything is contradiction: confusion on the surface, noise and secretiveness, mixed with an almost total lack of privacy. How can you be private with all those teeming millions around you? India is often exasperating and always absolutely fascinating. All this, plus an all-pervasive spirituality which is not necessarily religious but simply the product of a detachment which is uniquely and typically Indian. As a tourist you live, inevitably, in a cocoon and the dangers to your health and well being are minimal provided you follow elementary rules. As for what appears to us to be abject poverty, beggars etc, I have long ago come to one conclusion: the very fact that you are there, spending money, helps India and no single individual, least of all you, can help solve India's problems.

What matters is being there. What also matters is deciding where to go and what to do because there is no such thing as instant India. When Bombay swelters, Kashmir is freezing, and when the old hill stations are delightfully temperate, cool drinks are much needed on the southern beaches. Distances too enter into it and while you can reach almost every part of India daily with Air India or Indian Airlines, this is not a country but a continent. After many visits I have come to the conclusion that no one can really

Below: The City Palace at Udaipur, Rajasthan, as seen from Lake Pichola. It is a fine blend of Moghul decorative art and Rajput military architecture and, with its lakeside location, is just one reason why Udaipur is known as the "City of Dreams."
Bottom left: A bedroom in the Lake Palace Hotel, Udaipur: "every colour inspired by some poetic designer." Once a *summer palace of the Maharanas of Udaipur, the Lake Palace Hotel now ranks amongst the 10 most beautiful hotels in the world.*
Bottom centre: Originally introduced by Chinese immigrants, these traditional fishing nets at Cochin, Kerala, are still very much in use today. Counterweights are used to lower the nets into the water, trapping passing shoals *of fish and succulent prawns.*
Bottom right: Kovallam Beach, near Trivandrum, Kerala; one of the finest beaches in the world.

describe India — least of all in an article. So, unless you have unlimited time, you must choose and to help you do this I have carved up India into man-sized portions which you can at least begin to comprehend. The rest is up to you.

Let's go to Rajasthan first which is every tourist's romantic picture of India. The very name Rajasthan means the home of kings — and some kings they were, those wild Rajput princes who paraded through Indian history in a long colourful pageantry of chivalry and heroism. They rode fiercely into battle against all invaders and, in between, they carved out principalities — some the size of a European country, others a mere back garden. Names like Jaipur, Alwar, Bharatpur, Ajmer, Bikaner, Jodhpur and Udaipur are part of India's martial legend and although these private empires are today part of democratic India, they have kept an individual identity, a kind of flourish which you will surely enjoy. Of course you should see them all if you can, but you won't have time. So perhaps you should concentrate on two of them, Jaipur and Udaipur.

The first was the capital of the great Jai Singh. Besides being a leader of princes and a superb politician, Jai Singh was also a scientist and an astronomer. Jaipur, the pink city, is romantic, colourful and quite, quite beautiful. You must see the fanciful Palace of the Winds, of course, and the great complex of marvellous buildings known as the City Palace which is now a museum, and which contains priceless relics of the old Rajput times. Not far away from Jaipur is the legendary palace of Amber, the very heart of Rajasthan. Half palace, half fortress, it lies up a mountainside majestic and incredibly impressive. Inside the walls are the Great Hall of Victory and the lovely chamber of mirrors, and everywhere are carved panels of alabaster and marble and colourful wall paintings. Amber is a must for all tourists and like them you will probably climb up to it on an elephant's back, with a band of Indian musicians urging you along.

Udaipur is probably India at its maharajest. A luscious jewel of improbable wedding cake architecture set on a lake of shimmering silver. A city of potentates of no mean splendour, whose life seems to have been one long temptation from dishes of multi-coloured Oriental sweetmeats to ladies with mysterious eyes beckoning behind screens of sculptured marble — with a few wars in between of course to make the going worthwhile. Now the vast palaces stand almost deserted but, happily, not decaying — great structures of white, ochre and pale pink where every door was made to measure, every colour inspired by some poetic designer and in which every bathroom came from Piccadilly, complete with marble toilets and gold-plated taps. And then, in the middle of that enchanting lake are the island palaces — one of them now a world famous hotel — built by the maharanas of Udaipur purely for pleasure. Yes, they were maharanas here, not maharajahs. The palaces seem to float like jewels on the water and they are one of the great sights of India.

If you fly south of Bombay for an hour or so, you discover another kind of India. The first European to sail to India was of course Portugal's Vasco da Gama in 1497. Brushing aside Arab competition he began buying up the spices of the Orient in the ancient port of Calicut on the Malabar coast, and returned home to Lisbon a multi-millionaire. A dozen years later, another Portuguese, the great Albuquerque, sailed up the coast and captured Goa and for 450 years Goa remained more Portuguese than Portugal, with names like Sousa and Almeida getting pinned on darker faces. What

Goa has to offer today is the astonishing discovery of the great age of the European presence in India. Seventy years before the Spanish Armada sailed against England, the tough Portuguese were building churches and palaces in Goa and one is suddenly faced with gorgeous Manueline masterpieces right here on this tropic shore. Almost buried under masses of hibiscus and bougainvillea, Goa is India in the transitory glory of colonialism, and wisely the kind Indian Government is keeping up its alien heritage with real pride. Here is where the Great St Francis Xavier began his missions to the East and where his body still lies in the massive Bom Jesus Church. Even the new capital of Goa, Panaji, is Portuguese in spirit with pink, blue and green houses lining the banks of the Mandovi River. But Goa is very much a part of India's tourist future since it has become the country's best known beach resort. Most of its beaches are still undiscovered and hard to reach but two of them, Calangute and Colva, can be sampled — long stretches of fine white sand, aquamarine seas and fleets of handbuilt Malabar catamarans waiting for the tide. Yet Goa is merely the beginning of your Indian adventure.

You could try Kerala for another change of mood. This is flat country, completely tropical, intensely green from the dark green of the coconuts to the young, sharp green of the paddies and everywhere the land seems to merge with the waters of the inland lagoons — a potent mixture which is hard to resist. Kerala is India suddenly aquatic, peaceful and filled with brilliant colours. From Cochin, you can float for days on end along the waterways, drifting from shade to sunny side and being welcomed by simple people everywhere. Kerala people live on and for the water — fishing for mackerel and mullet and above all for Asia's most succulent prawns, using vast suspended nets which Chinese immigrants introduced years ago.

It was on the Malabar coast of course that East met West a long time ago. Greeks, Arabs, Portuguese, Dutch, French and British came here one after the other. Vasco da Gama died here in Cochin and was buried in the small St Francis Church, and it is believed that it was St Thomas the Apostle who first introduced Christianity to this part of the world. Stranger still is the discovery that Kerala is home to a small Jewish community — the famous White Jews of India — who came to Cochin after the Roman conquest of Jerusalem and who have been here ever since. Not many are left today and yet, visiting their ancient synagogue and talking to their venerable rabbi is one more proof of India's amazing universality.

I am not ashamed to say that after my first visit years ago, I fell for Kerala. The combination of tropic green and omnipresent water, the gentle air of unhurried daily life and above all the superb climate are more than acceptable. I had not seen anything, however, until I got to Kovallam, near Trivandrum, the capital of Kerala. Suddenly, there it was, one of five or six finest beaches in the entire world — a smooth tablecloth of blond sand lapped by an incredibly clear sea and backed by a belt of coconuts sheltering a fishing village. I recall walking down to the fishermen and greeting them. They greeted me back with flashing smiles. Hoping to get better pictures I began pulling the nets in with them, which gave rise to ripples of laughter. Nobody, it seemed, had ever seen a foreigner mad enough to work in the hot sun when he could lie and do nothing. One old man whose ancestors must surely have been one of the original Malabar pirates taught me the words of the Malayalam song

Below: Mahabalipuram, the temple city just south of Madras; every phase of Pallava architecture and sculpture is represented here. This is the Shore temple, built during Rajasimha's time (c.690-715). Bottom left: The Brihadisvara temple at Tanjore; built by Rajaraja (985-1012), it is the acme of Chola art. Bottom right: The huge "gopurams" of the Kumbeshvara temple at Kumbakonam. "Gopurams" are a regular feature in all temples of any importance in the south from the late Chola period onward.

they were singing. More laughs when I began repeating them. The sun rose higher and higher over this heavenly beach as we worked and the fish came in — mountains of quicksilver shining on the sand. I do not suppose I shall ever forget my first time in Kovallam. Nowadays of course things are different — you can stay in up-to-date comfort in the Kovallam Beach Hotel and have the best of both worlds.

Without even knowing it, we have crossed the invisible border — a line from Bombay to Calcutta — which separates ex-Moghul and well touristicated India from the legendary lands of the south, far less known to tourists although they are the real Hindu India. Here the people are darker of skin and speak yet other languages, Tamil or Telugu or Malayalam. Here is the land of the dance, superb art forms like India's world famous bronzes and a totally different geographical and historical orientation. Here, in Tamil Nadu especially, were the four great Dravidian kingdoms — Pallavas, Cholas, Cheras and Pandyas — whose influence once extended as far as Indonesia and Cambodia, yet another example of the astonishing diversity of this immense land.

In India, you never have far to go to see temples. Turn left and there is one, turn right and there are others. Nowhere, however, is there more temple togetherness than in Madurai, the ancient capital of the Pandyan kingdom. Eleven massive *gopurams*, those truncated pyramidal towers so well loved by Indian builders break the city skyline — vast structures of marble and plaster literally covered from base to summit with the sculptured likeness of gods and goddesses, all climbing together, holding hands, making love, giving orders and generally going through the immensely complicated rituals of Hindu mythology.

The biggest and best of Madurai are the five *gopurams* standing guard over the famous Menakshi Temple with, in the centre, the sacred Tank of the Golden Lotus. The best way to judge the size of a *gopuram* is to climb one, which needs a certain stamina. The one I once climbed in semi-darkness and up a treacherous spiral staircase was 52 metres high but the view from the top was worth it. The day's quota of 10,000 pilgrims were beginning to trickle into the Menakshi making for the tank, placing garlands of gardenia and lotus before innumerable statues or spilling into the Hall of a Thousand Columns.

Madurai is fabulous but for me it paled when compared with the effect of Mahabalipuram, the temple city just south of Madras. I was very lucky on one of my first visits — I arrived there on the night of the full moon which is a time of pilgrimage. By dusk, the tide of people began marching towards Mahabalipuram — buses and bullock carts, bicycles, tricycles and the occasional rich man's car all clogged the narrow lanes to the ancient temples by the shore — temples which have stood there since the time when Alfred the Great ruled England. But that night, as the traders set up their stalls, the palmists squatted down and the storytellers began unrolling their night-long tales, the camp fires of 40,000 people began to crackle in the night air and Mahabalipuram seemed the only possible background for the forever story of India. Beyond the great beach and its lonely surfside temple, the ocean gleamed like a sheet of silver paper, the moon rose high and full and soon it seemed to clothe the temples in the light of eternity. They stood, in superb isolation, supported by their myriad gods and goddesses and legendary beasts and as the moon rose higher the whole heavenly bacchanalia of Hinduism came to life

just as the Pallava kings had carved it out of time-defying stone. The vast frieze with its marching elephants gleamed like newly polished silver and in the dancing lights of the fires every statue and every carving appeared to mingle with the crowd and produce a piece of unforgettable cinerama.

Everywhere, people camped by villages, or families under the trees and on the beach, baking chapatis, drinking tea or simply watching. Girls washed their saris in the streams and hung them out to dry like so many multi-coloured banners across a belt of trees. Here a snake charmer held a rapt audience suspended on the thin strain of his flute. There a fortune teller passed tiny bits of paper to a circle of giggling girls and the drums went on beating till dawn. Then, as if moved by some silent command the huge crowd got up from the fires of the night and moved slowly towards the temples of the village. In India's extraordinary past, Mahabalipuram is but a drop in the ocean of time but for me personally it was the beginning of a great love affair with this part of India. Over the years, I travelled west to the little hill stations of Ootacamund (dear old Ooty) and Kodaikanal where the ghosts of the memsahibs still take tea on the lawn, and to the scenically beautiful wildlife sanctuary of Periyar, then to the great fortress of Tiruchirapalli (known to all as Trichy) and south again to that other fantastic temple at Rameswaram, one of the holiest places of Hinduism. I paid calls to Pondicherry which, after all these years, is still mistily French. Nearer Madras, Kanchipuram is not easy to miss — you can see the fantastic *gopurams* of its temples from miles away across the flat country. Kanchipuram is holy too because, like mediaeval Christianity, Hinduism is never short of heroes and legends — but it is also famous as the home of India's finest silk, so fine in fact that you can pull three or four meters of it through the ring from your finger, like great ribbons of multi-coloured gossammer.

At this stage, I know what the purists will say: I have not even begun to mention some of the great traditional sights of India. This is because they are, after all, well known but also for another reason: in India, real personal discovery is not always where the guidebooks say it is. Sometimes, in the strangest, most untouristicated places, one comes across something which hits you between the eyes and makes you wonder if you are not dreaming. Nobody for instance had warned me about the palatial splendours of Hyderabad and even less so about Mysore state, or, as they call it now Karnataka.

If someone were to ask you where the second largest dome in the world is situated, you might be forgiven for saying maybe Florence, or Vienna or Seville — but I have news for you on this score. The second largest dome in the world can be found in the small city of Bijapur, in the northern reaches of Karnataka. It is almost totally unknown and unrecorded at least in Western tourist literature, and I wager that hardly one Indian in ten thousand knows its name — Gol Gumbaz. It is enormously impressive, vast and monumental and measures 38m in diameter — only 4.6m smaller than St Peter's in Rome. It is flanked by four massive towers and when you climb to the gallery that girds the dome, be careful how you speak — the echo will repeat your words 11 times.

The man who built Gol Gumbaz in the early 17th century was Mohammed Ali Shah, a local sultan of Persian origin. By all standards he was not a very distinguished character but he obviously wanted to be remembered and he built himself the biggest mausoleum in the business. Bijapur is

Below left: Akbar founded Fatehpur Sikri, the "City of Victory", in 1571, where he erected several magnificent monuments; this, the tomb of Salim Chisti, is delicately wrought with latticework screens entirely of marble. Scarcity of water gave the city a life of only 17 years, and after Akbar's death the capital was shifted back to Agra.

Bottom left: Caparisoned elephant belonging to the Maharaja of Mysore, at an Independence Day parade.
Bottom right: The Red Fort at Delhi — "layers of Indian history."
Below right: Fascinatingly beautiful Kashmir.

another astonishing place, a treasure house of 50 mosques, 20 palaces and 30 other architectural curiosities. The fact that Gol Gumbaz exists is not half as surprising as the fact that it is where it is — at the end of a long dusty road, unsung and almost unknown and visited I would guess by no more than a score of tourists a week. This is the fascination of India — places which elsewhere would be great tourist meccas are here just a name on the map. You have to know.

Mysore is full of such places. I went to see Aihole, Pattakdal, Belgaum and Jamkhandi and given half a chance I would go again because Mysore is one of my favourite states in India. Pattakdal for instance, is a lesson in Hindu temple architecture, a whole complex of shrines dating back to the seventh century, resplendent with bizarre carvings in which the subject, frozen in movement, appears to have lived yesterday and all of them telling the great Indian stories of the Ramayana and the Mahabharata. Gods, dancers, kings, fortune tellers and legions of attendants tell in sun-warmed stone the great story of early Hinduism. Most poignant of all is probably Hampi, the present day shell of the once great city of Vijayanagar, a metropolis once so important that contemporary European visitors described it with awe as "as big as Rome."

Now let's go back for a while to the heartland of Moghul India. Delhi is the only one of India's great cities which seems to have always been at the centre of action. Hindu dynasties, Moghul conquerors and British imperialists all made Delhi their showpiece and today you get the feeling that here, among the temples, the palaces and the wide avenues, is the heart of this vast and diverse country. Bombay may work, but Delhi rules and it shows. There is a reason for Delhi's supremacy of course: it is the open door to the great plain of the Ganges, the turntable of India. Unlike other cities which grew out of religious or regional separatism, Delhi did not just happen — it was made.

And when, in August 1947, the Union Jack came down the flagpoles and the names of Clive, Wellesley and Curzon faded away with the last strains of alien music, Delhi did not die but was reborn as the true capital of the world's second largest nation. But, as you will soon notice, the British Raj may have gone but its ghost remains in Delhi, Indianised and assimilated but there nevertheless. You only have to ride along Parliament Street, Irwin Road, Kitchener Road or Connaught Place to know that it is still there. The innumerable *babus* of the Indian bureaucracy still tie their files with red tape. The policeman's ritual certainly did not come from the Moghul centuries. As for the post office, it could be anywhere from Winchester to Newcastle-on-Tyne. Yet, grand as it was, this British Delhi was a mere upstart — the eighth city on this spot. Around it you will see other ghosts, those of the six great Moghuls who toyed with India as they fingered their beads — Babur, Humayun, the great Akbar, Jehangir, Shah Jehan and Aurangzeb. And flowing around these ghosts is the unending tide of multi-coloured humanity that is India. Nowhere can these layers of Indian history be better understood than at the Red Fort. But before you even walk through these hallowed halls, sit outside one evening if you can and listen to the Red Fort's entrancing *Son et Lumière*. In the soft Indian night come the sound effects of India's magic history. The days of the great Emperor Ashoka ruling the world of his time with an almost Greek logic. The clash of arms and the first Moslem adventurers raging down from the Khyber Pass to the Bay of Bengal. The resurgence of Hindu power with Shivaji's Mahrattas and the Rajput lords and finally the arrival of the sober and orderly British. This is not just history but the majestic and often tumultuous progress of a great nation through the ages. You will find it more than romantic — truly entrancing.

Now by all means do enter the Red Fort itself and amidst the walls of red sandstone, the screens of marble and alabaster and the water channels and the fountains, you too will feel in your heart of hearts the words of that unknown Persian poet engraved in gold letters on the walls of the Hall of Private Audience: "If there be a paradise on earth, 'tis here, 'tis here, 'tis here..."Gone is the Peacock Throne, stolen by thieving Persians. Gone too is most of the ceiling which used to be of solid silver. But you can still see the traces of the priceless jewels once embedded into the walls. Go too to the charming and rather over-ornate Moti Masjid, the Pearl Mosque, which Aurangzeb built for his own use. Above all, take your time at the Red Fort. Sit and contemplate the gorgeous magnificence of India's ageless majesty.

Now go through the India Gate and along the Rajpath, surely one of the world's greatest avenues. It's an expedition just to trek across it and all around you are the permanent reminders of the Raj time — imperial architecture á la Hollywood, unbelievably grandiose and, let's face it, rather pompous. Yet in the end you will not begin to understand India if you do not get lost at least once in the twisted byways of old Delhi with its amazing bazaar, its kerbside peddlars, its curio shops and its multitudinous humanity. Above all, you will not fail to notice the unmistakable smell of India, so ably described by John Keay in his recent book: "One of the richest, strangest and most exciting smells imaginable shoot up the nostrils like a whiff of brandy. Urine and jasmine, cow dung, smoke and frangipani, low octane fuel and the acrid *bidi* cigarette combine with the baffling aroma of Indian cuisine to make the air almost tangible."

As far as one can tell no tourist ever goes to India without making a foray down to Agra. If Bombay is the future and Delhi the present, Agra is India's past — a past so romantic and so pregnant with memories that it can hardly fail to move even the most blasé traveller. Agra of course is the Taj Mahal, that monument to love built by Shah Jehan to the memory of his wise and beautiful queen, Mumtaz Mahal. Travellers and poets, artists and historians have described the Taj a thousand times and yet to my mind nothing equals the extraordinary experience of seeing it for yourself. If I have one secret to convey to you about the Taj it is this: for once, say goodbye to guides, avoid the tourist crocodile and build your own orchestration for the symphony to come. Walk around the outside slowly and gingerly, catching a glimpse of that incredible white dome here or the curve of a superb Moghul archway. Sit and think about it. Then be bold, walk right through the tall gateway and it will be like opening an oyster and finding a luscious pearl inside — the incredible whiteness and the unmatchable proportions of that noble dome with its flanking minarets rising to heaven like the notes of a flute and all of it mirrored with extraordinary precision in the rectangular pool. But you have not seen anything yet because the tombs of the illustrious husband and wife can only be believed when you have seen them — the latter with that moving statement: "God is everlasting, God is sufficient. He knows what is concealed and what is manifest. He is merciful and compassionate."

Kashmir has it all. Mountains, forests...and lakes. At Srinagar, below, the long, slim shikara is a familiar form of travel, while the houseboats, bottom left, are famous for their ornate interiors.
Bottom right: The spectacular Trichur Pooram festival; richly caparisoned elephants parade with ceremonial parasols.

108

Then you notice the inlaid decorations with cornelian, jasper, agate, lapis lazuli and bloodstone and if you look closer still you will see that a 2.5 centimetre square leaf in Mumtaz Mahal's tomb has 60 different gems in it. Such is the Taj. See it for yourself. See it by moonlight if you can or in the early morning as it rises immaculate and pure from the mists of the night and, as I wrote at the start of this article, you will never be the same person again.

India is India — a procession of moods, and not far from Agra is another one, that sleeping beauty of a city, Fatehpur Sikri. The colossal capital which Akbar built as a toy and where he sat playing chess with slave girls as living pieces surrounded by a luxury which, when described by the occasional European visitor, was totally disbelieved in the West. Nobody could be that rich, that powerful — but Akbar was. In my opinion, two of Agra's greatest sights are sadly overshadowed by the great Taj: one is Agra's own fort which combines Akbar's strength with Shah Jehan's unfailing eye for beauty and the other is one of my own great favourites, the exquisite mausoleum of Itmad-ud-Daula.

What else could one do in this part of India? The answer is simply: choose your direction. You could follow the burning path of the noonday sun, go back a thousand years or so to the heyday of Hindu India and visit the 85 temples of Khajuraho, with their curved togetherness of erotic scenes. As someone once said, Khajuraho is either pure pornography or just pure, depending on your own viewpoint. Or go east down the Ganges valley and even further back in time to Benares, the city which is today called Varanasi. Benares was already old when Jerusalem was a shepherd's village and Persepolis not yet on the map. To the average Westerner, Benares is strange, disturbing, uncomfortable and almost totally incomprehensible. But to stand at dawn near the ghats leading down to the holy Ganges is to witness the outward manifestations of a religion, a way of life which belongs to the hearts and minds of all Indians. The country's kaleidoscope does not end there by any means. It is also the amazing caves of Ellora and Ajanta, or, on the east coast, the superb carvings of Konarak. It is also that frenetic city of Calcutta with its millions of clever and argumentative Bengalis, its writers and its art schools. And if you should wish to see India nearer the abode of the gods, go to Darjeeling, get up with the sun and spend a while contemplating Kanchenjunga. But then again you might feel like a break on the beach and let us face it: it is only in recent years that Indians themselves have been persuaded by others that they possess some of the finest strands in the world — all the way from Goa in the west, around Cape Comorin and up the Coromandel coast, beach resorts are beginning to rise.

India goes on surprising everyone. It is surely a long way from holy Agra to the counting houses of Bombay but that is also India. A young, up-to-date, growing-up India. Bombay is India's materialistic mecca where the prevailing religion is making a rupee. Twenty percent of India's heavy industry is here. So are the enormous textile factories. Spurred by clever Parsees, worked by frugal Gujaratis and ambitious Punjabis, Bombay is rising from its one-time seven islands to become one of the world's really great cities. It draws people, teaches them to work and to get on until they own one of those mansions up on Malabar Hill or die in the attempt. In a world whose sinews are trade and commerce, Bombay was bound to succeed. It looks to the West over the Arabian Sea and the British, who inherited it from the Portuguese, knew what they were doing when they made it

the gateway to India, long before they built the monument of that name. But they could not have done it without those vast Indian masses and today, for those Indian masses, Bombay is a frontier town, the place where things happen, be it from nuclear energy to dairies and from banking to motorcars. For your information, they make more movies in Bombay than anywhere else outside the United States. Bombay itself is like that. In love with showmanship. Its own showmanship is visible enough if you walk along the famous Marine Drive all the way to the Gateway and the world famous Taj Mahal Hotel — Bombay rises, Chicago-like, on the backcloth of the greeny blue sea. But for the visitor, Bombay means one thing above all, the first taste of India, the first smell and one of Asia's greatest market places — which means shopping. Say what you want and Bombay's got it. Along the shopping streets they will sell you anything from shirt buttons to shirts, fashion handmade for you overnight, a suit tailored in 48 hours, gems by the shovelful, silks and cottons by the roll and if you want a Bukhara carpet why, of course they've got one, if only they could find it under that mountain of goods. Bombay is pulsating, exciting, cosmopolitan and effervescent and if you can survive that heady mixture, the rest of India will come almost as a rest cure.

But perhaps we should end up with a dream. When Moghul Emperor Jehangir was on his deathbed, his attendants asked him if there was anything he wanted. "Only Kashmir" he whispered. "Only Kashmir..." Indeed I have known old India hands who swore that when it came to it they would give up the whole of the sub-continent for only Kashmir. I would not go that far myself but I am ready to admit that the great vale country is immeasurably beautiful — and fun too, especially if you can have a houseboat. The Dal Lake houseboats near Srinagar have of course been a tradition since the days when the higher ranks of the Raj made them popular. They are unlike any other contraption in the world — veritable floating palaces, sometimes 45 m long, elaborately decorated and with walls of rare timbers and gay canopies of cotton flapping in the breeze. They are exceedingly comfortable, often with two or three bedrooms, living rooms, sundeck and a kitchen boat tied up at the back where expert Kashmiri cooks will work on anything from local dishes to mutton stew. There they lie, amidst beds of floating lotus blooms — quite unforgettable. All have fanciful names, like Triumph, or Paradise, or even Valhalla — I wonder where they got that one. And even Loves Lies Ableeding. The last houseboat I had was called New Eagle. Mornings, I used to hail my favourite *shikara,* called "Happy Days — guaranteed spring interior cushions", and have myself paddled to the far side of the lake where canny Kashmiris collect water grasses, hump them together in little clumps, anchor them with sticks and then grow the best fruit and vegetables in the East — luscious red tomatoes, fat watermelons and pumpkins wallowing on the edge of their aquatic home. I loved watching young Kashmiri girls, in red and yellow trousers, padding from one to the other, weeding and plucking. When the wind rose, the little gardens began floating away with their owners in hot pursuit and all the time the majestic Himalayas looking on, their profile grandiose, their snows unmelting, their virginity unsullied. Around this lake and others are the gardens once so well loved by their Moghul planners, places like Nishat and the legendary Shalimar where man, water and nature have combined to create real and lasting beauty. Then there are

the higher valleys of Kashmir, like Gulmarg and Pahalgam, where wild flowers sway gently in the mountain air. Nowhere else in this teeming country is there such perfection of nature, such peace, such boundless natural riches.

Yet Kashmir is only a tiny corner of the giant Indian canvas — a great mosaic of colour, history, art and beauty — and every piece of it a sensation which even the most jaded traveller cannot easily forget. There is much else on this canvas that you must discover for yourself for this is what travel is all about. I leave you here and if it is not a sacrilege on the part of a red-faced Westerner, I too join the palms of my hands below my chin in salutation and say *Namaste*. May your Indian journey be the journey of a lifetime.

HARNESSING TECHNOLOGY
FOR ENGINEERING AND CONSTRUCTION
WORLDWIDE

Adding value to Nature's wealth.

15 Portland Place, London W1A 4DD, England. Tel: 01-637 2821. Telex: 22604.

A Davy Corporation company

Davy McKee
OUR STRENGTH IS YOUR STRENGTH

THE FICTIONS
OF INDIA

Reginald Massey

Consider the following titles: *Damfool Smith Sahib, The Best Indian Chutney — Sweetened, Ganges Mud, The Adventures of an ADC, The Rajah's Second Wife, Coffee Coloured Honeymoon, Did She Love Him?, The Real India, Dust Upon Wind, Dogsbody: The Story of a Romantic Subaltern, The Empire of the Nairs, or the Rights of Women: A Utopian Romance, Gunner Jingo's Jubilee, Fleas and Nightingales, Jungle Jest, The Romance of a Nautch Girl, Indrani and I, With Rifle and Kukri, With Sword and Pen, Old Deccan Days, The Secret of the Zenana* and *Badmashes.* Now none of these is my invention; they are actual books written by actual people, not one of whom was an Indian. They bear names to match their titles — names such as Thomas Bland Strange, Max Joseph Pemberton, Alfred Frederic Pollock Harcourt, Cyril Argentine Alington, Charles Hanke Tod Crosthwaite, Dudley Hardress Thomas and Septimus Smet Thorburn. Let me also record for posterity the splendidly named authoresses Eliza Fanny Pollard, Maria Henrietta Crommelin, Flora Annie Steel, Theodora Edward Hook, Mary Eliza Isabella Freer and the prolific Fanny Emily Farr Penny. It is these and others like them whose vivid imaginations have stamped forever their picture of India onto the minds of English speaking peoples.

Millions the world over got their entertainment and thrills from these purveyors of popular fiction who could certainly tell a rattling good yarn. They churned out endless tales of maharajahs and monkeys; shikar, suttee, sanyasis, and snakes; fakirs and fakes; treasures in temples, turbulent tribesmen and thugs; dashing cavalry officers and faithful native orderlies. The Indians in these books were not by and large pleasant — indeed, with many of them one would not relish a midnight encounter — and those few who were

noble were sickeningly so. A stock figure was the funny Indian who gushed out fractured or convoluted English rather like the princeling at Bunter's school. In some novels this character was over corrected to become the handsome Oxford-accented English gentleman with a divine tan. Cultivated behaviour, because it arose from a different ethos, was not understood as such and therefore represented as bizarre or at best eccentric. No Indian was seen as normal and so far-reaching was the effect of these fictions that the images they created persist to this day.

Nothing about Hindustan was real — it was all larger than life, exaggerated. The picture was confused and confusing but always provocative, mysterious and intensely exciting.

I have advisedly refrained from starting with the obvious books and their authors for they are the tips of the iceberg or — since we are talking about India — the everests of expression.

The foreign interest in India — sometimes healthy, others morbid and obsessive — is as old as the Himalayas. Outsiders have possibly been enticed by moods and aromas to which we have become so accustomed that we hardly notice them. My own experience bears witness to this phenomenon: a few years ago I toured India after a considerable period abroad and realised that I was seeing things that I hadn't *seen* before although I vaguely remembered their existence from my childhood. Indeed, what can they of India know who only India know? That is why the travelogues of foreign visitors are so fascinating. The seventh century Buddhist pilgrim Huien Tsang, for example, noted the large number of courtesans at the Surya temple in Multan; the scholar Al-Biruni (11th century) in his work *India* catalogued the country's achievements in science and art and, three centuries later, another Arab, Ibn Batuta, recorded that there were two thousand musicians in the service of Sultan Mohammad bin Tughluq. The *Memoirs* of Babar, the founding father of the Moghul Empire, are a mine of information and later, in the 18th century, the missionary Dubois wrote his justly well known, and often unjustly vilified, *Hindu Manners, Customs and Ceremonies*. What has disturbed Indian prudes — faithfully following as they do their late Victorian masters — was his graphic account of the *devadasis* of south India.

We do not burn books or their authors but like the British we disregard the uncomfortable ones. One would think that after three-and-a-half decades of freedom we would have acquired the intellectual maturity to consider honestly the assessments of commentators such as Katherine Mayo, Beverley Nichols and V S Naipaul. Our verdict must be on the basis of reason, not emotion. India might not be a continent of Circe nor even an area of darkness but I'm sure that anyone who essays a discovery of India will always come up with something rich and strange. And also, most surely, something ugly and unpleasant.

The novel form came to India with the English language and significant imaginative writing tells us more about a people than statistics and census data. In George Grella's words, "Because it arises from and speaks to emotions, because it deals with the spirit of man, because it delights as well as instructs, fiction can help us know India in deeper and broader ways than the reports of scholars and scientists." He continues: "Dozens of books about early 20th century Indian conditions of class, race, climate, and history cannot replace the world of Mosque, Cave, and Temple created in a novel like E M Forster's *Passage to India*." How true. But for my money the master will always be Kipling. Poet, careful craftsman and wizard of words, he conjured up time and again the vast kaleidoscope of Mother India and her many millions and wrote of them with an acute understanding of the cultural context within which they functioned, although he clearly believed that this left much to be desired and could only be improved by the ennobling effect of British values. As a storyteller he was unbeatable. Jingoist? Apostle of imperialism? True: but he too was a prisoner of his cultural conditioning. Need one be an Anglican to appreciate the Authorised Version? Many a Hindu and even Roman Catholic, I daresay, has benefited by a perusal of that book.

Following Kipling's example, writers like Henty and Talbot Mundy fired the imagination of generations of Britons with books such as *The Tiger of Mysore, For Name and Fame, Red Flame of Erinpura* and *King of the Khyber Rifles*. And in our own times India has provided material and locale for the very considerable talents of J R Ackerley, W S Maugham, John Masters, Rumer Godden, Louis Bromfield, Paul Scott, M M Kaye, Ruth Prawer Jhabvala, H R F Keating and a host of others too numerous to list here.

Thus far the discussion has dealt with foreign writers: in other words, those who did not — or who do not — belong to any of the ethnic groups native to India. However, Indians have been using English for the purposes of creative writing for almost a hundred and fifty years and examples of such work first appeared in Bengal where the British influence was strongest. Derivative though much of this early poetry, prose and fiction inevitably was, it certainly heralded the Indian renaissance. It should come as no surprise that since these Indians were writing in English they were anxious to be recognised in England. This was not so much a matter of an inferiority complex, although this had set in, as a natural process. If by some linguistic miracle I were to write my next book in Russian I could be pardoned for wanting to know how the Academy in Moscow rated my work. And so it was that Tagore's English version of *Gitanjali* was taken up by Yeats, Sarojini Naidu was championed by Gosse and later writers followed a similar path. The Americans went through the same process and no less a poet than Robert Frost sought the encouragement of Englishmen like Rupert Brooke and Edward Thomas.

Today matters stand differently. Although many Indian writers still prefer to be published in England and America for international distribution and therefore monetary advantage, none worth his salt visits England for testimonials or a patronising pat on the head. Mulk Raj Anand, D F Karaka, Raja Rao, R K Narayan — who did procure a useful preface from Graham Greene many years ago — Khwaja Ahmed Abbas, Bhabani Bhattacharya, Kamala Markandaya, Khushwant Singh, Ved Mehta and now Salman Rushdie have written novels of quality and churlish labels such as "Indo-English" or "Indo-Anglican" do not befit their status. Writers are writers and these are Indian writers. That is all.

Paradoxically, an ever increasing number of Indians have begun to write in English since 1947 for it was not until Independence that English was finally established as an official Indian language. This is wholly to the good for it has channelled the Indian genius to flow into fresh, new and virgin fields. The harvest has been rich and often unexpected because English is to India today what Latin once was to Europe.

Radhakrishnan I think it was who said that the British legacy to us consisted of Shakespeare, the King James's Bible and the limited liability company. The first two concern language and for this we must be thankful: for of all the appliances of expression ever devised it is the English language that stands pre-eminent. It is tooled for both science and the soul. Supremely malleable, it is fitted for enquiry and reflection. Indeed, the argument for independence itself was conducted in English — "Liberty is my birthright: and I will have it!" could not have sounded the same in any other language. Nor for that matter that memorable utterance at the midnight hour when we made our tryst with destiny.

RICHNESS AND VARIETY OF THE PEOPLES

Bridget Allchin

The first thing about the peoples of India that strikes the outsider is their Indianness. Indianness is a quality that overrides many differences. Once encountered it is something clearly sensed and readily recognised but it is very hard to define. It can only be described as cultural character. An inhabitant of India, or for that matter of any part of the Indian subcontinent, is as readily identified as an inhabitant of Western Europe, North America or China — all like India major subcontinental units, each with its own pronounced cultural character. To perceive their character is one thing but to analyse or define it, quite another. This is particularly so in the case of India for within its parameters are such a bewildering variety of different groups and communities of people.

On reflection it becomes clear that the inhabitants of India must owe their distinctive character first of all to two basic features, one geographical and the other historical. Geographically the Indian subcontinent or South Asia is very effectively divided from the rest of the world by deserts, mountains and seas. None of them are uncrossable and indeed all are crossed by routes which at times have acted as highways of contact with the outside world, but they effectively define South Asia and prevent its cultural outlines becoming blurred. Historically and archaeologically the roots of Indianness go back a very long way. The literary, linguistic and scholarly traditions of modern India extend back to the early centuries BC. Although heavily influenced by Iranian, Moghul, British and general Western culture, the mainstream of Indian culture has continued unbroken. External influences have augmented rather than detracted from it.

Archaeological research of the 19th and early 20th century shows the roots of Indian village life, religion, agricultural practice and a number of traditional arts and crafts, go back to the mature Indus valley civilisation of the late third millennium BC. More recent research has shown the mature Indus valley or Harappan civilisation itself to have an even longer ancestry. Some of its most central and most Indian characteristics in turn have been traced back several millennia to older ancestral cultures of the Indus region. Therefore the mature urban culture of the Indus plains during the late third millennium BC so massively represented at Mohenjodaro, Harappa and other sites in Pakistan and at Kalibangan in India, itself is the end product of a process of evolution that began at least 2,000 years earlier in the western tributary valleys of the Indus on the borders of Sind and Baluchistan. With such an ancestry behind them it is not surprising that the peoples of the Indian subcontinent have a profound common cultural identity.

But to understand the diversity contained within this subcontinental cultural unity requires further consideration. Indians and outsiders alike tend to speak of India as though it were a single country comparable in size to France, Germany or the United Kingdom — each one of which was only brought together as a single entity during the last two, three or four centuries. In fact India is as large as the whole of Western Europe. In addition to being large, India is a land of extremes: extremes of climate ranging from deserts to tropical forests; fertile plains of incredible productivity, and the highest mountains in the world; extremes in terms of geological processses actively at work that maintain the height of those mountains and contribute to the

117

Some of the different types of turban worn throughout India: Rajasthan, in the north, below left; Mizoram, in the east, below centre; a dancer in Karnataka, in the south, below right; a Sikh from the Punjab, bottom left.
Centre right: The dhoti is a traditional dress to be found throughout south India.
Bottom right: Folk dress in Rajasthan.

catastrophic floods, droughts and other natural disasters to which its people are subject. In such a situation the people of India have had to adapt themselves to many widely differing environments. Diversity and variety within and around the main stream of Indian culture is more readily understood when one realises that over many centuries agricultural communities have been utilising the local potential in each part of the subcontinent. This has had its effect upon every aspect of life ranging from the basic foods and the control they have exercised upon the regional and local cuisine, to aspects of social structure and to the size of communities, the siting of cities ancient and modern and other aspects of the demography and human geography of the subcontinent.

The basic unit of Indian society from the time of the Indus valley civilisation and probably earlier has been the village; capable in normal circumstances of providing from local resources all its requirements in terms of food, housing, textiles etc, and of producing almost all of the artefacts required to do this. Within the village itself and in some cases within a group of related villages are communities of cultivators, herdsmen and craftsmen such as potters and blacksmiths. Although essentially interdependent upon one another, each such group has tended to maintain its individuality and each to marry only within itself or within equivalent groups in other villages. In this way two kinds of traditional group identity have been established and maintained, the local and the occupational.

This pattern of village life has steadily extended into the more remote parts of the subcontinent, absorbing many local communities with simpler life-styles. It is part of the genius of Indian culture that this has traditionally been done without destroying their community identity. Thus the older traditions of local peoples have in many cases been added to and absorbed by the incoming village structure that carries with it the qualities of essential Indianness.

Indianness, however, is also something that reaches out beyond the physical confines of the expanding village settlements. Its influence is felt by and can be recognised in communities with different, often less complex internal structures in the deserts, hills, forests and mountains of the subcontinent. This expansion of the Indian village, with its complex internal structure, can be seen with hindsight from the standpoint of the observer in the modern world with all its ethnic and economic problems, as a kind of colonialism, also part of the Indian tradition. Like all forms of colonialism it has its faults. But in many respects it appears both more benign and more successful than that of post-Renaissance Europe which has tended to demand the break-up of indigenous groups, and has only allowed their members to enter the more advanced society as individuals. In terms of cultural conservation it has proved immensely successful and should make all those concerned with such urgent problems throughout the world pause and consider. The Bhils of central India or the matrilineal communities of the south-west coast may differ from the norm of Indian village society and may resist certain aspects of more orthodox Indian culture, but at the same time they are part of it. Association, through commerce and individual contact over many centuries, makes this inevitable. They too are encapsulated into the mainstream and add to the enormous wealth of local cultural and craft tradition.

Indian urban and village communities alike have from the earliest times traded in certain items both within the subcontinent and beyond. Trade has not only added to the richness and variety of Indian society at large by increasing wealth and providing exotic materials for making jewellery, textiles, etc, but it has stimulated the emergence of communities concerned with all its aspects: merchants; promoters of sea and land transport; craftsmen of every kind, and so on.

Incoming groups of merchants have also been encapsulated by Indian society as a whole at the urban rather than the village level. These include a whole range of communities who to this day maintain their identity and add their contribution to the mosaic of Indian culture: Jews, Arabs, Parsees are long established on the west coast of the subcontinent; Christians of various sects and denominations and Moslems from western and central Asia are more widely dispersed. The two latter have also added to the general cultural diversity by being instrumental in creating communities of mixed birth and others of indigenous converts, arising from their perhaps somewhat over-zealous evangelical tendencies. Moslems now form one of the largest religious minorities in India and there are more Moslems in India than in any other country of the world. Other communities absorbed in this way have come originally as military invaders and remained. All these people, while retaining their group identity, have perforce become Indianised in many aspects of their dress, diet and social customs.

India is a secular state and among its people many of the major religions of the world are substantially represented. The majority of the population are Hindus. Hinduism alone has many aspects, and associated with each are a whole range of festivals and forms of worship, many of them colourful and exciting; they are expressive of forms of worship and a whole range of emotions and are associated with different seasons of the agricultural year. Some are specific to certain regions or communities while others, such as Diwali, the autumn festival of lights, Holi, the festival of spring, with its feasting, present giving and squirting of coloured water, and Makara Sankranti or Pongal, the mid-winter festival of north and south India, again with bonfires and, in south India with the new season's rice, are India-wide. In addition Moslems, Sikhs, Jains, Buddhists, Parsees, Christians, Jews, etc, and all the sects and sub-divisions of each, have their practices and festivals which add greatly to the richness, colour and variety of Indian life. Indeed it has not been unknown for as many as five religious festivals or holidays to follow one another consecutively, each one a public holiday! If there is one thing that the people of India share it is that they all tend to be religious, and all their religions tend to have public festivals, most of which are thoroughly enjoyed, both by their own adherents and by the population at large. Religion and social life are closely interwoven. Religious motifs also play an important role in the traditional arts and crafts of the whole subcontinent.

The dazzling range of religions in India is matched by the range of languages. By far the most numerous and widely spoken are the languages of the Indo-Aryan group: linguistic descendants though not necessarily physical descendants of languages spoken by the Indo-Aryan tribes who arrived in India from the north-west between three and four thousand years ago. These are spoken from the Pakistan frontier in the west right across north India to the Ganges Brahmaputra delta and for some distance up the Brahmaputra valley, and down into the Deccan (ie about half way down the peninsula). Hindi, the national language,

*Below left: Colourful
traditional Rajasthani saree.
Below centre: Typical style of
dress in Kashmir.
Centre left: Festival dress from
the Punjab.
Bottom left: A Moslem
coppersmith, with
characteristic round beard.
Below right and bottom right:
People bathing at Benares.
(Benares photos courtesy of
Rajesh Bedi).*

120

is the most widely spoken, being the mother tongue of the densely populated central Ganges valley region. Urdu, written in the Persian script, is the close cousin of Hindi used by Moslems and in its time the administrative language of Moghul and British India. Other major languages of north India, Bengali, Punjabi, Gujarati, Marathi, etc also belong to this group. The second major group is the Dravidian, spoken in the southern peninsula, of which the chief representatives are Tamil, Telugu, Kannada and Malayalam. The other language families of India are less numerous and in many cases lacking a traditional written literature, although rich in oral traditions.

All along the northern boundaries in the Himalayan valleys are languages of the Tibeto-Burman group. In eastern central India the Munda languages are spoken by such groups as the Santal tribes of inland Bengal and Orissa.

English is still an important language widely spoken at an inter-provincial level but not by so many people as Hindi or Urdu. It remains the language of a much higher level of administration, diplomacy and relations with the outside world, and is particularly important in higher education, technology, science and research. It is also the medium of much excellent literature today, and it is noteworthy that a recent major British prize for fiction in the English language, the Booker Award, was made to an Indian novelist writing in English.

The cultural richness and variety of the peoples of India is expressed in every aspect of their life-style. One of the first things a newcomer to India notices is women's dress. Even in the large cities where saris are worn almost exclusively in the India-wide modern style with the alternatives of modern versions of Salvar suits and other forms of dress, there is a dazzling range of textiles, jewellery and embroidery to be seen worn with casual elegance by shoppers and professional women. In the country the regional styles of wearing saris and other kinds of dress, combined with locally made textiles and styles of jewellery, distinguish each region's state and even in some cases individual districts. The traveller comes to know when he has crossed a cultural and sometimes also a linguistic or state frontier by the bearing and style of dress of the people, particularly the women, he encounters on the road.

No one who has once seen a group of Maharashtran women walking along the road in their subdued but distinctive plain green, blue or deep red saris with deep contrasting borders can fail to recognise them again. The exceptional length of a traditional Maharashtran sari and the distinctive way it is worn, either hanging freely or, when working in the fields, drawn up between the legs to appear like baggy trousers, is soon recognised also. Saris in north, east and south India are not worn so long as those of Maharashtra and are generally put on in the orthodox manner, pleated in front, draped round the back and the end thrown over the left shoulder or covering the head. Regional character is sometimes expressed in the way the sari is draped, as in Gujarat, or by a different form of dress as for example in the lungis worn by some groups in Kerala on the south-west coast.

In north-west India the traditional Rajasthani colours, vivid reds and yellows, or deep midnight blue and deep red, are unforgettable. Rajasthan is outside the area in which the sari is the traditional form of dress. The full skirts with many metres of cloth pleated into a band at the waist, small choli blouses and large chaddars worn by most Rajasthani women are well suited to life in this arid environment. It is often necessary to walk long distances and travel on camels, to both of which these clothes are well suited as they allow the necessary freedom of movement, and the chaddars can be worn in such a way that it gives protection from sun and dust. The salvar-kameez and dupatta, the traditional dress of Punjabi women, is equally distinctive. It is eminently suited to the more northerly climate with its greater extremes of winter and summer and the active life of most Punjabi country women. In its modern form it has also spread widely throughout India.

Men's dress too has its regional and community differences. Today, with certain notable exceptions such as Sikhs with their distinctive turbans, hairstyles and beards, these have tended to be dropped or become merged into a more limited range of India-wide styles. These range from the salvar-kameez of the Punjab - the counterpart of Punjabi women's dress - to the dhotis and lungis worn by Hindus and Moslems respectively in all the warmer parts of the subcontinent. Both these garments consist of lengths of uncut cloth worn in a distinctive manner by various communities much as saris are. Another form of traditional masculine dress are pajamas (the origin of the British and European nightwear of the same name). Jodhpuri pajamas are another type of cotton trousers with more tightly fitting legs. Both forms of pajama, worn with long high-necked, single-breasted tailored coats with many buttons (achkan) and Gandhi caps, have come to be regarded as national dress. More widely worn in urban contexts and ever gaining in popularity are various adaptations of Western trousers, bush shirts, etc.

Turbans or pugarees and caps of various distinctive styles and colours are worn by men in rural communities throughout the subcontinent and these in time the traveller comes to recognise.

The character of regional dress is closely linked to the wealth of regional textiles, tapestries, carpets and embroideries in all of which the subcontinent abounds. Each of these is a subject in itself, but no account of the people of India would be complete without some mention of the arts and crafts — especially those associated with textiles that are such an integral part of Indian culture. Wool, cotton and silk are all produced in India today, and all are used with immense skill and artistry in both traditional and innovative ways. Cotton cloth was woven in Harappan times, we know from archaeological evidence. We also know that it was dyed and that it was exported to ancient Mesopotamia. Textiles are not durable in the archaeological sense, and only survive in exceptional conditions or as impressions on clay or other substances. Therefore we cannot know about ancient Indian textiles, the kind of things we know for example about early Chinese ceramics. We can, however, infer from various sources of evidence that much artistic expression found an outlet in this field anciently as it does today.

In India, Gandhi's insistence upon the protection and fostering of all arts and crafts was an important factor in enabling them to survive the early years of industrial development. Now this period has been weathered, and the growing Indian professional classes provide a ready market to maintain their production and traditional craftsmen and women are prospering once more. All arts and crafts play an immensely valuable role in tourism and are increasingly popular as exports, as shops in Britain and Europe bear witness.

Embroidery too is important and contributes to the richness and variety of the dress of the people of India. But to appreciate it fully one must not only see the people but go into their homes where it is used to great effect, as are tapestries and carpets, carved woodwork, painted papier mache and many other crafts. All this however is beyond the scope of this chapter, and along with music, the performing arts and other equally fascinating and absorbing aspects of Indian culture must be left to other contributors to this volume. In conclusion one can only say that their extraordinary flair for varied expression in all these fields is something that people of the subcontinent share. It is part of their Indianness, and the dazzling variety of traditional crafts is part of the expression of the variety and richness of their cultural heritage.

ANTIQUITY AND CONTINUITY

F R Allchin

The outside visitor to India, today no less than in the past, is struck by the impression it presents of the individuality of her people, their character and culture. Should he go on to think about the history of that character, he is likely to conclude that it has all the marks of great antiquity. During the 19th century Western scholars attempted to discover the age of the Vedas and hence — they believed — of the beginnings of the Indian tradition. However, it was the archaeological discoveries of the 1920s and 30s and particularly the excavations at Mohenjodaro and Harappa, which provided for the first time a solid archaeological basis for the view that India's civilisation *was* of great antiquity. Soon after the first excavations, Sir John Marshall was able to announce to the world the discovery of a new and hitherto quite unknown civilisation in the Indus valley. This announcement carried back the knowledge of the first Indian cities to some 4,500 to 5,000 years ago; but, even so, the origins and antecedents of these cities remained shrouded in mystery. The cities seemed to appear from nowhere, in their fully developed form, and Stuart Piggott in his *Prehistoric India* (1950) wrote of their having "no known beginnings, no tentative early phases." Further discoveries have been made in both India and Pakistan during the past two decades, and these provide us for the first time with a more or less complete account of the genesis of the Indus civilisation.

In our present state of knowledge the earliest evidence comes particularly from one site, Mehrgarh, on the banks of the Bolan River near Sibi, not far from the point where the river emerges through a gorge, from the valleys of Baluchistan on to the Indus plains. Here the French Archaeological Mission to Pakistan has in recent years been ex-cavating a settlement that came to an end around the time when the Indus cities first appeared, and which had then lasted for perhaps 5,000 years before that time. That is to say, the settlement was already older than the interval which separates us from the beginnings of the mature Indus civilisation. The earliest, Neolithic, stage dates from *c.* 8-7000 BC. At that time we find in Mehrgarh a community already equipped with stone tools, soon also using stone blades set in wooden hafts with bitumen to make composite knives and sickles; beginning to make houses and compart-mented storehouses or granaries of mud brick; and cultivating wheat and barley. They appear to have had from the very start sheep and goats and perhaps also cattle, although during the first stages the number of cattle increas-ed dramatically, suggesting that we are witnessing the start of a new development. Among their crafts were basket and mat making. Remains of the people themselves occur in numerous burials, in one case involving a skeleton outlined with stone knife blades. Something quite unexpected is that almost from the beginning there is evidence of long distance trade, in the form of beads of turquoise and lapis lazuli, both apparently imported from northern Afghanistan or central Asia, and of sea shells imported from the Indian Ocean. Thus was a pattern of trade established which was to persist for many millennia. Already before 5000 BC the first objects of copper appear, in the form of beads, and after that time larger objects of copper gradually become more common. Around the same time the first pottery of baked clay is found — later to become so common a product of all the village settlements. Even earlier are the first small models of humans or animals in clay. These too in course of time were to be baked in an oven and turned into a long

Mohenjodaro: a masterpiece of urban planning, with straight streets criss-crossing the city, top left.

The Great Bath at Mohen-jodaro, bottom left.

Below left: This limestone bust of a royal priest wearing a trefoil-patterned garment across his shoulder was discovered at Mohenjodaro.
Below right: Early image of a bullock cart: this terracotta toy cart, complete with driver, was found at Mohenjodaro.
Bottom right: Artist's impression of how the city of Mohenjodaro may have looked in its heyday.
The continuing image of the mother goddess: the terracotta figurine, centre left, was found at Mohenjodaro; the one on the bottom left comes from Mathura, and is dated 3rd century BC.

series of terracottas. The painted decoration on the pottery, often recalling the patterns on modern textiles, and the terracottas represent the principal surviving traces of the art of these early settlements.

These developments took place at Mehrgarh and at other sites in Baluchistan and along the Indo-Iranian borders. Around 3500 BC a new and important development took place, in that agricultural settlements began to be established on the Indus plains themselves. These first settlements extend from the Indian Ocean and the Indus delta, through lower and upper Sind, into the Derajat and Punjab, right up to the Himalayas, and even farther into the northern valleys of Kashmir and Swat.

At first these newly settled areas are clearly distinguished from each other, and appear to represent several separate movements of colonisation, leading to the appearance of independent cultural provinces. But simultaneously a second tendency is noticeable, leading towards ever greater similarities of style between the material products of the regions, and probably representing a convergence towards a common life-style. From around 3000 BC onwards this tendency becomes ever more clear and must represent a growing process of communication, trade and contact between most parts of the Indus plains. This process we can now recognise as the formative period of the Indus civilisation. Originally named "Pre-Harappan" it now seems more appropriate to call it Early Harappan or Early Indus, as undoubtedly it represents the period of incipient urbanism which lays the foundation for the full urbanism of the succeeding Indus civilisation. During the Early Indus period we begin to find signs scratched on pottery which, although they are not actual letters or inscriptions, are surely the indications of a growing consciousness of the need for writing. So too do we begin to find small seals of stone or bone which probably indicate the need for securing and marking the ownership of storehouses, granaries, or bales of merchandise. These things find their logical development and fulfilment in the Mature Indus civilisation. Another exciting indication provided by recent discoveries is that many features of the mythology and religious beliefs of the Mature Indus civilisation also have their roots in this Early period.

Thus it now begins to emerge that the population base and level of technological know-how needed by the Indus civilisation had evolved slowly over a very long period in the Indus plains or on its borders. From c. 2500 BC onwards this process finds its logical fulfilment in the Mature Harappan civilisation. For the next five centuries or so the whole Indus valley and several adjacent areas witnessed a truly remarkable cultural uniformity and presumably common life-style. How this was achieved, in social and political terms, is still not at all clear, but it appears to have involved very large-scale trade and distribution throughout the whole area. Certain centres appear to have been responsible for the production of goods which were later distributed very widely: stone blades produced in the vast factory sites at Sukkur-Rohri; carnelian beads from Lothal and Chanhu-daro; conch shell bangles from Balakot and Chanhu-daro; metal objects from as yet undetermined centres; etc. Such interaction over so large an area cannot have been maintained without the use of writing and accurate methods of accounting, and hence the still unread script and the Indus seals must have fulfilled an important role.

The resultant life-style seems moreover to have been already typically "Indian", and many of its features survive even in modern times. The example of the Indus bullock carts is well known. Yet more remarkable is the discovery of a ploughed field surface at Kalibangan, the site in northern Rajasthan so carefully excavated by the Archaeological Survey of India, dating from the very beginning of the Mature Indus period and showing a pattern of crossed furrows representing no doubt the simultaneous planting of two crops, which is found till today in this locality and no other part of India or Pakistan. The meaning of this must be that here we have precious evidence of an agricultural mode which has been passed down from one generation to another over four-and-a-half thousand years! Many of the special features of the planning and construction of the Indus cities and their houses can be paralleled in modern towns and villages of the Indus area.

When we remember that the Indus life-style was the end product of several thousand years of gradual build-up of population and cultural tradition in the Indus valley and on its edges, we can see that the matrix it provided must have been, as Gordon Childe so aptly remarked: "deeply rooted in Indian soil. The Indus civilisation represents a very perfect adjustment of human life to a specific environment .... It is already specifically Indian and forms the basis of modern Indian culture."

The archaeological discoveries we have been discussing have given an altogether new perspective to our view of early Indian civilisation. This demands that we should think afresh about many things, some of which have been long taken for granted. For instance, it used to be thought that classical Indian civilisation was in essence "Aryan," the culture and tradition brought to India by the Indo-Aryan speaking people who entered South Asia during the second millennium BC. The discovery of the Indus civilisation upset this view, since it provided proof of a full urban civilisation already flourishing before the date when the still tribal Aryans were thought to have arrived. The more recent discoveries render it still less tenable. How can the earlier view be true, when so much clearly derived from the already established agricultural society of the Indus valley? Archaeology cannot at present supply a very precise answer to this question, since it is still not definitely established at what date the first Indo-Aryan tribes arrived in the Indus region: it is possible that it may have been several centuries earlier than was once thought, or even centuries later. But the new evidence provides us with a real challenge. How did it come about that Indian civilisation has regarded itself as essentially "Aryan" in origin? What can this mean and how can we reconcile the divergence between the archaeological evidence and the Indian tradition?

To begin with, let it be said that no-one these days can seriously doubt that the Indo-Aryan languages are a branch of the Indo-European family, and that they were first brought into India by the migration thither of tribes actually speaking them. A similar situation is believed to have existed in those parts of Europe and western Asia in which other branches of the Indo-European language family are found. It now appears possible that the earliest Indo-Aryan movements into South Asia may have taken place even before 2000 BC and thus that the Indo-Aryans may have reached the Indus region during the full flowering of the Indus cities. We may expect that in such an event they would have gained a military and political ascendancy over the people of the Indus region, as other Indo-European speaking groups are believed to have done elsewhere,

perhaps because they were armed with superior bronze weapons, and supported by horses and swift chariots. In such an event it is to be expected that there would have been a rapid process of cultural interaction between the two communities, probably involving the intermarriage of equivalent families, between for example the rulers of the tribes and the rulers of the cities, or the priests of the one group and those of the other. Such intermixture need not have happened equally in all sections of society. It is probable that some of the specialist craft groups would have remained reasonably uninfluenced by the new arrivals, and that some of the most downtrodden elements in the city society, menials, etc, would likewise have failed to make any such connections. The result of this process would have been to produce a society which was culturally speaking Indo-Aryan, that is combining elements of culture from the existing population with those of the newcomers.

One may, perhaps, find support for this thesis in the course of later historical episodes. For example, the Kushans at the beginning of the Christian era were a barbarous tribal people from Central Asia who invaded India and established a kingdom in the north and west. They soon became great patrons of the arts and of religion. So much so that some of the major developments of Buddhist religious sculpture and architecture in Mathura and Gandhara may be attributed to their patronage; and so that the flowering of Sanskrit drama and poetry also seems to have taken place within their courts. Similarly at a later date the Moslem invaders of Afghanistan and northern India early formed marriage alliances with ruling families, and came in time — in spite of the fierce intolerance of their religion — to achieve the splendid cultural synthesis of the Moghul period, in almost all fields of literature, arts and architecture. In both these examples we may observe that the underlying life-style of the mass of the population was probably little affected, and the archaeologist can find few traces, at best coinage or inscriptions, to tell him whether settlements were indigenous or mixed. There is little reason to doubt that the coming of the Indo-Aryan speaking tribes would not have involved greater changes for the mass of the population, either rural or urban, and more particularly rural. In the course of such a process can anything be regarded as exclusively Aryan, or exclusively Indus?

With this model in mind we may consider the Rigveda, the earliest Indo-Aryan texts to survive in India. Probably the Rigveda itself represents the hymns of several generations or more. It has been suggested that the oldest core, Mandalas II-VII, shows some earlier features than the later sections, particularly Mandalas I and X. We may expect the former to reflect more clearly the original Aryan ideology; and the latter to reflect the new synthetic Indo-Aryan. If such an idea is accepted, it means that already in the fountainhead of later Indian tradition a process of synthesis is in evidence; while in the life of the villages of India the mainstream of the life-style was already far older.

The archaeology of this period is still difficult to interpret, particularly for so long as archaeologists look for the Aryans, as though their settlements might be found in some culturally isolated and identifiable style. Once one accepts the new model of a process of cultural interaction between the Indo-Aryan speaking arrivals and the indigenous population, the growing body of archaeological data seems to become clearer. In two areas to the east of the Indus, one in the north, in Punjab, Haryana and northern Rajasthan,

and the other in the south, in southern Rajasthan, Saurashtra and Malwa, there was probably primary Aryan settlement. The period represented in these areas by the cultural traditions known as "Late Harappan" may be expected to belong to this stage. It is further to be expected that there would have been an onward spread of Indo-Aryan colonies from both these areas: eastwards from the northern region down the Ganges valley; and southwards and eastwards from the southern into central Indian and the Deccan. The timetable of these movements is still difficult to establish, but the broad outlines are reasonably clear.

The third point I want to make has to do with the onward transmission of the cultural stream, the origins of which we have been examining. I have been arguing that what we have witnessed was the emergence of nothing short of an Indian life-style and pattern of thought. I shall now go on to maintain that these were the direct ancestors of the life and thought of the modern population of India, recognisable from the beginning and at every stage thereafter in terms of their Indianness. It has often been maintained by both Indian and Western scholars that somehow the peaks which had been scaled in Vedic times, or in the time of the Upanishads, were never again to be reached and that all later developments of Indian thought must be regarded as declines, or as falling away from a once golden age. I believe that this is a quite wrong way of looking at things. The stream of historical development may much rather be likened to a river, in which, to use the analogy suggested by the Buddha, there is constant flux, constant change. Such a state is the natural condition of a living organism. If and when it ceases to be able to adapt itself and change, to take in new influences from outside, and to use them in its own way, it crystalises or freezes, it becomes a fossil.

This has not happened to the Ganges stream of Indian life and thought: rather it has gone on absorbing and synthesising ever-new cultural traits from outside, and developing its own innovations from within. Thus after the wonderful beginnings represented by the Vedas and Upanishads, Indian religious thought has still a long and splendid road to follow: the heterodox teaching of the Buddha provided the focus for a major current, releasing tremendous energy among generation after generation of Indian thinkers, but no less part of the mainstream; the development of the great sects, the Saivas and the Vaisnavas, also forms another major current, within which such jewels as the Bhagavadgita are to be discovered; the age of the Puranas represents the beginning of a further stream of popular religious fervour which in time gave rise to regional, vernacular movements, the Alvars in Tamilnadu, the Virasaivas in Karnataka, the Varkaris in Maharashtra, the Sikhs in the Punjab, etc.

Each one of these may claim to be a national religious movement in itself, but each is firmly within the broad flood of our Ganges of Indian life and thought; the theological systems of the great philosophers Sankaracharya and Ramanuja are yet another wonderful current. Of course, in the maintenance of such a long-lived character, many elements have been constant and unchanging: as we suggested above, the farmers around Kalibangan still plough their fields in the same way as did their forbears 4,500 years ago. The cow and the bull, the elephant, the pipal tree and its leaves, have all come down from the distant past as symbols which are of peculiar importance in the lives of ordinary people.

CUISINE– MORE THAN JUST CURRY

Henrietta Green

India means different things to different people, a vast subcontinent veiled in mystery, romance, religion and an incomprehensible foreignness. It means to me, however, above all else, irresoluble contrasts. Side by side exist staggering wealth and abyssmal poverty, palaces of stunning splendour and hovels of appalling squalor, paintings executed with exquisite refinement and horrendous crudity. The confusion explains in part my ambivalent feelings towards the country. Love and hate, pain and pleasure exist in an unending indelible impression which haunts you for a lifetime.

As for its food, it too can never be forgotten. Eat one — just one — perfect Indian meal and you are hooked forever. The sensuality and subtlety provoke and assault the Western palate, you stumble over new tastes, strange textures. "Wait," I hear you cry out horrified, "you are getting carried away. Indian food — subtle?" No doubt you remember that meal you ate at your local take-away which left you gasping for water as the raw spices caught at your throat. Well, the stuff of the local flock-papered palace is not what I'm talking about — what I remember is silver *thalis* laden with delicately flavoured foods, sweet and sour, pungent and bland. These are the contrasting elements of Indian dishes which together make a beautifully balanced and satisfying meal.

To compare our Indo-British concoctions (I wouldn't even grace them with the name of food — they're unappetising messes, usually of a truly repulsive grey-brown) to the lightness and splendour of true Indian food is an insult no cook would willingly bear. "Curries," that ubiquitous word, covers a multitude of ingredients; hands up anyone who hasn't at some time spiced up left-overs with a teaspoon of curry powder, a chopped apple and a handful of raisins and optimistically called it "curry?". But to eat real Indian food is to give your taste buds an experience equivalent to the once-in-a-lifetime-pyschedelic-trip. It really will (if I may coin a phrase) blow your buds.

The problem is how to describe Indian food when there is no such thing as a unified cuisine. How can there be when you are dealing with a country so vast that Britain could fit in its land mass 20 times over? It is populated by over 50 races, each with their own culture, language, dietry laws (the taboo of beef to the Hindus and pork to the Moslems are only a start) and traditions. There are climatic and agricultural differences to contend with — coconuts, for example, cannot be grown in the north, but in the south they are the staple diet and each region has its favourite foods. The diversities of Indian food is what makes it so exciting; travel a few miles in any direction and you may discover yet another regional speciality. It is known for pillaus, dosas, kormas, dhansak but there are thousands of other dishes which have never even reached our shores.

When I visited India at the behest of a generous publisher, my ideas on Indian food were shaken to my stomach. I had gone under the guise of researching herbs and spices. Distance and time were of no object — which was just as well when it can take 24 hours to cover that many miles — and the intention was to find out about the history and uses of herbs and spices in all their fields. It was not just an excuse to go on a glorious orgy of eating (although as a cookery writer it was important) but an opportunity to study their use in medicine, dyes, beauty and aphrodisiacs. Spices I soon discovered provide the link between all the regional variations of Indian food. Wherever you travel, whenever

The variety of a Bengali meal.

131

Below left: Mouth-watering Bengali dishes.
Food from Kashmir: Methi chaman and dam alu, below right.
Centre right: Chicken Kashmiri, with bay leaves, yoghurt, saffron, cinnamon, and cashew nuts, jeera and powdered coriander (dry phakchee seeds) and almonds.
Bottom right: A range of sweet dishes from Kashmir.
Bottom left: Dahi (right) plays an important part in Kashmiri cuisine.

you eat they are always employed to rouse the palate. No self-respecting cook is ever without her masala (her blend of spices prepared to a personal formula), no dish is ever served without that pungent aroma which is derived from a judicious addition of spices.

These spices — ginger, long pepper, black pepper, turmeric, cloves, nutmeg, mace, cinnamon cardamom, coriander, cumin and chillis — are the foundation of Indian cooking. Their original use was as preservatives (in the heat food decays rapidly), medicinal (the Ayurveda, the indigenous system of medicine, is littered with references to the curative properties of spices) and, of course, for flavouring. Try to imagine Indian food without its spices — it is like asking an Englishman to eat roast beef without horseradish sauce or a Frenchman to try his snails without garlic.

But it is difficult for us to realise that there ever was a time when spices were so important to the rest of the discovered world and were so eagerly sought out, that India's destiny was indivisible from them. Spices played an important role in the history of India; for centuries she was courted and invaded merely to secure a share in the lucrative spice trade. First came the conquering armies of the Greeks. Strabo, a geographer, wrote of a cargo of glistening nutmegs as jewels prized beyond the most precious gems. Their appeal lay in "the bile of their scent and taste" and the price they would fetch in his native land made them worth fighting for. Then followed the Romans eager to trade in amomum, bdellium and putchuk, their names for the spices which were indispensable to the wealthy Roman lady's toilette. With the decline of the Roman Empire, the Arabs dominated the spice trade. They faced great dangers and hardships as they crossed the vast deserts in their caravans of camels but the rewards of riches made the sacrifices worthwhile. In order to break their monopoly and to secure their own profitable share, the Portuguese in 1497 set sail in an attempt to discover a sea route. Vasco da Gama was in command and he braved the stormy seas of the hitherto unknown Cape of Good Hope, arriving the following year at Calicut. He signed an agreement with the Zamorin who pledged, "my country is rich in cinnamon, cloves, ginger, pepper and precious stones. That which I ask in return is gold, silver, corals and scarlet cloth."

But the Portuguese had to struggle to maintain their foothold and they were soon superceded by the French and Dutch. Then in 1612, the English established their first trading centre, The East India Company in Surat, and so the fighting continued between the natives and the conquerors and between the conquerors themselves. The spices were highly prized, ladies needed them for their pomanders, their gellatines and milk puddings; their perfumes and pot-pourris called out for the delicate fragrances and even the English Navy issued spice rations so as to disguise the taste of putrifying rations. The cuisine of virtually every nation owes some debt to the spices of India; the Italians eat manzo garafolato, a slowly cooked beef studded with cloves, the Spanish eat rice with saffron and cardamom — the list is inexhaustible and to think of food without its spices is like trying to imagine a world without sun.

Spices are everywhere in India; vast fields of ruby ripened chillis and the sunny yellow of mustard flowers. The stalls in the bazaars are piled high with ground turmeric, a bold yellow against the dark richness of cloves, or soft brown cinnamon sticks with their soothing scent contrasting with mounds of black and white peppercorns whose sharpness

make your nostrils tickle. They are the very essence of Indian cooking and are even included in a brides' dowry along with a chakki or grinding stone, which she uses for grinding and crushing her spices. An authentic cook will never reach for a tin of curry powder (actually it was concocted for the convenience of the British Raj) but will painstakingly prepare powders and pastes or masalas for each dish. Thus no two dishes will ever taste alike as the proportions of the masalas will vary and the freshness of spices is preserved. Masalas vary not only from region to region but also from cook to cook — it is all part of the exquisite surprise and delight of Indian food.

As, according to beliefs, "Food is a gift of the gods," it follows with undeniable logic that "to eat is a divine necessity." A meal should benefit the body — bland, balanced with spiced dishes so as not to over-stimulate the digestive system; nor should you overeat and leave the table feeling *tamasic* (heavy or bloated): rather, as an old saying goes, "eat till you are two-thirds full, leaving space for the lord." A satisfying meal usually consists of about three dishes — a vegetable, lentils or pulses, rice or some form of bread (roti) and some pickle or chutney and yoghurt. Meat, a sweet dish, or fruit and nuts and a digestive (pan or a handful of cardamom or aniseed) are often added, but for special occasions the menu will be even more elaborate.

The food is served on a *thali* (a polished circular metal tray) usually made from stainless steel, although gold and silver were once used. In the south, trays of woven banana leaves are often substituted which at least saves the washing up. Small bowls (katoris) containing pickles, chutneys or dahls (pulses) are placed on the thalis and can be added as they are required. Indians eat with their hands — or rather with their right hand — and once you have learnt the art, it seems a very sensible thing to do. Food is about taste, colour, smell and texture and there is no reason why we should not touch it. Rolling up a small ball of rice between your fingers is a rather satisfying experience as you become aware of the texture of the grains before you have even tasted them. There is a rigid etiquette involved in eating with your hands; just as we in the West never put our knife to our mouth. so should you never put your entire hand in your mouth. Equally it is frowned upon and considered the height of bad manners to dirty your wrists — it takes practice, but once accomplished it becomes incredibly easy.

In order to sample the authentic regional gastronomic delights, you really do have to travel and, if you do, there is another treat in store — the amazing railway station snacks picked up along the line. *Alu chat* (spiced potatoes), *samosas*, *bhel puri* (puff rice), all served in containers made of woven dried leaves. Specialist regional restaurants do exist in most major cities but they are not as good as the real thing — somehow the atmosphere, colours and smells are never quite right.

To define the food from each of the regions is a daunting task, so instead I offer up my impressions, my memories of surprising tastes which I had never even dreamed existed until I was offered them. With my courage in my hands, I ate in wayside shacks, shared meals in mud-lined huts, in sumptuous rajahs' palaces and in friends' private houses. Contrary to most peoples' expectations I suffered no diseases and took no special precautions, and survived the journey to tell the tale! From the north I retain the tastes of its strong Moghlai influence; creamy concoctions of lamb or chicken which had simmered for hours in ghee (clarified butter) and

This page: Tamilian thali-thoran, sambar, rasam, pugadh, poriyal, mysore pak, curd and plain rice, pappadams and poori, below left, and masala dosa with idly, vada, sambar, chutney and ghee, below right.
Centre left: A meal from Maharashtra. Some sweet dishes from Maharashtra, bottom left.
Bottom right: Skilful use of spices is the secret of successful Indian cuisine.

Opposite page: A variety of dishes that would make a luncheon or dinner feast. In the centre is tandoori chicken garnished with onion and lemon slices; then clockwise, beginning at the lower left, are dahi (yoghurt), fresh mustard fish, bhindi masala (okra or lady's fingers), palak gosht (mutton with spinach), chicken Kashmiri, nan (an Indian bread) and dahl (a lentil dish) garnished with red chillies.

a sensuous selection of spices. There was *rogan josh* (mutton cooked in yoghurt with ginger, coriander and cardamom), *mache kofte* (minced meatballs flavoured with ground almonds) and fine stews flavoured with pomegranate seeds. Then there was the vast selection of dishes prepared in the *tandoor* (clay lined oven), quails, baby chickens, pigeons which had marinaded for days in spices to give a subtle flavour. The vast wheat fields produced various *rotis* (breads) which were freshly cooked for each meal — *chapatis*, *nan*, *tandoori roti* and a special herb scented cake of unleaven dough.

From the west I have particularly fond memories of the best vegetarian food I have ever eaten; there were extraordinary vegetables whose names I could never pronounce, let alone now remember; each cooked with their own masala and often served for a contrast of tastes with *laddu* (pistachio-flavoured milkballs) or *shrikand* (drained curd spiced with saffron and cardamom). In Bombay I ate *dhansak* (chicken cooked with spiced lentils) as prepared by the Parsis and *kulfi* (a highly flavoured ice-cream) on the Chowpatty Beach. Goa offered food which seemed to combine both Portuguese and Indian styles of cooking. I even ate a *feijoida* (a stew of pork beans which differed from its European counterpart in that it was laden with spices). Fish and shellfish predominated, *prawn patia* (prawns simmered

in ghee and coriander) or whole baked fish wrapped in banana leaves and grilled on open fires were my particular favourites.

The further south I travelled the hotter the food; there was rice with *sambar* (a soup of toovar dahl with spices and curry leaves) or *iddlis* (steamed rice cakes) and *dosas* (feathery light pancakes made from rice flour and invariably served with a coconut chutney). Coconuts (both its flesh and milk) and fish are eaten in vast quantities and together they combine to form fragrantly flavoured dishes which are worth travelling those thousands of miles for.

In the east there is also plenty of fish but what it is most famous for and what I certainly enjoyed the most, was the stupendous selection of sweets; *rasgulla*, *gulab jamun*, *son-desh*, milky-white flavoured with rose water, *jaggerry* (cane sugar and chopped nuts). There were *kababs*, skewers of marinaded meat spiced with cumin and served with *puris* (fried bread and mounds of *pillau*.

I do not claim to understand the essence of Indian food anymore than I claim to have come to terms with the mysteries of the country itself. Suffice to say there is no food or country like it.

The first entry in our books would be a collector's item today.

State Bank of India has a commercial banking tradition that goes back to the year 1806.

Over the past 175 years we've been expanding and diversifying. Widening our operational base to cover key areas like merchant banking and, more recently, international banking.

Today, we are in the heart of international banking. Operating in 25 countries, covering all major financial centres.

As India's largest international bank, we handle over 55% of the country's foreign trade. And have the capability to offer a comprehensive range of international banking services.

State Bank of India
London Main Branch
G.P.O. Box 801
1 Milk Street
London EC 2P 2JP

State Bank of India
Growing worldwide

Bahrain ● Beirut ● Bristol ● Cairo ● Cayman Islands ● Chicago ● Colombo ● Dacca ● Dar-es-Salaam ● Dubai ● Frankfurt ● Hong Kong ● Jakarta ● Kuwait ● Lagos ● London ● Los Angeles ● Male ● Manila ● Nassau ● New York ● Nottingham ● Panama ● Paris ● Singapore ● Tehran ● Tokyo ● Toronto ● Vancouver ● Washington and others. And over 5900 offices in India.

And now INDIA

Your Destination in the 80s

Trade-wings LIMITED

30, K. Dubash Marg, Bombay 400 023.
Tel: 244334 Telex: 2494 Cable: Travel
Offices at : Bangalore, Baroda, Bhubaneshwar, Calcutta,
Cochin, Hyderabad, Madras, Madurai, Mangalore,
Manipal, Panaji (Goa), Nagpur, New Delhi, Pune,
Srinagar, Varanasi.

25 West, 43rd Street, Suite 1400,
New York (N.Y. 10036).

Tel : (212) 354-8328-9 Telex : RCA 223106
TRAVEL Cable: COHAKIM

Owners : Hotel Oberoi Bogmalo Beach, Dabolim (Goa).

India's Largest Travel Agency Network!

A photographer's dream; a shopper's Paradise; a historian's treasure-house. A land with a subtle and skilful blend of Persian, Muslim and Hindu culture.

A country of palaces, mosques, imposing monuments, of fantastic inlaid marble work. A journey through TIME and contrasting SPACE.

80s? A decade in TIME is not enough; INDIA.... it will always call you back.

TW/APM/81

Fly across centuries in minutes.

One of the wheels of the Sun-temple at Konark, in Orissa, symbolising the eternal cycle, (A.D. 1240-1280) superimposed on a B-737 engine.

That's Indian Airlines inviting you to an experience of India.

Discover a 5000 year old civilization in the swiftest and most comfortable way.

Jet in minutes from a 20th century metropolis to a 4th century kingdom in an Indian Airlines' Airbus or Boeing 737. Discover the rich texture of India's heritage....the paintings in rock-cut temples, the vibrant handicrafts, the traditional music and dances of this land.

Discover as well, graceful coastlines nestling unspoilt beaches, and unmatched flora and fauna.

Indian Airlines packs all this into a wonderful holiday with a network spanning 70 destinations... 62 in India and 8 in neighbouring Afghanistan, Bangladesh, Maldives, Nepal, Pakistan and Sri Lanka.

Just book your tickets through any of the international airlines' office or their agents. Or simply contact

Indian Airlines' Central Space Control at New Delhi.

And the fares!

Perhaps the lowest in the world. A 15 day 'Discover India' fare for just US $ 375. A 'South India Excursion' scheme—30% off on normal US $ airfare. And for all those under 30 years a 25% off on normal US $ airfares. You cannot get a better bargain.

Namaste...welcome to a rich experience of India.

IX ASIAN GAMES
DELHI 1982

Official Carrier to the
IX Asian Games, Delhi 1982

///1 Indian Airlines
So much for so little.

For reservations contact: Central Space Control, Indian Airlines, PTI Building, New Delhi-110 001, India.
Airimp code: DELRMIC Telex: 031-2576. 031-2131 Cable Address: CENTRESERV Member: Sita Communications.

HTD-IAC-7293

PERSONALITY
VERSUS PRINCIPLE

Philip Mason

My last six months in India were spent in Hyderabad, a state of roughly the same size and population as Spain. On Independence Day, August 15, 1947, Hyderabad was left in an extraordinary legal and diplomatic vacuum. The Indian states, of which Hyderabad was the largest, were supposed to choose between India and Pakistan, but the Nizam, the ruler of Hyderabad, wanted his country to be an independent sovereign state and would not accede to either. The issue was not settled till the spring of the following year.

Meanwhile, the vacuum made personal problems for someone like myself. I was a member of the Indian Civil Service, allotted to the UP, the province — now a state — which stretches along the foot of the Himalayas from Delhi to Allahabad. But in 1939 the UP had lent me to the Government of India and India had lent me to Hyderabad. It was agreed that I should go back to England on proportionate pension in November 1947. But to draw pension in England I had to have something called a Last Pay Certificate, not, as anyone might expect, from the government who last paid me, but from the UP, who hadn't paid me for eight years.

I wrote, asking for this document, to the office of the Accountant-General in the UP. No reply. I wrote again. Still no reply. I sent a telegram but nothing happened. But I knew Mrs Sarojini Naidu, the poet, the friend of Mahatma Gandhi, a veteran member of the Indian National Congress, who had just been appointed Governor of the UP. She had praised my novel, *Call the Next Witness,* and I had met her in Delhi at the Viceroy's house. I wrote to Mrs Naidu and told her of my difficulty. A friendly reply came by return of post — and with it the certificate. When I wrote to thank her, I ventured to guess that, in the India of the future, the wheels of government might roll even more ponderously than before when no personalities were involved, but that there would perhaps be a quicker response to the claims of friendship.

The point was brought home a few days later. There were air passages booked to England for my wife and myself and three children. But in those days we had to land in Turkey, for which we needed visas. Two days before our flight, the Hyderabad authorities told me they could not give me visas because their diplomatic status was still unsettled; I must get them in Bombay, where we changed planes and had a few hours to wait. It really seemed quite beyond reasonable hope to get visas in so short a time. But I made up my mind to try and on the bus from the airport I met an Indian resident of Bombay, who had heard me speak in the Legislative Assembly in Delhi about the future of the Indian Army. We made friends and he took me in his car to the Secretariat and refused to leave me until we had got the visas. We found an influential official whom he knew, we got the visas and I was back at the airport in time to catch the plane. Where else in the world could that have happened? It was the triumph of the personal element.

India before the coming of the British was government almost entirely by personal relations. Hindu or Moslem law regulated family affairs and the succession to property, but in public affairs the over-riding factor was personal allegiance to a superior; there was a hierarchy of chiefs, nobles or officials, each with a personal following, headed by a personal ruler. This was brittle in war; the history of India is full of battles that were lost because a commander was killed, or because he got off his elephant and thus started a

139

rumour that he was killed, or because someone decided to change his allegiance. It was this personal element in battle which more than anything else enabled the British to conquer India; they introduced a disciplined military hierarchy to replace the purely personal and won battles in consequence. The Indian Army of British days added British spit-and-polish, British ceremonial, organisation and discipline to the old Indian feeling of loyalty to a chief and welded them together into a living organisation capable of unshakeable fidelity. But the personal element was always strong; whenever there was trouble in that Army, you could be sure that bad officers — or simply new officers — had something to do with it.

In the civil administration, too, regulations came in with the British. But they were administered by Indian clerks and by subordinate officials to whom they were foreign in spirit and who therefore kept strictly to the letter of the law. The British in India were most unfair about this; we would tell funny stories about an Indian clerk's narrow interpretation of rules that we, the British, had introduced, forgetting that the clerk, left to himself, would never have dreamed of applying regulations at all. But almost every Englishman who stayed in India for any time would pay high tribute to the marvellous loyalty of Indian servants in an emergency and their gift for organising a satisfactory entertainment on the spur of the moment. The junior officials of a district had the same knack of producing at the last moment a firework display to welcome the governor or sleeping and feeding arrangements for a battalion of infantry.

The whole fabric of the British Empire in India was a compromise, a coalition between two sets of qualities. British and Indian people were strong in quite different ways, the British in discipline and obedience to law, in fixing principles by which conduct should be governed, the Indians in spontaneity and affection, in friendship and in response to affection. I cannot pretend that the fusion was perfect. Sometimes English people were insensitive, rude or ignorant; sometimes the legal system we introduced was too formal, too impersonal. It gave a man too many opportunities to ruin himself by litigation. But with all its imperfections, the huge creaking machine worked. As I lay in my tent in some outlying part of the district of Bareilly in Rohilkand, I was often wakened long before light by the rise and fall of the high-pitched creaking whine of bullock-cart wheels, as villagers took their families down to some fair on the banks of the Ramganga. It was the sound of wood turning on wood, mechanically very inefficient compared with what can be done with ball-bearings and grease. But it worked. And the Indian Empire worked, clumsily perhaps and sometimes slowly but with very little use of force.

When I was in Rohilkand, a division with six districts and between six and eight million inhabitants, the commissioner was British and so were three of his six district magistrates, and three of his six superintendents of police. Three district magistrates and three superintendents of police were In-

dian. Seven British and six Indian for the top jobs. Below that, I had charge of one sub-division, about a quarter of a million people; I was the only British subdivisional officer and the remaining sub-divisions, of which there were, I suppose, between 20 and 30, were in charge of Indians. The administrative framework below that was entirely Indian, except that each district had one reserve inspector, often a former sergeant from the British Army, to train the police in drill.

What was the force behind this tiny British administrative presence? The police, all Indian, were not more than a thousand or so to each district of about a million people. There was a battalion of British infantry, say six hundred men for the whole division, and a battery of gunners, another two hundred; there was the training battalion of the Jat Regiment of the Indian Army. In many parts of India there were no troops at all; we had more than our share in the UP. I was there from 1929 to 1932 — fairly turbulent years in the newspapers and the history books — but I do not think that in Rohilkand the military were ever asked to help the civil power in that time.

I make these points to support my argument that the old Indian Empire was a compromise between British and Indian ways of doing things and that it worked only because hundreds of thousands of Indians helped to make it work, while millions, and in fact hundreds of millions, accepted it passively. That could hardly have happened unless there was something acceptable to many Indians in the way British and Indian qualities fitted into each other, complemented each other and helped each other out. They were not rigidly opposed.

There was, for example, control of the police. There was a police-station with eight or ten constables, a head constable and a sub-inspector to every 50 or 60 villages. They worked through a headman in each village, a post of honour, unpaid, and a village watchman, who was paid a low wage and came from low in the social scale. There was always a strong personal element in the relationships throughout this network; there were always perquisites not strictly legal, fodder for the sub-inspector's horse when he came to the village, perhaps a basket of mangos for his wife; there would be a meal for the patrolling constable, grain and milk for the village watchman. Perquisites in kind were a sign of respect and goodwill and lubricated the whole machine. The superintendent of police and the district magistrate, if they were wise men, knew this and did not let it disturb them. A real bribe — a substantial sum of money paid to influence justice — was a very different matter and of course if that was proved it meant dismissal and perhaps prosecution. The line between perquisites — to be winked at — and bribery — to be severely punished — was a fine one but usually clear to common sense. And there was a similar line between real torture and the kind of threatening interrogation that took place when everyone knew perfectly well that the local bad character had had something to do with last night's burglary. A district officer who treated his subordinates with obvious suspicion and insisted on the strict letter of the law could paralyse the police and produce a spate of crime. A good district officer always walked a tight-rope between the legal and the personal.

Biologically, men and women differ because certain organs are developed in the one but vestigial in the other. Each has the organs of the other in an undeveloped form. And it is my belief (though it is unfashionable to say so) that there is often, though not always, a similar complementarity in temperament. That is why men and women do very often — more often than the newspapers suggest — get on well together. And I believe that there was often a similar kind of relationship between British and Indian. There was always ambivalence, there was often love and hate on both sides — as there often is between men and women.

There was ambivalence (though again it is not fashionable to say so) about independence. Of course, most Indians, in varying degrees, and after say 1919, wanted independence. But the feeling was often mixed with a touch of apprehension about what the future might bring, sometimes with appreciation of what the past had brought. It was rather like the feelings that sometimes arise between a man and a woman who have been married for some time but have amicably agreed to part. Yes, it is best; one of them has long wanted it and now both are agreed — but memories of things shared in the past are suddenly strong and there are moments of regret for the best of what could not be prolonged.

Appreciation for the past, I have written, and that there certainly was in the honeymoon period immediately after independence, though at least as strong was pleased surprise at British readiness to go. Dien Bien Phu and all that that meant for Indo-China was still to come, but many Indians had certainly feared that the British would be as obstinate about going as the French proved to be, both in Indo-China and in Algeria. There was justification for such fears; Churchill had declared his determination not to preside over the dissolution of the British Empire, and recent publications have made it clear that on India he was adamant. But a majority of his countrymen made Attlee Prime Minister and Attlee had a majority behind him in deciding that the time had come for the British to leave India. Pleasure at this decision contributed to the acts of friendship which I described at the beginning of this article.

But there was also, I believe, a consciousness among many Indians that we had contributed something of value to India. The Victorians were proud of the roads, the railways, and the canal systems they had built and these were considerable achievements. At the end of the century India was far ahead of China in railway communications and, Indian train fares being very cheap, carried vast masses of the people. Canals reclaimed whole districts from the desert. But I do not myself believe that these are the things about which British people should feel most pleased, rather about

something intangible, their contribution to the Indian way of looking at society and politics and law. It was during the British period that the idea of law was introduced as something higher than the will of a personal ruler and — later and more gradually — the linked idea that the mass of the people had some right to be consulted in making the laws. These were not really Asian ideas; the Chinese, like the Russians, moved almost direct from the personal rule of an emperor to the rigid tyranny of a bureaucracy. But by the end of the British period, there would be a public outcry if the British reverted to Moghul methods. Imprisonment without trial was felt by most Indians to be a grievous wrong, and it still is.

There was compromise about this, as about everything else. It was strange, to anyone brought up on British ideas — and this included many Indians trained in London at the Inns of Court — to find that in the ordinary administration of the district, a man could be brought before a magistrate under Section 110 of the Code of Criminal Procedure and called on to refute the charge that he was generally reputed to be of bad character. If he could not, he had to give security to be on good behaviour for a year — and if he could not, to go to prison for a year. The police took good care no one should come forward as security for him; he *did* go to prison. The proceedings before the magistrate were something of a farce. The magistrate and the sub-inspector of police had probably talked the case over beforehand; the sub-inspector had certainly talked it over with the leaders of the village, who had agreed to give evidence as to Janku's reputation, and *not* to give security for his good behaviour. It was a procedure in which the village as a whole acquiesced. And it worked. Petty burglaries in the neighouring villages would stop while poor Janku was inside — and usually start again not long after he came out. I don't believe real injustice often occurred under this procedure; if the sub-inspector tried it on a man who wasn't a crook, someone would whisper it to the district magistrate or the superintendent. But it is abhorrent to the true spirit of British law. It was a compromise between the legal and the personal system of government; the personal opinion of the sub-inspector was not enough by itself; he had to bring his witnesses to court and satisfy both the magistrate and the villagers. His judgement was regularised and put in order by legal means.

Democracy again is not an idea native to Asia except at village level, where it has always been strong. It came to India later than to Britain, but not by much. District boards and municipal boards were introduced in Victorian times; their powers were gradually increased and their chairmen, at first officials, were later elected. Voting for the provincial legislatures, and for the Indian legislature, was also something to which people had become accustomed before independence and in India, as nowhere else in Asia, the vote is understood as a means by which the people express their will. Voting is manipulated on personal lines; personalities are often better understood than policies — but the fact remains that the people of India voted Mrs Gandhi out of power and voted her in again when they did not like the alternative and when they thought she might have learnt a lesson.

Peasants there have been in India since time immemorial, peasants who cultivate the soil; there have also been rulers and fighters, priests, holy men, shopkeepers and money-lenders. But the educated middle classes in a modern sense, the businessmen and officials, the clerks, lawyers, doctors and politicians, grew up in British times.

Here let me pay tribute to a group often forgotten, the Provincial Civil Services. I said that I was in charge of a sub-division of Bareilly district and that the rest of the 20 or 30 sub-divisions of the Rohilkand division were held by Indians. They were members of the Provincial Civil Service. They had university degrees; some of them had missed getting into the Indian Civil Service only by a few marks in a competitive examination. In every district, they were the district magistrate's deputies; three or four or five of them had charge of sub-divisions, where they could settle disputes about land and supervise the land records, where they were magistrates and could sentence to two years imprisonment. Another would be in charge of the treasury and another of the district magistrate's office. They were the back-bone of the administration and, throughout India, in nine districts out of 10, it was they who made possible the peaceful transfer of power.

The Provincial Civil Services inherited a tradition going back to 1833. Their sons often became leaders of the new India — for one example, Pandit Govind Ballabh Pant, the first Premier of the UP. They, like all the new educated middle class, have been inevitably and deeply influenced by the English language, by English literature and English customs. Public education began in India in Bombay as far back as the governorship of Mountstuart Elphinstone in the 1820s before the state had undertaken any education in England, well before Macaulay's famous minute on educating Indians in the English tradition. As in England, scientific education came late and was grudging, but the tradition in which the middle classes were brought up was English and they cannot be indifferent to England; they must love us or hate us.

They have often done both. There have been a succession of crises in British and Indian relations — as there have been in British and American. Long after the American War of Independence, there was a tradition in the United States that when a politician appealing to his public could think of nothing else to say he would "twist the tail of the British lion," or in other words abuse the British. That feeling persisted with Indians as with Americans after independence — even though the Indians had to fight no War of Independence. But the tendency of Indians to put personal relations first made them expect the British to behave as friends when we felt we should make an impartial judgment.

This misunderstanding arose almost at once, and led to a crisis in relations with India and another with Pakistan. There were strong feelings both in India and Pakistan about the state of Hyderabad, already mentioned, and also about Kashmir, questions left unsettled at the time of independence. Hyderabad — with a Moslem ruler and about a million Moslem subjects, but with at least 15 million Hindu subjects, and surrounded by Indian territory — most Englishmen would have judged should accede to India. Kashmir, with a Hindu ruler and an overwhelming majority of Moslem subjects, by the same principles should go to Pakistan. But, rightly or wrongly, British official policy was to be neutral in both matters. Many Indians (and Pakistanis too) resented this indifference to the claims of friendship. A friend should give support when it is needed, not act as judge — that was the feeling. And that was the feeling too about the war with China, the war with Pakistan, the crisis over Bangladesh. Yet, somehow, some degree of friendship survives.

We can neither of us forget our past. For nearly two-hundred years, Englishmen, Scots and Irish, went to India as administrators, soldiers and businessmen; they came back with words and customs strange to the British of the island, some of which spread and have become part of our own life. The custom of washing the whole body, for example, unknown in Stuart England, became widespread in Victorian times, and was imported from India. Today, the surviving British officers of the old Indian Army revisit their regiments to be greeted with immense warmth and hospitality, to see the old Mess silver on guest nights, to hear the old words of command on the parade ground. And here in England, Indian influence is penetrating many aspects of daily life. In clothes, the Hindu peasant skirt, the *ghaghra*, is spreading; Indian rhythms creep into popular music and a whiff of curry is to be detected even in recipes so far from Oriental as fish chowder and parsnip soup.

I wonder too whether Indian customs of thought about people have not influenced us, just as we influenced them? Indians were divided from ancient times into hereditary castes which had some link with occupation. Is it altogether fanciful to think that our civil servants have become more like the Brahmans of India than they used to be, and that neither the French nor the Americans have civil servants who form so enclosed a caste? Are not our army officers strangely like Rajputs, the hereditary warriors of India? No, like a couple who have lived together in married life for many years, we have influenced each other in a hundred subtle ways, and however much we may fly into tantrums or be reconciled, we can never altogether escape the ties that bind us.

The Taste of Quality...

Air India's inflight service has a reputation which is famous throughout the world – especially the cuisine. We at SAS CATERING are proud to contribute – being responsible for providing meals on Air India's services to India and New York from our Heathrow Flight Catering Unit.

SAS CATERING

CINEMA-NEW HORIZONS

Marie Seton

For decades, India has produced an enormous annual output of entertainment movies, the volume only competing with Japan, and far outstripping Hollywood even in its palmy days. The criteria for this vast production was soon dominated by the popular Hindi pictures originating in Bombay, the only films certain to gain national commercial distribution. The most successful were flagrantly copied in the numerous regional languages.

In comparison with other films being internationally distributed, Indian movies were inordinately long, at least 14 reels at 305 metres per reel, and sometimes as long as 18 reels. (A 35 mm film runs roughly 10 minutes to 305 m). No matter what the theme — mythological, historical, or contemporary romance or social picture — convention insisted on an X number of songs and dances. Such a convention was lifted haphazardly from Indian theatre, folk and classical. In order to appeal to the widest and most varied audiences, these movies threw in, and still do, everything — romance, melodrama, comedy with much slapstick (a mixture common in the plays of Shakespeare!). With very few exceptions even the most interesting and thought-provoking stories stuck closely to theatrical production. They never escaped from stage sets, usually with painted backcloths. The camera was static and the style of acting and make-up was more suited to theatre than the sensitive eye of the motion picture camera. These conventions continued long after film-making in most of the world's film production centres broke with theatrical traditions to explore the potential of the *cinematic* medium for the creation of entertainment and films that could be classified as art. This exploratory trend began in Western countries even ahead of the 1920s and before the invention of the sound film in the latter years of that decade.

The pattern of Indian movies having proved a success at the box office, there existed no commercial incentive to force change. The same conventional trend was maintained as to subject and style after Independence in 1947. But in Bengal where there was a powerful literary tradition, plus some theatre with innovatory ideas largely stemming from the creative Tagore family, film production developed a more literate attitude in the thematic sense. Something similar encouraged the Marathi cinema then rooted in Poona at the studios which would later house the Film Institute of India and the National Film Archive.

Fairly soon, and chiefly for economic reasons, talented Bengali and Marathi directors and cameramen, along with some actors, gravitated to Bombay, the centre of the ever-expanding Hindi industry. The films they were able to make in this intensely commercial environment did something to refine Bombay films from a technical point of view, even as to subject. Still the insistence on songs and dances, no matter how unsuited to the stories, plus the use of stage-like sets when natural locations would have been far more effective cinematically, remained a straitjacket on the evolution of better and more expressive film-making.

Nevertheless, over the three decades from 1940 to 1970, stimulants mainly from outside the film industry have appeared to contribute encouragement to the development of a truly *cinematic* film production over the vast terrain of India, each state with its differing regional language. As might be expected, the embryo beginning was the founding in 1947 of the Calcutta Film Society, which started off by purchasing the most famous of international film classics — Sergei Eisenstein's *Potemkin* — a compendium of "film

146

language" as to camerawork, directing non-professional players, and editing.

One of the initiators of this first Indian film society was Satyajit Ray, who was by then trying his hand at scenario writing. Since the release of his first film, *Pather Panchali* in 1955, Ray has been India's most distinguished and famous film director. Though not a teacher — he's always been too busy making films or writing stories — he has served as a catalyst, the study of his films through the proliferation of film societies and the setting up of the Film Institute at Poona (now Pune) in 1961. His huge "opus" almost exclusively using Bengali dialogue to plough the life of Bengal, past and present, has inspired students belonging to different linguistic states to *explore* and reveal that which is characteristic of their home territory, or true to their own creative imaginations.

It must be stressed here that the government of India, despite the snags of bureaucrats with inadequate knowledge or appreciation of cinema, has aided the development of styles of film-making designated New Wave. Over the decades from the 1950s the government has sponsored a series of international film festivals which have stimulated and expanded awareness of cinema's expressiveness for audiences in general, and would-be film-makers in particular. The setting up of the Film Finance Corporation substantially aided the production of better films, particularly for regional areas, and individuals wishing to make Hindi pictures beyond the commercial. Moreover, much that has taken place has been helped by the gradual relaxing of the code of censorship, a pre-requisite for the growth of more intelligent and realistic films.

I, who have been an involved witness-participant in much of what has happened in Indian cinema since 1955, must say that a most constructive helper, usually from behind the scenes, has been the present Prime Minister, Mrs Indira Gandhi. Fortunately her private interest in the arts compelled her in 1956 to jump in to become a founder of a film society in Delhi. Subsequently, once the Federation of Film Societies came into existence in 1960 to aid and co-ordinate the growing film society movement ranging from Assam to Kerala, Mrs Gandhi became a hardworking vice-president under Satyajit Ray. As Minister of Information and Broadcasting, although frequently hampered, she did her utmost so far as the Ministry's multi-headed cinema projects were concerned.

Obviously, in a brief survey, I have to leave out very much more than I can mention.

As to films with Hindi dialogue, the breakthrough to a new style came from two students of direction from the institute at Poona, Mani Kaul and Kumar Shahani, who revealed a high degree of individuality long before they graduated with the first batch. Belonging to the Hindi area, instead of rushing to Bombay to join the Hindi industry, they both set out to make two films far too esoteric in style to meet with commerical success. Nevertheless, Kaul's *Uski Roti*, a strikingly curious and interesting interpretation of a Punjabi village woman awaiting the return of her husband, and Shahani's *Maya Darpan*, a haunting though mystifyingly confused portrayal of a woman's life of isolation, broke up Hindi conventional cinema for other later non-conformist directors who, with low budgets mainly on loan from the Film Finance Corporation, began to produce less obtuse "art" films.

The most notable of these directors is Shyam Benegal, who against the odds blasted his way into commercial distribution. Having made something like 600 documentaries and commercials, in 1974 Benegal ventured to direct his first feature film *Ankur (The Seedling)*. It not only gained some degree of international release, but introduced a new young actress, Shabana Azmi, born to become a star, as the village servant to a smugly ruthless city executive. From the moment of *Ankur's* success, Benegal has never ceased directing films, many being highly successful in box office terms. Like Bengal's Mrinal Sen, Benegal's capacity to find finance has been assisted by the fact that both these directors are proficient in several Indian languages so that they could rove around regional production centres as well as using Hindi.

For at least five of Benegal's films, the cameraman was Govind Nihalani. Belonging to the Kannada cinema with its capital at Bangalore, in 1973 he photographed the first Kannada film to be distributed abroad. *Kaadu (The Forest)*, a singularly intriguing depiction of the conflicts and secrets of a Karnataka village. This was the first picture to be directed solo by Girish Karnad, who had been president of the Oxford Union ten years earlier. In 1961, he had turned dramatist; in 1970 he became a scenario writer and actor, and for the year 1974-75, became the director of the Poona Film and TV Institute. It is the increasing entry into film-making of people with such backgrounds which has done much to culturally enrich Indian film production and to some extent modify the crudities of commercial entertainment films.

To return to Hindi films: In 1980, Karnad and Benegal's cameraman, Nihalani, directed his initial feature film, *Aakrosh (Cry of the Wounded)*. By late May, 1981, when I saw *Aakrosh* in a packed cinema in Delhi, he had almost completed his work as director/cameraman of the second unit for Richard Attenborough's long delayed film, *Gandhi*. *Aakrosh* impressed me as a bold, powerful film, sharply political by implication: an innocent tribal man is found guilty of the murder of his wife through the corrupt influence of elite officials guilty of her rape and murder. It was screened at the Cannes Film Festival and at the 1981 London Film Festival.

As Ken Wlaschin of London's National Film Theatre observed in his introduction to New Indian Cinema in the 1979 London Film Festival: "Quality cinema has been mostly limited to Bengal (the state of Satyajit Ray). The situation has changed considerably in the 1970s with new directors emerging from many language centres and even from the dominant Hindi industry."

Before leaving films in Hindi, one picture of the mid-1970s must be mentioned — the brave study of what it was like to be a Moslem family in Agra during the 1947 Partition. *Garm Hawa (Hot Winds)* was the last performance of the actor, Balraj Sahni, who had consistently appeared in every earlier film of merit produced against the odds in Bombay. The non-Moslem director, M S Sathyu, came from Karnataka to brave the controversy that his compassionate picture was bound to meet from Hindu fundamentalists. No film until *Garm Hawa* had as truthfully attempted to portray the disease of communalism. Everybody knew of the horrors of the Partition, and that communalism has not been liquidated. This film was an act of courage.

Courage accounts for the dynamic development of Indian films since Ray blazed a trail far beyond Bengal in 1955. He had dared to risk his then fairly lucrative career as com-

THE FILMS OF SATYAJIT RAY

1. "Pather Panchali", 1950-55. Chunibala Devi, a very old former stage actress, discovered by Ray living in a Calcutta brothel, created the memorable character of Old Indir with inspired artistry. To keep her going, she had to have a pill of opium each day. She died only after the triumphant recognition that "Pather Panchali" was a masterpiece.

2. "Aparajito", 1956. Pinaki Sen Gupta, the second Apu; his curiosity aroused in Benares. "Aparajito" won the Golden Lion at the Venice Film Festival; Ray regarded this film, the second of the Apu trilogy, as a considerable advance in direction on "Pather Panchali".

2a. A death in the family. Karuna Bannerji as the stoic wife and Kanu Bannerji as the ineffectual Brahmin father, in "Aparajito".

3. "Apur Sansar", 1959. Aparna, the first role of 14-year-old Sharmila Tagore, is prepared for her wedding. When the bridegroom arrives, he is found to be insane. Her mother refuses to permit the marriage. Apu, present through a friend, marries Aparna to save the ruin of her life, this being the propitious day that she must be married, or remain unwed for life.

4. Ray's "Mahanagar" (Big City), 1963. The universal problem of the wife as breadwinner. Subrata Muzumdar (Anil Chatterjee) and Arati (Madhabi Mukherji). The shot is taken from behind the cooking pots; a saree, used as a curtain, hangs between the verandah and father's room. Centre right is a vague vista of houses (an enlarged photograph reproduced on a big screen set at an angle).

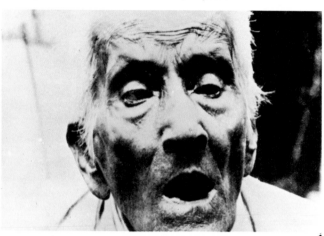

1

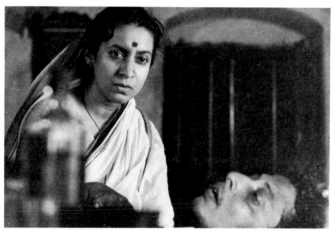

2A

2

3

4

5. Ray's "Charulata", 1964. Soumitra Chatterjee as Amal, at first the joy-bringer to Chanie (Madhabi Mukherji), but finally the ruin of her married life.

6. Ray's "Goupi Gyne and Bagha Byne", 1968-69. Based on a story by his grandfather Upendrakishore (1863-1915), pioneer of Bengali printing, the film reveals Satyajit Ray's inventiveness for fun and satire.

Pictures 7-12
Ray's "Chess Players" (Shatranj Ke Khilari), 1977, his only film with Hindi dialogue, based on a short story by Premchand.

7. Amjad Khan as Wajid Ali shah, the poet-musician ruler of Oudh, an honourable man in love with the Arts and inept as a king, his time being given to dancing and dramatics.

8. The confrontation: The East India Company's Resident, General Sir James

Outram (Richard Attenborough), also an honourable man in a situation that he personally detests, comes to demand Wajid's crown. Wajid refuses and offers only his hat. The take-over goes ahead.

9. Outram warns his ADC (Tom Alter) that he will pay a price if he continues to defend "the bad king".

5

8

6

7

9

149

10. *The pained Wajid faced by...*
11. *...Outram doing his duty with a stiff upper lip...*
12. *Wajid, realising his courtiers have kept him in the dark, upbraids them.*
13. *Mirza (Sanjeev Kumar) breaks off his game to pray like the good Moslem he is. Ray expanded the original story with the chess addicts' game becoming the grim political* *game of the British swallowing up Oudh in 1856, almost on the eve of the Mutiny.*

10

12

11

13

mercial artist with a British advertising firm, staking everything his family possessed to direct *Pather Panchali,* rejected by every producer he approached. This film — it took a decade from conception to completion — the first of the Apu trilogy put India, via Bengal, on the map of world cinematography. Ray's subsequent films and those of his fellow Bengalis like Ritwik Ghatak and Mrinal Sen, served as encouragement to the central government to liberalise its attitude towards cinema beyond the production of documentary films.

Before the completion of the epoch-making film, *Pather Panchali,* as if directed by premonition that something unusual was stirring in Indian cinema, the Indian Education Ministry took the risk of inviting me, (I had written a biography of Eisenstien, and salvaged his unfinished Mexican film under the title of *Time in the Sun,* which the audio-visual department had bought), the plan being that I should lecture around the subcontinent on the then virtually unknown subject of film appreciation.

I arrived as Ray's film was being released in Calcutta, with 36 film classics and the request from the British Film Institute to try to discover an Indian film fit to screen at the National Film Theatre. I first saw *Pather Panchali* in Delhi at 10 am. From then on I climbed out on a limb declaring that *this* film was destined to be recognised as a film classic; that if it ever reached an international film festival, it was bound to win an award. *Pather Panchali* did get to the 1956 Cannes Film Festival, where it won the first of its innumerable awards.

Ray's films illustrated to everyone desiring to make a new type of film, particularly the more intelligent students at Poona, the feasibility of going and tilling one's home ground in the hope of breaking the artificiality of current commercial production. Ray used locations rather than sets wherever possible; he combined professional and non-professional actors who acted as human beings rather than puppets. Above all, Ray's scenarios, written by himself, were perfect in construction, whereas the conspicuous weakness of Indian film-making lay in the erratic, poorly structured scripts. (The reason for this was partly the oddity of financing which I cannot explain, not having the space here).

It took time for the early batches of institute students to escape (some naturally never did) the hypnotic influence of the commercial entertainment of the Bombay-Madras movie-making circuit. But there were enough who graduated with the determination to return to their home states and struggle to free regional film-making from the fetters of imitating Bombay or Madras, both being divorced from any known local environment, past or present. In the southern, Dravidian language states — Madras (Tamil), Andhra (Telegu), Karnataka (Kannada), Kerala (Malayalam) — producers, distributors and film-makers lacked faith that audiences, largely rural, would ever support attempts to introduce a better standard of film-making.

Here it must be stressed that no breakthrough would have been possible except for the enthusiasm stirred and persisting from 1955 with the founding of film societies in the northern and southern states. The proliferation of membership screenings of outstanding films generally supplied by embassies and the presentation of film festivals of different countries influenced the growth of a new audience. Ray's "opus" of Bengali society was frequently shown along with the best of Bengal's production.

By 1970 it was in Karnataka that P R Reddy directed a new style picture, *Samaskara,* in Kannada. He discarded the entrenched conventions of songs and dances and glittering stars. A serious film disruptive to traditional castism, *Samskara* was banned for a year. But Reddy's unorthodox film ignited an explosion of creative cinema activity in a linguistic area where there were many multi-talented people akin to Girish Karnad, mentioned earlier. Kannada cinema's saga, with its inventiveness as to how to overcome difficulties in financing and distributing better films, had begun.

The advent of the New Indian Cinema, especially in regional languages, owes much to people of more than single talent, Ray, in Bengal, being a prime example. In Karnataka, over-all appreciation of film has gained from the fantastic enterprise of K V S Subbana, agriculturist, publisher, avant garde theatre man, rooted in a remote village of 300 souls near the small town of Sagar, where he founded a film society. In the former he has built a rural theatre where performances and seminars are held. In 1967, Subbana arrived to attend a month's crash course in film appreciation at the Poona Institute, so did other dynamic people who went off to inspire diverse projects as far away as Assam. Subbana wrote and published a book devoted to Eisenstein's *Potemkin.* Issues of his Kannada magazine have been devoted to film. It is the spreading of ideas in regional languages as to what cinematography is all about that not only helps the makers of serious films, but aids audiences to understand so-called "difficult" examples.

Over the decade 1970-80, Kannada cinema has evolved into one of the vigorous regional styles, one that has developed a distinctive neo-realism and also a combination of fusing "social observation with entertainment in what has been termed 'folk cinema,' " according to Shama Zaidi, script writer of *Garm Hawa,* and responsible for both the dialogue and costume designs for Ray's only Hindi film, *Shatranj ke Khilari (Chess Players)* with Richard Attenborough as Outram, the British Resident to Oudh. Starting with *Samskara,* two other Kannada pictures — *Chomana Dudi* (1975), and in 1958 the highly disturbing *Ghatashraddha,* the ritual ex-communicating "immoral" Brahmin widows, the first film of 26-year-old Kasaravalli — received India's award for the best film of its year.

Equally dramatic change and rapid development has taken place in Malayalam film production in Kerala, a most singular state, the neatest of all where nothing in its intricate socio-religious patterns runs true to form. India's second smallest state, it is the least accessible since it runs as a thin strip down the south-west coast facing out towards Africa. New ideas have ever been streaming in while its natural products, especially spices, have been carried forth to the world. Legend claims that King Solomon's ships dropped anchor close to the present capital, Trivandrum. Further north along the coast, an ancient Jewish community took root. Phoenicians, Greeks, Romans, Arabs, known today as Moplahs, came; even Chinese whose hats both Kerala fisherman's headgear and house roofs conspicuously resemble. It is believed that in 53 AD Christ's Apostle, Thomas, arrived and made converts known today as Syrian Christians. Then followed the Dutch, Portuguese and French, finally the British. This constant exposure to diversity might explain two striking statistics — that in Kerala literacy in 1975 was 80 per cent and 43 daily newspapers were published! The art form for which this state is famous, is the unique dance drama, Kathakali.

Gaudy melodrama reigned supreme in Kerala cinemas

14. Shyam Benegal's "Ankur" (The Seedling), 1974, Hindi. Anant Nag, of the Kannada cinema, is the city man who, coming to stay in his family's village house, sets out to seduce his married servant girl, beautifully acted by Shabana Azmi.

15. Having married a real memsaheb, Surya (Anant Nag) brings her home and she administers humiliation to his servant-mistress. The film evolves beyond this triangle to become a document of the alienation of city people from villagers. Benegal's first film made Shabana Azmi a star; playing a totally different type and class of woman, both petulent and seductive, she appears as Mirza's wife in Ray's "Chess Players".

14

15

16

M S Sathyu's "Garm Hawa" (Hot Winds), 1974.
16. In Agra, Amina, the daughter of the quietly dignified Salim Mirza, walks peacefully with Shamshad, the son of a family friend, through one of the great Moslem monuments. Their hope is to marry. But communalism tears the communities apart as Independence comes.
17. Salim Mirza (Balraj Sahni) is assaulted…

18. Violence breaks loose between Hindus and Moslems. The Moslem families depicted by the director — he is a Hindu from Karnataka — are torn apart, Shamshad and his family going to Pakistan. The film is a movingly truthful picture of exactly what happened in one city to a group of individuals during a period of nightmare involving millions of human beings.
19. "Akrosh" (Cry of the

Wounded), 1981. The first feature film directed by the cameraman, Govind Nihalani, who, belonging to Kannada cinema, photographed many of the most interesting, as well as working with Shyam Benegal. Derek Malcolm wrote in "The Guardian": "The film is made with considerable force and fluency, and bravely pinpoints:..the endemic corruption…. The lack of a really first-class script mitigates

against the power of both acting and direction. That said, it remains a highly promising debut."

17

18

19

**REGIONAL CINEMA —
KANNADA AND
MALAYALAM**

20. P R Reddy's "Samskara",
1970, the first Kannada film
to break with convention and
spark off in the state a deluge
of New Wave film-making.
Girish Karnad turned script
writer and actor, appearing in
the leading role.

21. Girish Karnad's first solo
film written and directed by
himself, "Kaadu", 1974.

Govind Nihalani, as
cameraman, evoked im-
pressively the secret,
superstitious forces, the power
of magic which embroil a little
boy, Kitti, acted by G S
Nataraj with utter conviction,
and his aunt, Kamala, when
their own lives are put under
the pressure of the uncle's
adultery.

22. "Kaadu". Fear of what
they have done in the
forest…Kamala was inter-

preted by the Bangalore
"housewife", under the name
of Nandini, married to the
dynamic Bhaktivatsala, then
president of the Karnataka
Film Chamber of Commerce,
who had initiated a campaign
for a new style of film.
Nandini had never acted
before. The first Kannada film
to be released in London.

20

21

22

until 1964 when a unit I'd encountered at Poona went home to see what they might do to change things. First they started a film society, which evolved into the Chitralekha Film Co-operative and over a decade spread film societies throughout the state to create audiences for better films. By 1975 I saw the further development of an umbrella scheme — a studio to provide not only all essentials for making films, serious ones and experimental ones, but also handle distribution, plus studies in collaboration with the National Film Archive, the head of which is a Kerala Nair.

The chairman of Chitralekha, Adoor Gopalakrishnan, in 1972 finally created a new type of Malayalam film with his first feature, *Swayamvaram (One's Own Choice)*. A plausible and convincing film, it was awarded the President's Gold Medal as the best feature film of the year. His next film *Kodiyettam (Ascent)*, the slow awakening of a drifter, bagged all the major awards for Malayalam films in 1977.

Of the increasing roster of Keralan directors, several are Christians, and two, John Abraham and G Aravindan, truly avant-gardist. *Uttararayam (Throne of Capricorn)*, Aravindan's first film, so excited me in 1974 by its search into the mind and spirit of its Nair characters, that I thought this film was a *must* for the next London Film Festival. I went to Calicut to try to meet its director. He was not to be found. I discovered that Aravindan, the son of a noted Nair humourist, was a painter and cartoonist, trained in classical music, his background somewhat resembling Satyajit Ray's. No copy of *Uttararayam* reached London. His next picture, *Kanchana Sita (Golden Sita)*, based on the Ramayana, was a highly individual and imaginative interpretation — Sita, Rama's wife, never appears, her different moods being depicted through the aspects of nature. His 1978 film *Thampu (The Circus Tent)*, in startling contrast to its predecessor, in seeming defiance of form contemplates with endless patience the visit of a quaint group of circus people to a little village, and the villagers' reactions. *Thampu*, which haunted David Robinson of *The Times* with its magical qualities, reached the London Film Festival, so did Aravindan's totally enchanting 1980 fantasy for children, and no less for adults, *Kummatty (The Bogey Man)*, who befriends the children of a remote village, turning each, as a joke into an animal.

Over the last quarter-century irrespective of the rubbishy pictures still churned out, the new horizons that have opened for Indian cinema from Ray's Bengal in the north-east to Kerala in the south-west with the exceptional work of Aravindan and a whole youngish generation of talented people, is a saga of defeating every obstacle. An independent cinema now exists, no longer an optimistic dream, but concrete reality, one that is a credit to all who have contributed to its creation. To round off this all too brief survey, which cannot give an adequate impression of the diversity and daring of the themes attempted by those who have thrown in their lot with New Wave Indian cinema, I must comment on the role of women in Indian film-making in 1981.

Many of the outstanding performances, even in commercial hide-bound movies, let alone those that escaped from the cliches, were given by actresses. Every woman that had the good fortune to be directed by Ray, professional or non-professional, created a memorable character. But women appeared to be confined to acting until 1981. Only with the National Awards for the Best Film did the changed role of women become evident. For example, the Best Art Direction went to Meera Lakhia for the award-winning Gujarati pic-

ture, *Bhavni Bhavai*, "perfectly creating the glamour of a royal palace juxtaposed with the grim austerity of hutments" occupied by Untouchables.

Five women emerged as producers — Rosamma George, the Second Best Feature Film of India, *Oppol*, from Kerala, for "boldly presenting a woman's love for her illegitimate child... and for offering social acceptability to the mother and child, thereby giving a new perspective to the values prevalent today." The Best Malayalam Film, a first picture, *Yagam* was produced by B Chandramani Bai, the wife of the director, for "presenting the dilemma of a romantic revolutionary...and successfully building up the sense of doom underlying the human relationship throughout the film." *Anirban*, the second picture of the director, produced by his wife, Preeti Saikia, was judged the Best Assamese Film for "depicting man's attachment to life through the story of an unfortunate married couple...(and) for providing a touch of realism by a delicate representation of a piece of lower middle class existence." Of the trio of producers responsible for *Chann Pardesee*, one was a woman. It represented "a departure from the usual trends prevalent in Punjabi cinema." Finally, it was a woman, Krystyna Khote, who produced *Daldal*, a "powerful indictment of a social malaise — bonded labour — very sensitively handled and well researched," which was judged the Best Information Film.

Indian films are escaping from the "escapism," which first struck me as so "un-Indian" that they looked as if made by foreign units without roots in Indian culture. Now, very noticeably, the standard singing-dancing-weeping, passively victimised heroines, are changing into actively independent women making their own choices, as is increasingly reflective of life in India. I've indicated that Satyajit Ray pioneered the movement towards a new type of film-making, but without suggesting to what an extent his films — 29 to the beginning of 1982 — pay tribute to women who are full-fledged human beings and act in accordance with their own convictions.

Consequently, it is not surprising that the two women directing feature films written by themselves, entered films as actresses directed by Ray. Ever seeking new talent, in 1969 he introduced into the Bengali cast for one of his favourite pictures, *Aranyer Din-Ratri (Days and Nights in the Forest)*, a Sikh girl, Simi, to interpret with delightful cheek the tribal girl who outwits her would-be city seducer. Having been inspired by Ray, Simi Garewal became fed up with Bombay stardom, even international offers, and started to direct a low-budget picture last October. *Ardhanginee*, she says, explores the role of "the new Indian woman, whom men don't know how to cope with." Aparna Sen, when she was a fourteen year old — Ray had known her from birth — created the deliciously temperamental tomboy, "Pagli," in *Samapte (The Conclusion)* for the Ray trilogy of Tagore short stories titled *Teen Kanya (Three Daughters)*. As Aparna matured (like Sharmila Tagore she became a Bombay star), she appeared in several later Ray films.

Growing bored with Bombay where she established a relationship with the couple who would aid her first directorial venture — Shashi, the highly intelligent star, younger sprout of the dominant movie family of Kapoor — he had turned producer of two of Syham Benegal's films — and his wife Jennifer Kendal, the elder sister of Felicity, Aparna hied back to Calcutta with thoughts of the Anglo-Indian teacher

23. "Swayamvaram", 1972. Written and directed by Adoor Gopalakrishnan, and the film which introduced the idea of a new type of Malayalam cinema. With the help of the film societies pioneered by Gopalakrishnan, the movement for better films has flourished and multiplied. Unfortunately, stills to illustrate what has happened are very scarce and hard to come by.

24. G Aravindan's "Kanchana Sita" (Golden Sita), 1977, was his second picture. To give a sense of reality to the story taken from the Ramayana epic, Aravindan had the bold idea of having the five major characters acted by tribals known as the Ramachenchus. They claim they are the descendants of the family to which Rama belonged. The film was shot in colour on location in the Andhra Pradesh area associated with Rama, where the landscape has probably changed very little from the time of the epic. The tribal actor shown plays the role of Lakshmana, Rama's ever-faithful brother.

25. "Kummatty" (The Bogeyman), 1980. Aravindan's fourth film, of which Derek Malcolm wrote in "The Guardian," and quoted for the film's screening in the London Film Festival, "I haven't seen a film in ages which has quite the same power to charm without causing the slightest feeling of being taken in by well-crafted sentimentality."

BACK TO BENGAL
26. "Ekdin Pratidin" (Quiet Rolls the Day), 1979, is Sen's 18th film. He has directed two since. Ken Wlaschin's comment on this picture sums up the impression it leaves. "There have been

23

25

24

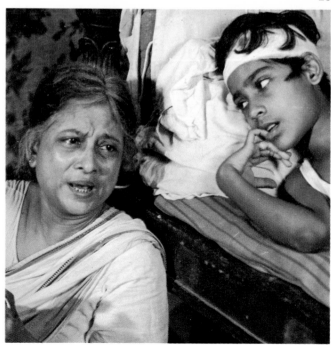

26

many films about the oppression of Indian women but been none with the determination to show just what being a 'modern' independent woman in India today really means....Sen has carried the discussion into the double standards of judgement presently in effect in India, even in liberated circles." The tensions of a family and neighbours are stripped bare as they await the return of the breadwinner, the eldest daughter. She arrives only with the dawn, giving no explanation...Many of Sen's films have been overtly propagandist and to the Left. 27/28. Aparna Sen's "36 Chowringhee Lane", 1981. The first film to be written and directed by Aparna, who, as a very young teenager, made her film debut in 1961 in Ray's "Teen Kanya". Her father is the film critic, Chidananda Dasgupta, founder with Ray of India's first Film Society of Calcutta.

Photos 1, 3, 16, 19, 20, 24, 25, 26: courtesy of Indian High Commission, London.

Photos 2, 2a, 4, 5, 6, 7, 8, 13: courtesy of Marie Seton.

Photos 9, 10, 11, 12: courtesy of Sir Richard Attenborough.

Photos 15, 18, 21, 22: courtesy of Contemporary Films.

Photos 27, 28: courtesy of Chidananda Dasgupta.

27

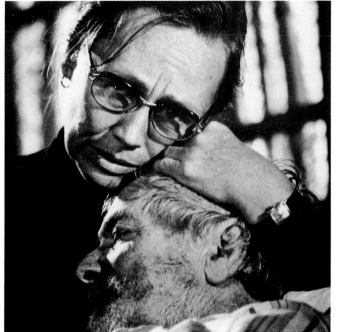

28

who had taught her. The result is the English dialogue film, *36 Chowringhee Lane,* in which Jennifer Kendal gives a superb performance as the ageing and lonely Violet Stoneham, whom a young couple, first brightening up her existence, end by exploiting her dismal flat as a place to meet and make love. Once married, Miss Stoneham painfully learns that she is extraneous to their luxurious lives. All the solace left to her is Shakespeare. With a stray dog for company, Aparna Sen ends her very interesting and terribly apt film, with Jennifer Kendal (as marvellous an interpreter of a woman older than herself, as Karuna Bannerji was as the stoic mother in *Pather Panchali*) reading aloud from King Lear!

The only honest award that could have been given to Indian cinema in 1954, was that it was about the world's most un-cinematic, the most commercial and gaudily dated. From this, it has, against all the odds, now evolved into an increasingly dynamic, *cinematic* national, or rather multinational because of the different regions, genuinely expressive of India. This is a remarkable achievement.

Mercury's Indian Adventure

MERCURY TRAVELS (INDIA) LIMITED

Jeevan Tara Building
Parliament Street
Post Box No. 312
New Delhi-110 001
Phones : 312008, 321403
Telex : 3207
Cable : MERCTRAVEL

Branches At : Bangalore, Bombay, Calcutta, Hyderabad, Madras, Srinagar, Varanasi.

Overseas Offices : Newyork, Frankfürt.

Flight of fancy

Albright & Wilson salutes the Festival

Albright & Wilson contributes to the industrial and domestic welfare of India through its trading links over many years.

It has two long-established Indian associate companies: Albright Moraji and Pandit Ltd. is a major producer of detergent raw materials; Bush Boake Allen (India) Ltd. is a leading supplier of flavours and fragrances.

ALBRIGHT & WILSON International in chemicals

Albright & Wilson Limited
1 Knightsbridge Green London England

MACAU
Another world 55 minutes from Hong Kong

Macau combines the excitement of 24 hour-a-day roulette-wheels with the serenity of cobble-stone streets and old-world surroundings.

The magnificence of 17th Century St. Paul's Cathedral lives on in the facade that survived a fire and typhoon in 1835. Modern-day splendour is reflected in the Hotel Lisboa— from the giant chandelier that dominates the foyer, to the vast gambling halls that play host to thousands every day.

The Lisboa's ten restaurants offer the best of Japanese, Portugese, European and Chinese food. The Shopping Arcade. Children's Playground, ten-pin bowling alley, coffee shops,

swimming pool and cocktail bars make the Hotel an international favourite.

Away from the casinos, close to the harbour, is Hotel Sintra. Here the emphasis is on comfort and relaxation, ideal for those who enjoy the warmth and friendliness of a family hotel.

The luxurious Boeing Jetfoils cruise from Hong Kong to Macau in 55 minutes. A hydrofoil takes just 70 minutes — or for those with time to spare, there is the enjoyment of the 2-1/2 hour ferry ride.

Macau has a magic all its own. Once you've discovered it, you'll want to keep coming back.

TRAVELLING IN INDIA, TRAVELLING WITH INDIA

Sir John Thomson

Philosophers of history and science like R G Collingwood and Karl Popper have been teaching us — if we were not aware of it already — that we only get answers to the questions we ask. In the same way, we tend to see only what we are looking for. But we are open to surprises. During five years of extensive travelling in India, people, places and events have surprised us into consciousness of our misapprehension. We have been revising our assumptions; and, in the manner of those who have seen visions, we often wish to tell travellers new to India to look and learn, before they conclude that they have seen what they assumed they would see.

McLuhan has taught us — if we did not know it already — how vulnerable we are to literacy and to post-literate visual media: how much of our experience has become mediated, even by the camera we hold between ourselves and what we are looking at. In India the traveller can move for days beyond the reach of modern media. The first assumption that crumbles with this experience is the tendency to equate education — in the sense that includes culture — with literacy.

The large proportion of India's people who remain illiterate are nevertheless for the most part deeply cultured. Literacy has been felt to be irrelevant and indeed inimical to the deepest culture, which must be memorised and then internalised so that it becomes as much part of a person as breathing. The religious teacher keeps the scriptures in his head: family Trivedi is so named for being able to recite three of the Vedas from generation to generation. The sculptor memorises the shastras that tell him the proper proportions of each image; his inspiration will vary in excellence from piece to piece, but his basic patterns have

become an automatic part of him. The genealogist may write in his register the names of your latest children, but he will have your family tree in his head for generations back. The storyteller from Bikaner can entertain you for five nights running with the tales of Bapuji, an epic sung in verse and handed on from parents to children. The classical musician can create improvisations for hours on ragas — modes — whose form he has memorised as a child but whose potentialities and subtleties grow as he grows; and he holds also in his head a grammar of rhythms that he can elaborate in breath-taking complexity.

Literacy is a necessary tool for dealing with the bureaucracy and some technology, and India's formerly illiterate people are learning to read when and because they now need to. But let no one suppose that, where literacy has not been found to be a necessary technique, culture and appropriate education are therefore lacking.

Thus, the traveller never feels in India that the illiterate are "savages." Yet quite often he will conclude that a higher percentage of literate people would indeed be appropriate to the education that is needed in modern conditions. Literacy — and numeracy — is an important defence against the extortionate ways of the itinerant packman or the local money-lender. And their high level of literacy has something to do with the enormous contribution which girls from Kerala make to the nursing services of India. Even more important, literacy, especially literacy among women, evidently tends to have a limiting effect on the size of families.

These comments point to what would be an obvious conclusion were it not so frequently missed, namely that what is probably the oldest continuous civilisation in the world is

Top left: A Brahmin meditating over his books, in front of a shrine at Puri.

Far left: Contemporary India — present and past exist side-by-side.

Left: Continuity - market day in a Kerala village.

163

Below left: Jacobite Syrian Christians at Kerala. Hindus at prayer, below right and centre right. A man and "his" god, bottom left.
Sunset prayer at Jama mosque, Delhi, bottom right.

indeed cultured and much-educated, but is in need of adaptation if it is to deal with all its problems, especially its modern ones. Fortunately India, which has been remarkably resistant to revolutions, has through the ages shown an equally remarkable ability to adapt. We have been very impressed from village to factory by the Indian's readiness and ability to learn (except perhaps when he is didactically expounding).

Though adaptation is needed, it is necessary to beware of change for the sake of change — an attitude that has become almost a passion in the West. It is important to remember that people in India are living at many levels and that for some the old ways are still the most appropriate.

The Western traveller tends to assume that history is sequential and that the present has buried the past. He needs to travel for only a few kilometres along any Indian road to realise that *contemporary* has a special meaning here. Bullock carts and cycle rickshaws and farmers raking out seed to dry in the sun all share the national highways with the heavily loaded lorries and buses and India's sturdy private cars. Many ages, many technologies co-exist: tribal communities of hunter-gatherers and bullock-based agriculture are literally contemporary with the latest hydro-electric irrigation schemes and chemical technology.

We remember how moved we were, when we were very new in India, to meet our first tribal people in Palamau game park in Bihar. This is country very like landscape we know well in the foothills of the Appalachians in Pennsylvania and West Virginia. In Palamau there are footpaths, where footpaths naturally should be but in North America are no more. And along the Palamau footpaths walk quiet people, at home in the forest as aboriginal people are no more at home in America. Those *Santhals* of Bihar turned out to be the beloved hedonists of our nursery tales by Helen Bannerman, Little Black Sambo and his family. His tigers are being protected, in the nick of time, by the Forestry Service and Project Tiger. His forests are shrinking disastrously fast. But India has been large enough, and the technologies and the germs of successive invaders have been gentle enough, for there to have been a degree of peaceful co-existence.

Travellers in India have a unique opportunity to assess the quality of life in communities which in the West have slipped over the historical horizon. What makes a life-style satisfactory? As one British teenager told us, after sharing the work and the festivals of a village in Uttar Pradesh for a year, " You learn here how much you can do without, and how to celebrate with what you have."

Indians themselves are very local people. Except for pilgrims and members of the central government's military and administrative services, few Indians move outside of their family place or their caste. (The Westernised business community whirls back and forth across the subcontinent but most know little of other communities.) In a country as large and at least as varied in races and cultures as all of Europe, we find ourselves wishing that Indians knew more about one another and about this contemporary wealth of their society.

Travellers prepare themselves for visits to famous monuments by studying their history and archaeology. And it is not inappropriate to visit the monuments of Agra or Ajanta or Khajuraho in an air-conditioned coach from a five-star hotel. We are not intruding; we are in fact re-creating, bringing alive in our imagination lives and achievements that are otherwise empty of content, beyond our ken.

But if the object of our journey is to visit people, to enter places that are alive, then we go as guests or as pilgrims seeking enlightenment. We go to share, to experience a way of life that is interesting because it is different from our own. The tourist industry bears a heavy responsibility when it introduces visitors whose material standards are very different from those of the people they are visiting. Nepal has suffered considerable cultural shock; we are worried — perhaps unnecessarily, for the season is short and their self-confidence is strong — about the friendly people of Ladakh and their carefully balanced subsistence economy. Our children have managed to travel simply through rural India, sharing the life-style of the people they meet, and they have been received with the kind of friendly hospitality that makes the world a happy place.

Pilgrimage has for centuries been India's typical motive for travelling. As in mediaeval Europe, there is a great infrastructure of inns and *dharamsalas* and *chai-khanna* stalls to provide for the modest needs of those who visit the holy places. And what a lot of holy places there are: sacred rivers, sacred mountains, here the shrine of a saint (saints of all religions seem to be venerated without discrimination), there a famous local deity (the great gods take on local names and attributes if properly invoked.) As a friend from Orissa says, if you paint a stone holy red, even if it's in the middle of the road the Public Works Department won't move it. The size of pilgrimage crowds, who gather to commemorate a special holiness and acquire a special merit, has to be seen to be believed.

But the Indian does not have to leave home in order to celebrate. Public festival is an art-form of endless variety throughout India, and of dependable satisfaction.

There is in India no boundary between the sacred and the profane. Liturgical worship belongs to India's minorities, in her mosques, several of which are " the largest in the world," in her churches, some of which are older than memory, named after Thomas the Apostle, who is believed to have founded the earliest Christian communities in India. (There are roughly 62 million Moslems in India and about 15 million Christians.) Hindu worship is unliturgical, individual, private. Hindu temples and shrines are visited at all hours of the day and night; prayers, offerings, perambulations are done privately. Most homes and many workshops have a shrine. The housewife says a prayer as she draws a rice-flour pattern on her doorstep each morning. Every stitch in a Punjabi embroidered shawl may have been a prayer.

But a warm climate brings people together out of doors, and a continuing closeness to the seasons and the agricultural work cycle gives life to the festivals that mark the annual events: Pongal to thank the animals and bless the plough; Holi to go a little mad over the coming of spring; car festivals to celebrate harvest and take the local deity, in gratitude, on an outing; Dussehra to celebrate Rama's return to his kingdom after defeating the wicked Ravana, the annual triumph of good over evil; Diwali to thank and propitiate the goddess of wealth.

We have been impressed again and again by the involvement of whole villages whose traditions remain intact — and *76 per cent* of all Indians still live in agricultural villages — in this round of festivals which punctuate the cycle of work as season follows season. Many Indians live close to natural

Early morning mist lingers
over Periyar Lake, below;
elephants in the jungle at
Periyar, bottom left. A young
spotted deer, bottom centre.
Bottom right: Project Tiger;
saving an endangered species.

disaster, but also close to divinity; close to hardship but also to joy. We have also been impressed by the tolerance of rural Indians for every form of worship. In India one is constantly aware of the assumption that divinity is all around us, and the same for all of us. It is lovely to be a guest in an Indian festival crowd.

How to preserve this closeness to nature and this natural assumption that work is an offering acceptable to God? How to further the agricultural green revolution and provide non-agricultural work for the growing number of landless labourers, without losing the contentment belonging to this cycle of work and worship?

India's stability has been based on a hierarchical system of common law that has regulated everything from diet to consanguinity. Everyone has his place from birth: his rights and his duties are clear to him and to his whole community. Statute law has been needed only to apply extraordinary punishments for breach of law and order, and to collect taxes.

India today is still largely a common-law society, but with a growing number of people who are displaced from their traditional birth-roles, whether by political or natural disaster, by education voluntarily pursued, by the simple devastating pressure of numbers, or by the lure of glossy urban goodies. India also has a contemporary government which has passed a large body of new statute law. Minimum wages, land ceilings, legal aid, drought relief — all the mechanisms of a modern state in which individual mobility is the norm — all these exist by law; but the habits for using this new machinery are slow to form.

The traveller in India will see plenty of refugees and migrant workers who have lost their traditional places and whom the benefits of statute law and new kinds of social organisation have not reached effectively. He can also visit imaginative and lively experiments in peaceful change: not charity in the old sense of passive giving and receiving, but projects that teach new self-awareness, new techniques of cooperative self-government, self-sufficiency and confidence in new roles, both technical and social. We could not begin to list all the quiet good work we have seen, but a short list would include the women's union, SEVA, in Ahmedabad where rag-pickers and head-loaders have learned how to run their own bank instead of resorting to money lenders; the Oxfam project in Kalahandi District of Orissa where landless villagers have learned to use the government's food-for-work programme to build themselves several huge earthworks for reservoirs that will irrigate unreclaimed land; the school for "gifted children" in Pune, where "gift" can mean any one of some 10 categories of skill and leadership, and a lively group of children from all sections of society are both given a sound liberal education and trained in self-confidence, social commitment, and appropriate vocations (while the expenses of running the school are largely raised by an electronics workshop run inside the school itself); an amazing number of villages "adopted" by Lions or Rotary Clubs, by industrial firms large and small, by religious or other charitable organisations, or by one arm or another of government, where, with every degree of success, projects like adult literacy, family hygiene, appropriate technologies such as biogas and solar energy, the use of new agricultural programmes, new crafts and light industries, are all promoted; a network of mobile nurseries and schools that serve the construction workers of Delhi on the sites where they both camp and work, by keeping their children safe and busy while both parents carry bricks and concrete; a mobile technical college in Gujarat that carries courses in mechanics and light engineering to villages, on contract, complete with necessary equipment and a teacher who is dedicated enough to stay for the required six weeks or six months.

Indians are notoriously self-critical, and like to indulge in a fatalistic tone that is perhaps the dark side of their wise conservatism. But we have noticed the growing self-confidence of people at all levels of society even during our time in India. Indians do tend to suspect others of selfish motives. We would like to pay tribute to the impressive amount of unselfish and unpublicised good work we have met.

One last note, on India's wildlife and forests. We have much appreciated our visits to game sanctuaries like Palamau, Ranthambor and Manas, and the bird sanctuary at Bharatpur; we have much enjoyed the company of their dedicated wardens. We realise that these places are all under terrible pressure from local people who need more and more land for pasture, more wood for fuel. The economic argument is loud and clear. But we are even more clear that it would be a false economy to sacrifice these final refuges of India's natural ecology to the immediate pressure of population. They have already proved their worth, as places of education above all.

Public awareness of environmental problems, especially of the effects that the destruction of the forests has had on climate, soil and water supply, has grown, not a moment too soon, during our time here. Forestry officials, who have always been called *conservators*, now remark wryly that this title is inappropriate unless they move ahead much faster with their schemes for social forestry. This some of them are doing, teaching villagers who have always carried their fuel from the "commons" to begin to become self-sufficient in forest crops that provide fuel, fodder and building materials. They are promoting share-cropping on government-owned forest lands in return for caretaking (we saw this in Gujarat); they are successfully replanting bare hillsides with a typical mixture of forest trees which, we saw on the hill in Madhya Pradesh, was repaying the trouble of building a stone wall against the animals by growing a lush crop of grass for cutting under the new trees. Trees thus protected grow wonderfully fast in India's strong sunlight, her best source of energy.

But we also hear with horror of new paper factories that will use bamboo as raw material in Tripura and Assam, and of a project to replace more of the mixed jungle in Madhya Pradesh, which provides tribal people with work and food, by a further pulp-wood crop of conifers. All across the northern hills, we have seen road-cuttings and paddy terraces sliding downhill for lack of trees to hold the soil; we see the silt-laden rivers and canals carrying away India's most important resource, her top-soil, after every mountain thaw and monsoon rain.

The race between good management and further, possibly irreversible, exploitation of India's natural resources will be a desperate one. India's human resources will need to be educated and mobilised to preserve her natural ones. The traveller soon sees that she is fortunately rich in both, but to win the race India will have to employ her talent for adaptability and make good ecological practice part of her village culture.

WOMAN AND BEAUTY

Tambimuttu

The story of Woman's creation has been variously told; but the following account is my favourite. In the beginning Brahma created man. But when he came to the fashioning of woman he found that he had no more solid materials left. So Brahma took:

The clustering of rows of bees, and the joyous gaiety of sunbeams, and the weeping of clouds, and the fickleness of winds and the timidity of the hare, and the vanity of the peacock, and the hardness of adamant, and the sweetness of honey, and the cruelty of the tiger, and the warm glow of fire, and the coldness of snow, and the chattering of jays, and the cooing of the kokila, and the hypocrisy of the crane, and the fidelity of the chakravaka; and compounding all these together, Brahma made woman and gave her to man.

Eight days later the man returned to Brahma: "My Lord, the creature you gave me poisons my existence. She chatters without rest, she takes all my time, she laments for nothing at all, and is always ill; take her back;" and Brahma took the woman back.

But eight days later the man came again to the god and said: "My Lord, my life is very solitary since I returned this creature. I remember she danced before me, singing. I recall how she glanced at me from the corner of her eye, how she played with me, clung to me. Give her back to me," and Brahma returned the woman to him. Three days only passed and Brahma saw the man coming to him again. "My Lord," said he, "I do not understand exactly how it is, but I am sure that the woman causes me more annoyance than pleasure. I beg you to relieve me of her!"

But Brahma cried: "Go your way and do the best you can." And the man cried: "I cannot live with her!" "Neither can you live without her!" replied Brahma.

And the man went away sorrowful, murmuring: "Woe is me, I can neither live with her nor without her."

Another Indian myth relates how woman was created out of the reflections of man gazing into pools of water when, like Narcissus, he sought company for himself.

The woman as soon as she was made began to cry, and she said, "Alas! Alas! I am and I am not." Then the Creator said: "Thou foolish intermediate creature, thou art a nonentity only when thou standest alone. But when thou art united to man thou art real in participation with his substance." And thus, apart from her husband a woman is a nonentity, and a shadow without substance; being nothing but the image of himself reflected in the mirror of illusion.

These myths don't, however, tally with the classical conception of woman, that had its origin in the earliest customs and beliefs, passing through the Epics, left its mark on the classical, mediaeval and modern periods. Even the stern and austere Brahman version of the Law Book of Manu (the first version according to Sir William Jones existed about 1580 BC) gives her an honoured place:

Then only is a man perfect, when he is three people united
— The wife, himself, and his son; so have wise Brahmans said:

"The husband is even one person with his wife."
Married women should be honoured with solicitude
With gifts from fathers, husbands, brothers and
*   brothers of husbands*
When these desire abundant prosperity.
Where women are honoured, there the gods are pleased
And where they are not honoured all sacred rites are
*   fruitless.*
Houses cursed by women of the family, to whom as
*   their due*
Homage has not been given, will perish entirely:
Struck down, it would seem, by a magic sacrifice.
Where the husband is contented with his wife, in every
*   family.*
And the wife with the husband — happiness reigns
*   forever.*

Throughout the maze of literary and artistic creation at various periods we catch glimpses of the Indian ideal of female beauty which seems to have remained constant. To begin with, it has been defined in memorable sayings:

"Thy well-combed hair, thy splendid eyes with their arches curved almost to thine ear, thy rows of teeth entirely pure and regular, thy breasts adorned with beautiful flowers."

"Thy body anointed with saffron and thy waist belt that puts the swans to shame."

"Moon-faced, elephant-hipped, serpent-necked, antelope-footed, swan waisted, lotus-eyed."

Through the amazing proliferation of poet's metaphor and simile, it is still possible to get an idea, however faint, of the type of woman meant.

We come across many descriptions of the ideal woman in the two great epics, the *Mahabharata* (c 300 BC), and the *Ramayana* (c 1000 BC). Tapati, the daughter of the sun god, has "lotus-leaf" eyes … deep-black and big … thighs like banana-stems (the texture of the skin is meant) …" "She has "swelling, long lips."

Broad hips were then the ideal, a delicate skin, and long, black almond-shaped eyes:

Oh! Leila!
In your eyes are three things,
Black diamonds of Hindustan,
Figured silks of Lahore,
Flames of Fusi-Yama:
The mountain flames are their brightness,
The figured silks of Lahore their dusk,
The black diamonds of Hindustan their colour,
Oh! Leila!

Nepalese Song.

Much attention and art has been given to the eyes, which are the most prominent feature of Indian women. Very thin, plucked eyebrows seem to have been the fashion from the earliest times:

You look: and black arrows of bees shoot out;
Bend your eyebrow; and Cupid shatters his deadly
*   bow!*

Kalidasa, fourth to fifth century*

*Tr by the author

To obtain eyes "like fishes with their long, flashing glide" and increase the size, a fine pencil mark was made outwards from the corners of the lids. To increase the depth of eyes the lids were stained blue with the juice of the wild plum. To make them dark and bright *surm* or collyrium (sulphuret of antimony) was applied on the eyelashes even as it is today. A silver stick or brush is dipped into the collyrium and passed along the lids and beyond the angle of the eyes to give them the large almond shape which is the delight of the painters, sculptors and poets:

Her lovely eyes shone white beside
The surm that dyed them, bees, as it were,
Mistaking them for spotless water-lilies.

Vidapathi, 15th century*

From the Epics, as well as the sculptures and frescoes, we learn of the ever-recurring convention of the fulsome breasts of a beautiful woman that make her bend with their weight. Also fulsome is her belly, exquisitely ringed with three folds of the skin, an ideal which is seen to advantage, for instance, in the much reproduced first century BC sculpture from Bihar of a female attendant, at present in the Patna Museum, or in the following quatrain by Bhartrihari:

Fair is her body as a deserted river
Whereon the moonbeams quiver;
About her waist three furrows in a row,
Like circling billows go.

Seventh century**

Her ankles are slim and the insteps of her feet highly arched. As one poet has put it, beautiful feet have insteps so arched that water flows under them. In fact the convention had become so set by the time of the *Ramayana* that we are told Sita stood gracefully on "her twelve," without further amplification, by which is meant of course her 10 toes and two heels connected by the arch of the foot. The heavenly hetaera, Urvasi, had all these auspicious characteristics:

When the moon had risen, and early night had come, the broad-hipped one went forth and sought out the house of Pritha's son. Shining with her soft, curly, long hair, wherein she wore many jasmine flowers, the heart-breaker went her way. With the moon of her countenance, and the delight of the movements of its brows, and the sweetness of the words tripping from her mouth, with her charm and her soft loveliness, she seemed to be challenging the moon as she walked along. As she went along, her breasts, scented with a heavenly salve, dark-nippled, rubbed with heaven's sandalwood, and shining from her necklace, were shaken up and down. Through the upborne burden of her breasts, and the sharp movements of them she was bowed down at every step, she with the surpassing splendour of the centre of her body, gloriously girdled around by three folds. Below shimmered, spread out like a mountain, swelling high like a hillside, the place of the temple of the god of love, ringed by dazzling splendour, adorned by the girdle's band, tempting with heart-stirrings even the divine Rishis... Her feet, in which the ankles were deep embedded, and whose toes made red and long-stretched expanses, glittered, being hung with small bells, and arched like the turtle's back.

The Mahabharata c 300 BC***

*Tr from the Sanskrit by Ananda Coomaraswamy
**Tr from the Sanskrit by P E More
***Tr from the Sanskrit by J J Mayer

The artists of the Kangra Valley, during the latter half of the Moghul period, produced paintings which in a unique blend of the sensuous and the spiritual, glorify woman's beauty, revelling in the loveliness of the female form and the delights of love:
Below left: "Ragini Telangi".
A girl is seated on a "chauki", having her body massaged

with oil. One of the attendants holds a "thali," with oil in a bowl, while the other rubs the girl's arm. The nude is never painted in Kangra painting for its own sake, but it is subjects like these which provide an opportunity for the artists to paint the beauty of the female figure.
Below right: "Ragini Kamodi".
The yearnings of love. A

female attendant is dyeing the soles of the girl's feet with henna, a cosmetic which is also applied to the palms of the hands. The girl reclines against a bolster in a languorous mood, with her arms raised, displaying her bust and her delicate, attractive body. She smiles, her eyes full of the unsatisfied longings of love.

The big hips and big bosom were of course accompaniment to the wasp-waist: the perfect hour-glass figure which was until very recently the European and American ideal:
O paragon of women! Thy waist was
Too slender and curved even at Thy birth;
It's now a vanishing line what with Thy
Heavy breasts! It's now come to be fragile

Like the tree on the bank of a gushing stream
That has washed all earth from its roots away.
Kama has wanton made Thy golden breasts
Hard so that they might tear Thy bodice, and
Expose Thy arm-pits. But, he could not harm
Thy waist; for it's safe bound by three cardamon lines.
Shankarachariar, eighth century*

*From the Sanskrit. Quoted from The Bride's Book of Beauty

Since it may be thought Indians pay too much attention to human anatomy, it should perhaps be mentioned that they associate the divine with its perfect proportions. It is also necessary to bear in mind the style of clothing favoured in South Asia which was a direct outcome of the climate:

Dress of characteristic South Asian type leaves the upper part of the body generally free and covers the lower, up to a little above the knees with a simple garment of mostly white and unsewn cotton. Wrappers of various kinds were generally worn over one or both shoulders thus providing for an easily enfoldable protection in the case of sudden cold spells, especially in the winter. The method of two garments, of which one is generally not worn, or carried as a fold only, is a characteristic adaptation to the quickly changing temperature and sudden spells of the otherwise tropical climate of South Asia. The beauty of well-trained and sun-tanned chest and shoulders was further stressed by the frequent use of white flower garlands, or shining metal jewellery, on the bare skin. In that way aesthetic attention was concentrated on the natural beauty of proportion, line and colour of the human body, rather than on the display of costly material in unnatural shapes, such as have been characteristically developed in the dress fashions of Europe, Northern Asia, including classical China and Japan...thereby upsetting the body's inner harmony and meaning. If man was made in the image of God, the south Asian artist has perceived something of the divine in the proportions and positions of the body which do not bear heavy clothing. Buddhist and contemporary sculpture reached certainly the peak of utilisation of the human body as a symbol for the eternal.*

In the Epics we are told that a beautiful woman is arched in six places: at the back of the hands, the top of the feet, the belly, the breasts, buttocks and eyes; she has seven things fine and delicate: skin, hair, fingers, toes, and the joints of fingers and toes; three things deep: voice, character and navel; five things red: palm of hand, corner of the eye, palate, tongue and lips. A similar catalogue of charms is given of the heroine Draupadi:

Her ankles do not stand out, and her thighs are firm and hard. Three things in her are deep (voice, understanding and navel), six high-arched (nose, eyes, ears, nails, breasts, the joint of the neck), five red (the palms of the hands, the soles of the feet, the corners of eyes, the tongue, the nails); she speaks unclearly as the swan, her brows and eyes are round-arched, red as the bimba fruit are her lips, her neck is like shell, her veins are hidden, her face is like the full moon. Glorious she is as a mare from Kashmir.**

In the Epics, too, we find the earliest mention of the idea, popular among the poets, that a woman should have the graceful walk of an elephant.†
The Agni Purana repeats the same theme centuries later:

*U R Ehrenfels in United Asia, *Bombay, 1950*
**Tr by J J Mayer

†*In the East where woman's garments permit freedom of movement and sympathetic co-operation of the muscular system this is an apt comparison. In the West the natural swing of the hips, only possible in conjunction with the free, lithe play of the muscles of the foot and torso, is restricted and becomes jerky...The elephant has an exquisite sense of balance and most supple joints, and can even make obeisance with profound dignity.*
F H Andrews *in* Journal of Indian Art, *London.*

*And so the Lotus-Eyed One, to Him of the lotus eyes
Walked up, with the proud step of the elephant,
And the Dark One, with tear-filled eyes, spoke to him
the Dark One.*
Mahabharata*

A woman, beautiful both in the formation and development of her person, and walking with her full and rounded thighs and hips, in the gait of a she-elephant in rut, and possessing eyes agile and full of desire like those of a pigeon intoxicated with the wine of youth, should be deemed specially fortunate...
Agni Purana**

Though the elephant is considered clumsy by the people who do not know him, he is as graceful as a ballerina, as anyone who has seen him walk slowly along the narrow bund of a ricefield would know. He is so much a symbol of strength, grace and symmetry in India that women's arms and thighs have often been compared to elephant's trunks.

The ideal woman's voice has been defined with care. The soft, low and musical — the "husky" voice seems to have been the most admired. Draupadi spoke "unclearly as the swan," as we have already seen. In commending the Lotus and Art-types of women as the best among the four types mentioned, the classical works on the subject compare their voices to the swan's and the peacock's. Though the voices of these birds are by no means pleasant to hear the poets have admired them because of the pitch. It is for this reason the voice has also been compared to a parrot's:

*The ineffable sweetness of your words seems the voice
of a parrot caged in your throat,
And so the God of Love has placed the bimba*** fruit as
your nether lip just to tempt that bird from within.*
Muka: Arya Statkam (15th century)****

We find that the Indian woman was fond of cosmetics. From the earliest times she used various fards to keep her complexion clear and transparent. Mudpacks for the face were in use during the time of the Buddha (563-483 BC) and the *Ananga Ranga* besides mentioning different beauty creams for the face describes hair-oils, restorers and dyes; formulae for various skin-foods; depilatories; and remedies for the removal of pimples, freckles, etc. The place of lipstick in her toilet was taken by the shell of green walnuts, betel leaf, or the bark of the walnut tree. Nails were coloured red with henna and pink with myrhh, or petals of red roses steeped in vinegar:

*When she puts henna on her hands and dives in the river
One would think one saw fire twisting and running in
the water.*
Dilsoz, 18th century*****

The soles of the feet were reddened with scented lac, and very pretty they look nowadays too since the custom persists among dancers:

*Tr by the author
***Tr by Manmatha Nath Dutt*
****The Momordica Monadelphia is a fruit about two inches long; when ripe it becomes vermilion-red.*
*****Tr from the Sanscrit by K Chandrasekharan and V H Subramania Sastri*
******Tr by Powys Mathers*

Below left: "The village beauty." A beautiful village girl guards the paddy field. A mauve fillet covers her head and a garland of flowers enhances her beauty. On the terrace of the house in the background is Krishna, seated with an old woman, a messenger, who describes the beauty of the girl to him: "A garland of water-lillies adorns her breast, And flowers of sann-hemp bedeck her forehead; Thus standing, that lovely damsel, with elevated bosom, Keeps watch on the field." Below right: "The radiant beauty." Surrounded by utensils, a pile of brinjals stored against the wall, a beautiful girl is cooking. Her jet-black tresses reach her waist; her face is serene and beautiful; her simple white dress enhances her loveliness. In the background, Krishna, the cowherd, is sitting under a tree. The female messenger is describing the girl: "Clad in a newly-washed garment, the Nayika is cooking; The kitchen is shining with the radiance of her lovely face."

*Cloud, tired of wandering, rest on balconies perfumed with flower's pollen,
And bearing marks of red lac from their dainty feet walking on them!*

Kalidasa, fourth to fifth century*

The Indian perfumes, mention of which we find in the Epics, were of course exotic. There were perfumes for different hours of the day, for different seasons, for different kinds of dresses and for different types of women. To quote *Bride's Book of Beauty,* the cool attar of *Keora* is a well-known perfume for the summer morning and goes with summer dresses and a fair, slim form and a reflective temperament. The attar of roses is suited to mid-day, goes well with velvet and reflects to advantage a vivacious, dark brown, full face. The delicate attars of *Motia* and *Chambeli* are suited to the shades of afternoon and the evening, violet, blue or green dresses. And they become mature women of 30 or 40. The fascinating aroma of *Molsary* is subtly conducive to rest in the tense, heavy Indian summer. It goes with rustling silks…The attar of *Kasturi* is appropriate for the hours of work, and should be used on yellow or saffron robes. It is specially suited to men and women who profess the arts which require deep meditation. The attar *Champa* is a perfume for the open air and the garden…is young and innocent. The attar *Henna* is a sports scent. The attar *Fitna* goes with highly emotional natures. The attar *Pantiz* is a gay and naughty perfume with an active and tingling freshness. The

*Tr by the author

172

attar *Musk* evokes a tenuous emotion like that aroused by flowing water, music or any pure form, tinged with a faint uneasiness:

Even now I remember her on her beds
Her body exhuding a fragrance of musk
Mixed with the curdy essence of santal:
Whose eyes while she was being kissed
Like two birds inserting beak into beak,
Looked beautiful, with their lashes
Shut fast, in her ecstasy.
I still remember her at the great moment of love
Her slender shape and restless eyes;
Her body balmed with musk and blend of saffron,
Her mouth with camphor-scented betel;
And O her lovely lower lip!

*Bilhana, 11th century**

As for the mode of dressing, we find that silks, wools, cottons, and garlands of pearls, precious stones, or flowers were used in such a way as to emphasise the symmetry of the form. Jewellry was used on the hair, ears, the breasts, nose, around the neck, the waist, arms, wrists, the ankles:

Woman Playing with a Ball
Clearly do I see, O ball, your intention
Set on kissing the lower lip of that young lady,
Since struck by that red-lotus-like feminine hand,
You bound back to her, again and again.
Keeping her breasts' covering, slipping down, time and
    again, in its place,
And in its proper place, every ornament that was in
    disorder;
Singing softly one song or other, running here and
    there,
She is driving forward the ball set with jewels.
Her breasts made visible with their covering slipping
    down;
Charmingly visible her thighs, with their garment
    upwards flying;
Her limbs' beauty seen to advantage, by jewels on her
    body disarrayed...
Here and there wandering, with each step, she makes
    the hearts of youths also to wander.
From your hands' touch, O celestial one, this ball fired
    with great affection,
And as if begging for leave to flirt with you, falls first
    at your feet;
And taking your side-glances for your consent to it,
The ball now further tries to kiss your mouth.
First holding in her hand, her dress become loose, her
    girdle dropping off,
Then with chin swung backwards, pressing over
    shoulder, the skirt of her dress,
This maiden, with tossed flowers in her hair, thick
    tresses dancing, as she whirls about easily,
With her whole body sweating, is playing at her sweet
    will with the ball.
Holding the ball in her hand which looked dulled like
    the moon, overpowered by her face's beauty,
Slightly inclined her head, through bashfulness and
    curiosity:
Who is it she has made the receiver of those long
    side-glances,

Springing from eyes vieing with blade of golden
    champak — tip darkened with black bee on it?
These sports of the doe-eyed, skirts dancing free, at
    each shift braids getting disarranged,
In which, each time the right hand's tossed, bracelets
    create a great din;Panting, blurred words from lips;
heads of hair shatter
    with ball thrown lightly to hands of the other side,
And garlands of flowers swing free —
Such sports of the deer-eyed, playing with a ball,
Give a lot of amusement!

*From the Sanskrit. Author unknown**

Maidens in cloth of fine weave, woven by hand
And too fine to be distinguished by the eye.

*From Manimekalai.***

Silk weavers who do tremendously fine work
In the weaving of silk cloths, of wool and of cotton.

*From Silapathikaram.***

And there was of course the red spot of kum-kum on the forehead that is to this day worn by women:

Fair-face, red brow-spot, there—
Behind, the heavy jet-black hair —

*Vidyapati, 15th century****

The hair was cared for elaborately with the use of oils, unguents and pomades. It was shampooed and dried with the aromatic smoke of aloes-wood, just as women in India, today, dry their hair with *bokhur* smoke.

Often pomaded, wavy, thick black hair
Sweet with it, and the fragrant smoke of
The scented black core of aloes-wood...

*From the Tamil of Pattu-pattu, first century AD***

The coiffure was of the most amazing diversity of styles: worn in masses of ringlets in front; two large buns on either side of the neck, decorated with flowers, pearls and precious stones; peaked buns on top wound with strings of pearls and flowers; side tufts; buns; rolls etc. To describe the hair styles of ancient India would in itself need the scope of a book:

Weaving lovely strands of flowers, of many
    colours,
Delicately, in our black braids, gathered on top.
The woman with bracelets, whose braided hair
Falls like the elephants' trunk, down her shapely
    back.
Salt-selling women who walk about
Their coiffure in the five different modes.

*From Pattu-pattu***

Many methods for curling the hair were in use. One consisted of winding thin strips of banana leaf into the hair. The quickly drying leaf curled up in the Indian climate producing a crop of curls. Thus was born the earliest known method for curling the hair.

The Vedic hymns (1500 BC) tell us that women swathed their hair in the "gossamer" of lotus fibre which was soft and lustrous, adding to its sheen.

*Tr from the Sanskrit by the author and G V Vaidya

*Tr from the Sanskrit by the author and G V Vaidya
**Tr from the Tamil by the author
***Tr from the Sanskrit by Ananda Coomaraswamy

GOPITEX GROUP

Manufacturers, industrial entrepreneurs, exporters & importers.

Head office:

79, Wyndham Street, G.P.O. Box 2366, Hong Kong.
Tel: 5-232406, 5-221343, 5-244405
Cable address: 'GOPITEX' Hong Kong
Telex: 74308 GOPI HX

Branches & Associates

1 GOPI TEXTILES & INDUSTRIALS LTD. (TAIWAN BRANCH)
P.O. Box 55-69
China Daily News Bldg., 14th floor
131 Sung Chiang Road
Taipei, Taiwan
Cable: 'GOPITEX'
Telex: 23172 GOPITEX
Tels: 5810963, 5620377, 5638872

2 GOPITEX (SINGAPORE) PTE. LTD.
Suite 1809 18th floor
Shenton House 3 Shenton Way
Singapore 0106
Cable: 'GOPITEX'
Telex: GOPITEX RS 36363
Tels: 2239824, 2221928

3 GOPITEX KOREA
C.P.O. Box 2206
Bumhwa Building, Gr. F.
70-1 Bukchang-Dong, Chung-ku
Seoul, Korea
Telex: 24924 GOPITEX
Tel: 283518

4 GOPI TEXTILES & INDUSTRIALS (INDIA) PVT. LTD.
P.O. Box 11083
Rewa Chambers, 1st floor
31 New Marine Lines
Bombay 400 020, India
Cable: 'GOPITEX'
Telex: 113637 GOPI IN
Tels: 296498, 296557

5 GOPITECH (KENYA) LTD.
P.O. Box 41223
Nairobi, Kenya
Cabe: 'GOPITECH'
Telex: 22716 VIPIN
Tels: 20721, 336715

6 GOPITEX (NIGERIA) LTD.
P.O. Box 3364
Aba
Imo State
Nigeria
Cable: 'GOPITEX' ABA

7 GOPITEX (U.K.) LTD.
15 Spear Mews
London SW5 9NA
United Kingdom
Cable: 'GOPITEX'
Telex: 946437 GOPI G
Tels: 01 370 6862

8 TRANS-OCEANIC TENDERS & TECHNOLOGY LTD.
3rd Floor, Cardinal House
171 Wilson Avenue
Toronto, Ontario
M5M 3A2
Canada
Telex: 065/24642 MENDEZ TOR
Tel: (416) 481-2276

And you thought India was a last resort...

Amritsar – Golden Temple

Goa – Fort Aguada Beach Resort

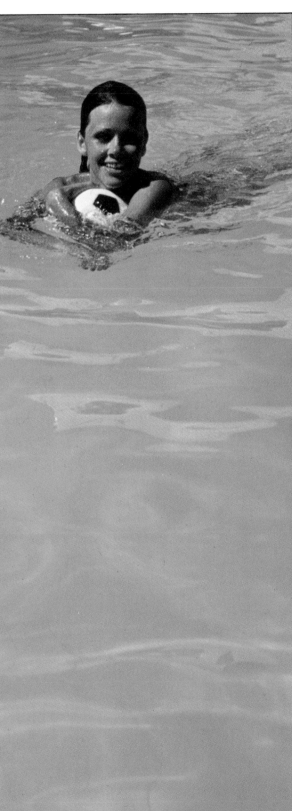

When you've wintered in Hawaii, wined in Cannes, sailed in the Seychelles, sunned in Antigua, what else is there to indulge yourself in?

India.

Because in India, everything is indulgent.

The sun-drenched beaches run for miles and the soft sands never seem to run out.

As if one ocean was not enough, in India you can swim in the warm waters of three.

The hotels are not just hotels. They're palaces and forts and palm-fringed cottages.

All with the kind of silently superb service, even the very rich are hardly accustomed to.

And when you drag yourself away from the beach, there are ancient temples to feast your eyes on, colourful bazaars to assail the senses, wildlife sanctuaries that will amaze you with rare and different animals, and more exotic experiences than you could ever fit into a lifetime.

Indulge yourself in India.

It's everything you've been longing for. And more.

Kovalam

For further information on holidays in India contact:

The Government of India Tourist Office, 21 New Bond Street, London, W1Y 0DY.

india

Scindia recalls the maritime heritage of India

When boats docked at Lothal

Indians in every age since the dawn of history, have been renowned for conveyance by water. The vast Indian coastline was studded with hundreds of ports, small and big.

The Harappan port-city of Lothal on the Gujarat coast played a great part in the Indo-Sumerian maritime trade of the Bronze Age.

This well-developed port of the Indus Civilization had a large brick-built dock with a water-locking device to ensure deeper draught for quicker turnround of ships. Warehouse and repair facilities were adequate. Enormous quanta of cargoes emanated from and terminated here.

The port of Lothal was an important link in the chain of economic development of ancient India.

Today, Scindia carries India's gifts to countries far and near. Reviving the sea-faring traditions of our past.

The Scindia Steam Navigation Co. Ltd.,

Scindia House, Narottam Morarjee Marg, Ballard Estate, Bombay 400 038.
Telephone: 268161, Telex: 011-2205

Scindia Steamships (London) Ltd.,

Kempson House, Camomile Street, LONDON EC3A 7AS.
Telephone: 01-283-1200, Telex: 884761

Sista's-SSN-854/81

TEXTILES IN HISTORICAL PERSPECTIVE

John Irwin

In India, the so-called "decorative" arts reflect something fundamental in the traditional way of life: certainly more than the mere wish to be carefree and sociable. No one who has been among the colourful crowd in Indian villages and market towns can ignore this impression. Costume and jewellery are not the only clues. It is expressed in the way the poorest farmer will find a fitting moment to ornament his bullock's horns with silk tassel; and in the ubiquity of the flower-garland as a symbol of dedication. India is perhaps the only country in the modern world to support a large profession of garland-makers.

The spontaneity and instinctive good taste which characterise the traditional way of life cannot, of course, be considered apart from the tradition of handicraft of which it is a part. Accustomed as we are to a sentimental view of handicraft as a reaction from mechanisation, we must remember that in India this tradition survives — however precariously — in its own right. We are too late to stem the tide of mechanisation; but we still have time to develop a better understanding of the way of life the handicraft tradition represents.

The Western industrial designer who caters for constantly changing fashion and is the self-conscious creator of designs he regards as his own, has no real counterpart in handicraft tradition, where convention is binding; and habit, rather than self-conscious invention, governs the approach. This is not the same as saying that designs were static — only that the changes were slower and more akin to growth, as observation and comparison with any historical collection will show

For two thousand years or more, Indian history had been closely bound up with her pre-eminence as a producer of textiles for the commodity market. Imagery of the loom is a feature of her poetic tradition. In the Vedas, for instance, day and night are said to spread light and darkness over the earth as weavers throw a shuttle on the loom. In many parts of the ancient world, Indian fabrics were proverbial. As early as 200 BC, the Romans were using a Sanskrit word for cotton — Latin *carbasina,* from Sanskrit *karpasa.* In the time of Nero, delicately translucent Indian muslins were fashionable in Rome under such names as *nebula* and *venti textiles* ("woven winds"), the latter exactly translating the technical name of a special type of muslin woven in Bengal up to the modern period. The *Periplus Maris Erythraei,* a well-known Roman document of Indo-European commerce, gives to the main areas of textile manufacture in India the same locations as we find in a 19th century gazetteer, and attributes to each the same articles of specialisation. The quality of Indian dyeing, too, was proverbial in the Roman world, as we know from St Jerome's fourth-century Latin translation of the Bible, in which Job is made to say that wisdom is even more enduring than "the dyed colours of India."

The lasting influence of Indian textiles in the English-speaking world is revealed in such names as *calico, chintz, shawl, pyjama, gingham, dimity, bandhana* — and these are only a few among the textile terms which were exported by India with her fabrics, and which are still common in English usage. How did she manage to exert supremacy over such a long period? This is a question requiring answer if we are to understand Indian textiles in their historical perspective.

Initial answer can be found in abundance and cheapness of raw materials. India was the original home of cotton,

Woman at the spinning wheel-
handicraft tradition still
survives, below.
Weavers at their looms;
imagery of the loom is a
recurring feature of poetic
tradition, bottom.

woven there from prehistoric times. Fragments of cotton cloth survive among the archaeological remains of Mohenjo-daro, dating from the end of the third millennium BC; and even more significant is the fact that one of these fragments shows signs of having been dyed with madder, the use of which presupposes a knowledge of mordants. Until as recently as the 17th century AD, India alone had mastered the complicated chemistry of cotton-dyeing, which involved proper permeation of the fibres, as distinct from mere application of pigments to the surface. (The same problems did not apply to the dyeing of non-vegetable fibres such as silk and wool, the dyeing of which had already been practised in other parts of the world, without depending on Indian example.) Silk-weaving is mentioned in Indian texts as early as the third century BC, although the implication is that at this period only wild silks were used: there is no evidence that the cultivated silkworm reached India from China before the early centuries of our present era.

Another, perhaps equally important clue to India's traditional textile skill is the social one of caste, since it would be difficult to imagine some of the complicated and laborious techniques employed outside the context of long-established caste division of labour, which produced enormous advantages for the passing on of skills, especially those based on empirical knowledge rather than theory. Here we use a word of Portuguese origin — caste — for want of an alternative, although it tends to misrepresent Indian craft organisation, having, as it does, some irrelevant meanings and associations. The Indian caste system as reflected in textile manufacture, combines features of both tribal and guild organisation. It would be difficult to imagine any craft system more calculated to encourage specialisation and the accumulation of hereditary skill.

In some respects, castes had functions comparable with craft-guilds of the West; but whereas the latter lasted only *hundreds* of years, Indian caste conventions persisted for *thousands*. Even physique was changed by so many generations of specialised craftsmanship. This was tragically shown in the 19th century, when tens of thousands of Indian weavers were thrown out of work by the competition of the power loom, and found that their fingers and hands, so delicately adapted to their craft, were useless for other manual occupation. As a result many of them starved, and their deaths are recorded in a famous minute of Governor-General Lord Bentinck which began: "The bones of cotton-weavers are bleaching the plains of India…"

A convenient classification of fabrics made in India for Indian use can be made on the following basis:
(1) skilled work of professional weavers and dyers who usually worked close to large market towns:(2) articles of luxury made under court patronage or in the court tradition:(3) folk embroidery and (4) fabrics of the aboriginal tribes.

Among those in the first group are brocades, *bandanna* work or tie-and-dye, muslins and painted and printed cottons. Brocades include examples of the famous kincobs (*kimkhabs*) of Benares and Ahmedabad, woven silk and gold and silver thread on looms not very different from the brocade handlooms of the West. There are also *himru* brocades of mixed cotton and silk, woven primarily for Mohammedans, who were not allowed to wear garments of pure silk.

Tie-dye or *bandanna* fabrics represent one of the oldest Indian techniques. It consists in tying tightly with waxed strings portions of a silk or cotton cloth before dipping it into the dye-vat. The strings are afterwards untied, the parts which were protected remaining uncoloured to form the pattern. This technique lends itself most effectively to patterns composed of all-over spots, or circles or groups of spots. Gujarat and Rajputana are the main centres of tie-dye work. Here, the cloths are known as *chunaris* and are classified according to the number of knots in the repeat. Crude tie-dye work on coarse calico comes from many parts of India, especially Assam and the Deccan.

The so-called *ikat*-technique is another kind of tie-dye. (The widespread use in textile literature of the Javanese work *ikat* must not be allowed to conceal the fact that, as far as Asia is concerned, India is probably the source of the technique.) In the making of these cloths, the warp and weft threads are dyed separately by the tie-dye process before weaving. *Ikats* are made in several parts of India; besides the well-known *patola* marriage saris of Gujarat, notable examples are the cotton shawls of Orissa and *telia rumals* of the Deccan. Traditional patterns are geometrical in kind: trellis-work, lozenges, chevrons — the special effect being the subtle merging of adjoining colours. Some of the floral scrolls and human figures sometimes appearing in 19th century designs are not traditional and may be taken as a sign of decadence.

Another kind of tie-dye cloth is the *mashru* of mixed silk and cotton, in which the warp only is tie-dyed before weaving with characteristic patterns of wavy lines.

Printing and painting on cotton are the arts for which Indian textiles have been chiefly famed abroad. The distinction between *painted* and *printed* is of more than technical interest. In the *painting* of cotton, the dyes and mordants are applied freehand with a brush. Thus each design has the character of an individual drawing, with the human and sensuous touch. In printing, on the other hand, the use of wood blocks inevitably restricts the design to repeats, and only the most skilled master of this art can eliminate a mechanical effect. Sometimes the two techniques were combined in the making of a single cloth.

The second classification is that of the textiles produced for the rulers and their courts, in which Persian influence is most apparent, especially in the use of a diaper: there is no evidence that it is featured at all in Indian textile design before the 16th century. By the middle of the 17th century it appears to have been completely assimilated in Indian decorative tradition.

Although the spread of Persian influence is undeniable, the term "Indo-Persian" should be applied with caution, if it is not to become meaningless. It is true that in the late 16th century, Persian craftsmen were encouraged to settle and to instruct Indians in the court workshops of the Moghul and Deccani rulers. As far as individual products of these workshops are concerned, the term "Indo-Persian" can often be legitimately applied. But beyond the immediate sphere of the court, Persian motives were adapted by Indian craftsmen for their own purposes and made subservient to the more earthy and dynamic qualities of Indian art as a whole.

There have been many periods in Indian history when her craftsmen have borrowed freely from the West, beginning with the Indus civilisation of the third millennium BC and extending to the growth of Islamic architecture in India from the 13th century AD onwards. But each phase of borrowing has merely illustrated the encompassing personality of India: her extraordinary capacity for combined assimila-

*Below left: Cotton, printed
with woodblocks and laid out
in the sun to dry.
A saree shop: Colourful dress
is part of the traditional way
of life, below right.
Bottom right: Pattern being
painted freehand onto cotton,*
*each design thus having the
character of an individual
drawing.
Opposite page: Satin coat,
embroidered with silks;
Moghul, 17th century (Photo
courtesy of Victoria & Albert
Museum).*

We worship the painted mandir tree
Which promises us granaries full of rice and paddy.
We worship the rice-paste drawing of the mandir,
Knowing that our homeland will be rich in gold and
silver.

These rituals are important for an understanding of the functional basis of popular art in India. They are fundamental in the living experiences of the people and reflect their whole attitude to life, giving rise to a culture rich in drama and imagination and deriving tremendous vitality from its group-character.

Nothing illustrates more clearly the religious or ritual basis of Indian textile motifs than the constant re-emergence in designs of the Tree of Life, which recurs in countless variations up to the present day, identifying the user or wearer of such designs with prosperity, or auspiciousness. From such examples it should be clear that art in the modern Western sense as aesthetic expression *for its own sake* is foreign to traditional societies. The very word we use — "art" — is non-existent in the social milieu we are thinking about. Throughout the ancient world, and in India until the recent past, each artistic operation had been a rite, never an act of beauty-creation for its own sake. Hence, our modern concept of "decorative art" would have been incomprehensible. One proof of this appears in the changing meaning of words used to express "ornament". The ancient Sanskrit words we translate as "ornament" — *bhusati* and *alamkara* — derive from roots meaning to "equip" — especially "equip with magical efficacy." Similarly, our English word, "ornament" from Latin *ornare*, and German "schmuck" — all originally meant "equip, fit out, prepare." They had no connection with the idea of embellishment, which came only much later. Sometimes, however, the words continued to carry both meanings, with seeming inconsistency, like the English word "charms," from Latin *carmen*: originally, this word was used only in the sense of "magical formulae," and we still talk of being charmed in the sense of "enchanted, bewitched," while using it also in the sense of "pretty, pleasing," which is foreign to ancient usage.

In discussing the popular basis of Indian textile design, we should not lose sight of an important distinction between folk-art, and the productions of tribal societies, which are worlds apart. Although folk-tradition sometimes draws on the memory of "primitive" ritual, it has other features which presuppose a background of settled class-society and the coexistence of an orthodox priestly culture. Typical of tribal traditions are the weavings of the Nagas of Assam. Unlike traditional weaving in Hindu India, tribal weaving is entirely the work of women, who weave as part of their domestic duties — the true Naga housewife being expected to produce the clothing needed by her family. The loom she uses is the single-heddle tension-loom of simple type, best known from its survival in Indonesia. The weaver sits on the ground, regulating the tension of the warps with the aid of a belt attached to a wall or simply to two small stakes driven into the ground. Patterns are made partly by using differently-coloured warp and weft yarns, and partly by insertion of separate pieces of coloured thread at intervals in the weaving — a technique that could be described as a very simple kind of brocading or loom-embroidery. A tribal costume proclaims the wearer's social position and prowess, and is invested with an elaborate code of meaning.

tion and invention. The influence of Persia in the decorative arts of the 17th and 18th centuries is no exception.

The third classification is the embroidery, traditionally done by women, and belonging to the villages. Styles are broadly regional, like the local traditions of folk-art to which they are related. In spite of commercialisation in some areas and at different periods, the regional characteristics are distinctive: and even today, with Indian folk-traditions everywhere in decay, it is still possible to identify at centres of pilgrimage the satin-stitch *phulkari* embroideries of the Punjab, chain-stitch work of Cutch and Kathiawar, cross-stitch work of Sind, and the *kantha* embroideries of Bengal. Each of these regional styles has its distinctive combinations of technique, colour and design: and each has its counterpart in commercial embroidery produced for the export market.

Another type of folk fabric is derived from *alponas* — the patterns which village-women of Bengal draw in rice-paste on the threshold of their dwellings. These drawings are not ornaments but symbols, and an understanding of their function helps to explain much about the forms of Indian decorative art as a whole. Briefly, *alponas* are drawings required for the enactment of rituals performed by women of the village at times of crisis. The objective may be the promotion of rain, success of the harvest, or the safety of the village against epidemic: the usual underlying idea is that when mimed in ritual the objective is more likely to be realised. When crops are ripening, for instance, ritual is performed with the help of a drawing of a tree. This serves as a fertility symbol. The tree is drawn on the ground in white rice-paste according to established conventions of design; it then forms the centre for the action of the ritual, when women sing in chorus:

Braj Kumar Nehru was born in Allahabad and educated at the University of Allahabad, The London School of Economics, Balliol College, Oxford, and the Inner Temple, London. He joined the Indian Civil Service in 1934 and till 1939 held various governmental appointments in the province of Punjab. He was then appointed Under Secretary in the Department of Education, Health and Lands, and later, officer on special duty in the Reserve Bank of India in the office of the Accountant General, Bombay. He then joined the Ministry of Finance, and in 1951 was appointed Secretary of the Department of Economic Affairs. Between 1949 and 1954 Mr Nehru worked as Executive Director in the World Bank and Economic Minister at the Indian Embassy in Washington. In 1958 he was appointed Commissioner General for Economic Affairs to handle India's external financial relations and in 1961 became Ambassador to Washington, a post he held till 1968. That year he was appointed Governor of the States of Assam and Nagaland and subsequently in 1972 of all the North-Eastern States of India. In 1973 he became High Commissioner for India in London which post he held up to 1977. He is currently Governor of the State of Jammu and Kashmir.

L K Jha was educated at Banaras Hindu University and later at Trinity College, Cambridge, where he studied economics under such distinguished men as Keynes, Robertson and Pigou. He joined the Indian Civil Service in 1936. After serving for four years in Bihar, he came to the Central Government in 1942. The posts he has held include those of Chief Controller of Imports & Exports; Joint Secretary, Commerce & Industry; Secretary, Heavy Industries; and Secretary, Economic Affairs. Mr Lal Bahadur Shastri appointed him as Secretary to the Prime Minister and he continued in that capacity with Mrs Indira Gandhi till 1967, when he retired prematurely from the ICS in order to become Governor, Reserve Bank of India. After three years as Governor, he went as Ambassador to the USA. From July 1973 to February 1981, he was Governor of Jammu and Kashmir. Currently, he is Chairman, Economic Administration Reforms Commission. Mr Jha has a number of publications on economic topics to his credit, including *Economic Development: Ends and Means, Shortages and High Prices — The Way Out,* and *Economic Strategy for the 80s.*

V K Narayana Menon MA PhD has been Executive Director, National Centre for the Performing Arts, since October 1968 and is also the Honorary Executive Director, Homi Bhabha Fellowships Council. He has held various posts with All India Radio (1948-1963) including that of Director of Calcutta, Madras and Delhi stations; Director, External Services; and Deputy Director-General. He was Secretary, Sangeet Natak Akademi (1963-65); and Director-General, All India Radio (1965-1968). Dr Narayana Menon has also held the following offices: President, International Music Council (UNESCO) 1966-68; Trustee, International Broadcasting Institution 1968-76; Member, UNESCO Advisory Panel on Space Communication 1965-68; he was re-elected President of the International Music Council in 1976.

Kapila Vatsyayan's dance specialisation is both practical and theoretical. She gained a PhD in Indology at the University of Banaras, Varanasi, in 1952, and has also trained as performer, teacher and notator in the classical dances of India, under India's foremost gurus. She has choreographed ballets and been active in the field of theatre for many years, having been responsible for introducing styles like Kathakali, Bharatnatyam etc onto international forums, and has lectured in many parts of the world, especially the USA, Indonesia, Japan, Thailand and Burma Dr Vatsyayan was Joint Secretary of the 26th International Congress of Orientalists, New Delhi, 1962-64, and is currently Joint Educational Advisor, Department of Culture, New Delhi. In 1978 she was elected Vice-Chairman, Sangeet Natak Akademi (the National Academy of Music, Dance and Drama). She has been responsible for the establishment of several institutions of the performing and plastic arts in Delhi. Her books include *Classical Indian Dance in Literature and the Arts* (Sangeet Natak Akademi), and *Traditions of Indian Folk Dance* (Indian Book Company).

Calambur Sivaramamurti's life has been devoted to the study and exposition of Indian art, as archaeologist, numismatist, epigraphist, historian and scholar of Sanskrit. He began his career as Curator of the Archaeology in the Madras Museum, he then joined the Indian Museum in Calcutta as Superintendent of the Archaeological Survey of India. Posted to the National Museum at Delhi, as its Keeper, he then became Assistant Director and finally Director. He has been the Honorary Advisor on Museums for the Government of India, has served on the executive committee of the International Council of Museums, Paris, and has been the Chairman of the Indian National Committee of the Council. He was also honoured by being elected the General President of the All India Oriental Conference. An early recipient of the Jawaharlal Nehru Fellowship, he worked on the theme of "Nataraja in Art, Thought and Literature," now acclaimed as a major contribution to Indology. Dr Sivaramamurti's monumental book, *L'Art en Inde*, originally published in French, has subsequently been brought out in German, English, Italian and Spanish editions.

Richard Lawrence Bartholomew has been Secretary of the Lalit Kala Akademi, New Delhi, since 1977. He was a teacher in Cambridge and Modern Schools, 1952-55, and then worked as a freelance journalist, 1956-58. He held the position of assistant editor of *Thought*, 1958-60; assistant editor, *Vak*, 1958-59; feature writer, *The Statesman*, 1957-58; art critic for the *Indian Express*, 1958-62; for *Thought*, 1955-60; and for the *Times of India*, since 1962. He was Director of the Kunika Art Centre, New Delhi, 1960-63; and Development Officer, Tibet House, New Delhi, 1966-73. He is a member of Lalit Kala Akademi, and has held one-man shows of paintings in Delhi and Bombay. Richard Bartholomew's publications include: *Husain* (co-author Krisha Reddy); *The Story of Siddhartha's Release* (poems).

Maheshwar Dayal joined the Atomic Energy Commission of India in 1955, and participated in the design and building of the country's first atomic reactors. He was also involved at that time in the initial studies of India's energy problems and the economic evaluation of the introduction of nuclear power. Subsequently he participated in the selection of the site for India's first nuclear power station and in its entire course through financing, construction and operation. In 1969 he was appointed Chief of the Station, and head of the department dealing with technical, economic and administrative matters of the new project. In 1970 he was appointed a member of the Atomic Power Authority of

India; and in 1974, was appointed Minister and Indian Representative to UNESCO at Paris. He became Advisor, Department of Science and Technology, Government of India, in 1979: Secretary, Commission for Additional Sources of Energy (CASE) in 1981: and in 1980 was elected General Secretary of the National Academy of Sciences, Allahabad.

V Ramalingaswami is at present Director-General of the Indian Council of Medical Research, New Delhi. He was previously a pathologist at the Indian Council of Medical Research, Nutrition Research Laboratories, 1947-54; Deputy Director, Indian Council of Medical Research, 1954-57; Professor of Pathology, All India Institute of Medical Sciences, 1957-69; Director, All India Institute of Medical Sciences, 1969-79; and President Indian National Science Academy, 1979-80. Dr Ramalingaswami specialises in the field of nutritional disorders. Another of his main interests is the moulding of Indian medical education, traditionally based on the European models, into patterns suitable for India and other developing countries. His work has exerted a wide influence both in India and abroad particularly in relation to community orientation of medical education.

Monkombu Sambasivan Swaminathan was Director, Indian Agricultural Research Institute 1966-72; Director-General, Indian Council of Agricultural Research and Secretary to the Government of India, Department of Agricultural Research and Education 1972-79; Secretary to the Government of India, Ministry of Agriculture, Department of Agriculture and Co-operation 1979-80; and is currently a member (agriculture) of the Planning Commission. He is also Chairman of the Science Advisory Committee to the Cabinet, and Chairman of the national committees set up for the control of leprosy and blindness. Internationally, Dr Swaminathan is Independent Chairman of the FAO Council, United Nations; and Chairman, UN Advisory Committee on Science and Technology for Development. He is President of the International Federation of Agricultural Research Systems for Development; President, Society for Breeding Researches in Asia and Oceania; and President, International Bee Research Association.

Pupul Jayakar has been closely associated with the development of handloom and handicrafts of India since Independence. A pioneer in the field of rural art and design, she was Chairman of the Handicrafts and Handlooms Exports Corporation of India Ltd (Government of India) from 1968 to 1977 and Chairman of the All India Handicrafts Board (Government of India) from 1974 to 1977. She has served as Chairman of the Central Cottage Industries Corporation from 1975; Chairman of the Governing Body of the National Institute of Design, Ahmedabad, from 1974-78; President of the Krishnamurti Foundation, India, from 1968 to 1978 and Chairman of the Calico Museum of Textiles from 1979. She is on the editorial board of the *Lalit Kala* journal and *Journal of Indian Textile History*. Pupul Jayakar is author of *God is not a Fullstop,* a volume of short stories, and was co-author of *Textile and Ornamental Arts of India,* Museum of Modern Art, New York. She is author of *The Earthen Drum — An Introduction to the Ritual Arts of Rural India,* National Museum; *The Buddha — A book for young people;* (Publishers Vakil & Sons); and has contributed a number of articles to *Marg, Lalit Kala* and *Journal of Indian Textile History.* She was awarded the Padma Bhushan in 1967 for her achievements in the field of handloom development, and is also a recipient of the Watumull Award. Mrs Pupul Jayakar is Chairman of the Advisory Committee for the Festival of India in Britain. She is also Advisor (Handlooms & Handicrafts), Government of India, and Vice-Chairman of the All India Handlooms & Handicrafts Board set up by the Government of India.

B N Goswamy, MA, PhD, is Professor of the History of Art and Chairman, Department of Fine Arts, Punjab University. Author of a dozen books and over 50 research papers, Dr Goswamy is well-known in academic circles in many parts of the world, having been associated as guest professor or guest lecturer with various prestigious universities, institutes and museums in Asia, Europe and the USA. A fellow of the Royal Society of Arts and Fellow of the Royal Asiatic Society, Dr Goswamy is associated with many learned societies and advisory committees.

Rene Lecler was born in Belgium, educated in France and is a British citizen. He has been travel editor of the magazine *Harpers & Queen* for the past 22 years and in the course of his duties has visited 101 countries so far. He is the author of the best selling bi-annual book *The 300 Best Hotels in the World* (Macmillan, London) and of *The World Shopping Guide* which will be published this year. He is known as one of Britain's best known experts on up-market travel and contributes frequently to leading periodicals in Britain and the United States. India, which he usually visits once a year, is one of his two or three favourite countries and he says: "India is not just a travel destination — it is an experience which no intelligent person should miss."

Reginald Massey, Indian writer, critic and film maker has lived in London for many years. His poetry has been widely published and anthologised and *Indian Dances — Their History and Growth* (Faber) and *The Music of India* (Stanmore), which he co-authored with his actress/writer wife Jamila Massey, are recognised works on those subjects. With her he also wrote *The Immigrants* (Hind), a novel about Asians in Britain. He is a Fellow of the Royal Society of Arts.

Bridget Allchin MA PhD is a Fellow of Wolfson College, Cambridge. Since 1951 she has travelled widely throughout the Indian subcontinent while engaged in various projects of research and fieldwork in Indian prehistory. Between 1969-74 she was Director of the Cambridge-Baroda project researching the prehistory and past climates of the desert and dry zone of north-west India. Since 1975, Dr Allchin has been Joint Director, British Archaeological Mission to Pakistan, and is a Founder Trustee, The Ancient India and Iran Trust (1978). Her books include *The Stone Tipped Arrow* (1966); (with F R Allchin) *The Birth of Indian Civilisation* (1968); *The Prehistory and Palaeogeography of the Great Indian Desert* (1978); (with F R Allchin) *The Rise of Civilisation in India and Pakistan* (C U P, in press).

Frank Raymond Allchin MA PhD FBA is a Fellow of Churchill College, Cambridge. He served with the Indian Army in India and Singapore (1944-47). Subsequently he taught Indian art and archaeology in the Universities of London (1954-59) and

Cambridge (1959-present). Since 1951 he has travelled widely in the Indian subcontinent, engaged in fieldwork as a UNESCO consultant. Dr Allchin has been Joint Director, British Archaeological Mission to Pakistan (1975-), and is a Founder Trustee, The Ancient India and Iran Trust (1978-). Author: *Neolithic Cattle Keepers of South India* (1963); translations of *Tulsi Das Kavitavali* (1964) and *The Petition to Ram (Vinayapatrika)* (1966); (with B Allchin) *The Birth of Indian Civilisation* (1968); ed with N Hammond, *The Archaeology of Afghanistan* (1978); (with D K Chakrabarti) *A Source-book of Indian Archaeology,* vol 1 (1979); (with B Allchin) *The Rise of Civilisation in India and Pakistan* (C U P, in press).

Henrietta Green, born in London, is a journalist who specialises in cookery. She is a self-taught cook who was inspired to write by a "a greedy interest in good and unusual food." She has travelled widely in Europe and India where she spent 18 months researching for a project on Indian herbs and spices. Henrietta Green has written two cookery books: *Fine-Flavoured Food,* published by Faber & Faber, and *The Marinade Cookbook,* published by Pierrot: She is cookery editor of both *The Sunday Express Magazine* and *Company* magazine.

Philip Mason had a distinguished career in the Indian Civil Service from 1928 when he was Assistant Magistrate, United Province, to 1947 when he completed three years as Joint Secretary to the Government of India's War Department. In 1946 he was made a Companion of the Order of the Indian Empire. After 1947 he held several high offices in British race relations bodies, including that of Chairman of the National Committee for Commonwealth Immigrants. He is a prolific author and has written several books on Indian affairs and race relations.

Marie Seton was born in the UK. Of pioneering spirit she is much travelled and internationally known for her writing on cinema and the arts (including contributing to many Indian newspapers and magazines, and broadcasting). The subjects of her biographies — Sergei Eisenstein, Paul Robeson, Pandit Nehru, and Satyajit Ray — have the link of all being motivated by the universality of their ideas, and ahead of their times. Her

latest, and only fiction book, *Song of the Atom,* appeared in December 1981. She has spent nearly 12 years in India encouraging the creation of the New Indian Cinema. *Time in the Sun,* her salvage of Eisenstein's unfinished Mexican film, is now in the archives of most countries, and continues to be shown. The first film sponsored by the British Film Institute was Marie Seton's *Drawings that Walk and Talk,* which traces the history of animation, starting with early man's cave paintings.

Sir John Thomson is the High Commissioner for Britain in India. His father and grandfather were both physicists and both Nobel Prize Winners. After leaving Cambridge University, Sir John joined the British Diplomatic Service. He has served in three Arab countries, in Washington and in Europe, but half his career has been at headquarters in London. He has been head of the planning staff in the Foreign Office and later of the assessments staff in the Cabinet Office: He has also been in charge of both defence and disarmament in the Foreign Office. Sir John took up his present job in India in January 1977.

Tambimuttu was born in Sri Lanka to the same family as Ananda K Coomaraswamy and is grandson of the poet S Tambimuttu Pillai. He arrived in England in 1938 at the age of 22, and within a few months had published the first issue of *Poetry London* magazine which, along with *Poetry London - New York,* was considered by many to be the most prestigious literary magazine in Britain throughout the following two decades. Editions Poetry London was the publisher of first books of distinguished writers such as Lawrence Durrell, Vladimir Nabokov, Keith Douglas, Anais Nin, Elizabeth Smart and Henry Moore. His fine production of books has been recognised by the National Gallery, the Victoria and Albert Museum, *Graphis,* and by international awards. Tambimuttu has featured Indian writers and themes in *Poetry London,* and served as the poetry editor of the Indian issues of *Atlantic Monthly* and *Poetry (Chicago).* He is currently compiling a *Golden Treasury of Indian Verse.*